D1554376

Trauma Cinema

Trauma Cinema

DOCUMENTING INCEST AND THE HOLOCAUST

Janet Walker

UNIVERSITY OF CALIFORNIA PRESS

BERKELEY LOS ANGELES LONDON

Chapter 2 of this book was originally published as chapter 7 in *Endless Night: Cinema and Psychoanalysis, Parallel Histories,* edited by Janet Bergstrom. Copyright © 1999 The Regents of the University of California. Reprinted by permission of the University of California Press.

Extracts from the following previously published essays by Janet Walker appear in revised form throughout *Trauma Cinema* by permission of the publishers and/or copyright holders:

"The Traumatic Paradox: Documentary Film, Historical Fictions, and Cataclysmic Past Events," *Signs* 22:4 (Summer 1997): 803–25. Copyright ©1997 The University of Chicago. All rights reserved. Revised as "The Traumatic Paradox: Autobiographical Documentary and the Psychology of Memory," in *Contested Pasts: The Politics of Memory,* edited by Katharine Hodgkin and Susannah Radstone and published by Routledge. Copyright © 2003 Janet Walker.

"Trauma Cinema: False Memories and True Experience," *Screen* 42:2 (Summer 2001): 211–16. Reprinted by permission of Oxford University Press.

University of California Press
Berkeley and Los Angeles, California
University of California Press, Ltd.
London, England
© 2005 The Regents of the University of California

Library of Congress Cataloging-in-Publication Data
Walker, Janet, 1955–.
    Trauma cinema : documenting incest and the Holocaust / Janet Walker.
        p.   cm.
    Includes bibliographical references and index.
    ISBN 0–520–24174–6 (alk. paper)—ISBN 0–520–24175–4 (pbk. : alk. paper)
    1. Documentary films—History and criticism.   2. Documentary films—History and criticism.   3. Holocaust, Jewish (1939–1945), in motion pictures.   4. Incest in motion pictures.   5. Psychic trauma in motion pictures.   6. Memory.   I. Title.
PN1995.9.D6W26   2005
791.43'653—dc22   2004014327

Manufactured in the United States of America

14 13 12 11 10 09 08 07 06 05
10 9 8 7 6 5 4 3 2 1

This book is printed on New Leaf EcoBook 60, containing 60% post-consumer waste, processed chlorine free; 30% de-inked recycled fiber, elemental chlorine free; and 10% FSC-certified virgin fiber, totally chlorine free. EcoBook 60 is acid-free and meets the minimum requirements of ANSI/ASTM D5634–01 (*Permanence of Paper*).

for Steve

.

CONTENTS

ILLUSTRATIONS

ACKNOWLEDGMENTS

How do authors choose their topics? I am convinced that the process is profound and mysterious. I set out to write a book that would deal, consciously, with disturbing material related to things I had written about before intuitively, unconsciously, with little control over what would bubble up. Naturally, there proved to be further layers. I am deeply grateful to those who helped me discover some of the sedimentary meanings of mind, memory, and representation.

A number of people took their precious time to read and comment on this manuscript or parts of it. I would like to single out my great friend and fellow documentary enthusiast Michael Renov. Our conversations, his writing, and the Visible Evidence conference and book series that he co-created with Faye Ginsburg and Jane Gaines have taught and inspired me over many years. I feel lucky to have enjoyed the benefit of his support and written comments on this project, which might not have come into being without what he offered. Janet Bergstrom, Katharine Hodgkin, Ann Kaplan, Julia Lesage, Susannah Radstone, and Ban Wang contributed excellent editorial suggestions on essays related to this work. Catherine Cole, Cynthia Erb, Jon Lewis, Joshua Hirsch, Lisa Parks, Constance Penley, Lynn Sacco, Diane Waldman, Chuck Wolfe, and the anonymous reviewers from the University of California Press read with insight and were generous with their responses. I would also like to thank Joshua Hirsch, Michael Renov, and Lynn Sacco for making their monographs available to me in manuscript form.

I also owe a huge debt of thanks to the independent film and video-makers whose inventive pieces are a true inspiration. I am thrilled that their works are now more widely accessible than they would have been in the days before the Internet, and I am delighted to direct readers to this book's video/filmography, where information about procurement may be found. Several of these artists talked with me at length about their films. Laura Bialis in particular was tremendously giving of her time, expertise, wonderful ideas, and *Tak for Alt* stills. She, Brody Fox, Sarah Levy, and Judy Meisel shared their experiences not only with me but with University of California, Santa Barbara (UCSB) Department of Film Studies students as well. When I was shy of asking yet again, Laura and Judy, along with Fred Meisel, assured me that it was their pleasure to visit my classroom, and they did so many times. All of us were deeply moved. Abraham Ravett, Michelle Citron, and Joshua Hirsch spoke to me with courage and candor about their autobiographical works. Thanks are due as well to Heidi Bollock, Jesse Friedman, Lynn Hershman, and James Whitney, who answered my queries about the films and videos they have made.

Along with these individuals, many others who share my passion for film, memory, and history have been willing and eager to exchange ideas. I would like to thank the following people for their own creative and critical projects and their engagement with mine: Allison Anders, Constance Atwill, Renée Bergan, Edward Branigan, Joshua Braun, Robert Burgoyne, Jackie Byars, Mim Carter, Denise Cicourel, Donna Cunningham, Cynthia Felando, Frances Guerin, Roger Hallas, Barbara Herr Harthorn, Judith Herman, Jill Levine, Diane MacKenzie, Alison Maclean, Harold Marcuse, Marléne Roberts, Michael Roth, Bhaskar Sarkar, Candace Schermerhorn, Bjørn Sorenssen, Charles Stivale, Rea Tajiri, Lenore Terr, Carol Whited, and Juliet Williams. Students in my documentary and historiography courses and colleagues at various talks and panels over the years have also helped shape this book by their thoughtful, informed, and lively responses to the sometimes wild ideas that prefigured it. If I have forgotten anyone, I would be grateful if you would understand and forgive the frailty of memory—the subject of this book.

The production of the book could not have occurred without the research skills and calm influence of Nick Pici, who compiled the bibliography and video/filmography and prepared the manuscript. Emily Davis served as copyeditor extraordinaire. Nina Seja lent her artist's eye and technical expertise to the illustrations. Thanks are also due to Dan Riley, Amy Hoppy, Nicole Taher, and Christy Zolla, who provided additional research and production support. Dean David Marshall generously allocated funds for research assistance along with bibliographic leads and advice about publishing. Kathryn Carnahan oversaw the disbursement of funds and helped immeasurably with day-to-day support and friendship. Eric Smoodin was the first to express interest in turning this manuscript into a book, and Mary Francis at the University of California Press followed up. I hereby thank each one, along with Kalicia Pivirotto, Kate Warne, Elisabeth Magnus, Leslie Larson, Colette DeDonato, and the others at UC Press who helped produce this book.

The UCSB Department of Film Studies is an exceptional place. It is my great fortune to have spent much of my adult life in these halls, where ideas flourish and mutual respect and friendship are the order of the day. I am grateful to my departmental colleagues on faculty and staff and to our students for being their brilliant, energizing, and sustaining selves. To my extended family and friends, I say thank you for your love and encouragement. And to my husband, Steve, and our daughter, Ariel, words cannot express my joy in creating our personal history together.

Polite society has a love/hate relationship with disaster. On one hand, people generally prefer to distance conversation from disturbing subjects like incest and the Holocaust. On the other hand, such things inspire perseveration. Assaults continue to be perpetrated both inside families and by one group against another that the first wishes to subjugate or wipe out. Some sources, from the current administration to action movies, choose to characterize violent aggression as coming from isolated "evildoers" and to see its passage as a finite event. But a less simplistic perspective recognizes a geography of closely and loosely interconnected conflicts around the world, from Afghanistan, Iraq, the Balkans, East Timor, Rwanda, Israel, and Palestine to places right here in the United States.

The social consequences of this heritage of catastrophe are yet to be understood, let alone ameliorated. People do not escape unscathed from the shooting, chopping, bombing, burning, twisting, thrusting, starving, cutting, and suffocating that they suffer, witness, or even perpetrate. The harm may be mental as well as physical, and it is inevitable that some will emerge from these experiences profoundly traumatized. Nevertheless, traumatized people carry on with their lives in relation to others, including strangers, acquaintances, friends, and family members. They bear and raise children who are the "memorial candles" of lost loved ones and vanished well-being.[1] Thus, the legacy of trauma is bequeathed.

Looking backward to what happened and forward to what could be, physicians and psychologists attempt to diagnose and heal bodies and minds. Historians also face in two directions, characterizing the details of lives and deaths at a temporal remove but doing it for present audiences and future benefit.

Film- and videomakers can also be helpers and historiographers. In this book, I endeavor to show how certain films and videos advance our understanding of the etiology and sequelae of trauma by elaborating the links between, and the consequences of, catastrophic past events and demon memories. The wild past does not come down to us purely and simply through a collection of eyewitness testimonies and tangible artifacts. These are important, surely, but they must be read.

The lap dissolve from the end of the twentieth century to the beginning of the twenty-first superimposed in our minds a series of media episodes that publicized the inadequacy of empirically based historical writing about catastrophic events. One frequently adopted reference point was the controversy that surrounded the planning of a Smithsonian Air and Space Museum exhibit initially designed to explore the use and effects of the two atomic bombs that the United States unleashed against Japan in 1945.[2] In the debate that erupted, all sides acknowledged that the United States had bombed Hiroshima and Nagasaki, but attributions of public historical meaning varied greatly: the bombings brought an end to the war, mercifully saving American lives; or the bombings were a capricious atrocity perpetrated by the U.S. government against Japanese civilians. Also at odds were opinions about how to represent—or whether it would be best for Americans not to represent—the devastated center of Hiroshima and that city's human casualties. Likewise, the media coverage of the events of September 11, 2001, and its aftermath emphasized the tremendous discrepancy between the perspective of Osama Bin Laden and his associates and that of most other people. Whereas most people were horrified to experience, witness, or learn about the assault on the United States, the notorious CNN-aired "Bin Laden Tape" showed the Al Qaeda leader reflecting gleefully on the beautiful orchestration and surpassing success of the attacks. As for the question of representation, the destruction of the World Trade Center was featured prominently in media outlets. Footage of the jet-bombs making contact was burned into our retinas by television images from every angle repeated continuously. Home movies of the devastation were projected silently in the background as news anchors and commentators delivered their incredulous reports. Cameras found families seeking loved ones, and later there was assiduous coverage of the cleanup efforts, of toxicity studies, and of the funeral rites of June 2002. The site continues to be subject to attention and inquiry as plans for the memorial construction go forward. Dubbed "Ground Zero," it carries the name given to the blast site in Hiroshima; but the difference in U.S. perspective has generated excessive coverage rather than the reluctance to represent that has characterized the historiography of the earlier Japanese Ground Zero.

In other cases of contested memory, especially those contingent upon personal recollection, the facts themselves have eluded discovery and verification. Binjamin Wilkomirski's book *Fragments: Memories of a Wartime Childhood* purported to be a memoir about a Jewish boy's early childhood experiences in the Riga ghetto and several death camps. Only several years later, after an investigation commissioned by the book's German publishers, was the work revealed to be a confabulation.[3] A scandal tailor-made for Holocaust deniers could not have been more perfect: Wilkomirski lies; Jews lie; the Holocaust never happened.

One of the most furious, prolific, and sustained of all the retrospective debates has concerned the legitimacy of repressed and recovered memories of incestuous childhood sexual abuse. Some say that recovered memories attest to the epidemic proportions of incest, while others contend that women's recovered memories of childhood abuse—for the rememberer is usually a woman—are mendacious, erroneous, iatrogenic (created by the therapeutic process itself), or even part of a feminist plot.[4]

When the practice of history is frustrated by the transience of evidence, by the subjectivity of individual memory, and by the realization, as other voices are heard from, that historiography is intrinsically interpretive, the allure of what Michael Frisch terms the "supply side" approach to public history may feel irresistible.[5] Proponents of this historiographic method maintain that we need facts, lots of them, to prove beyond a doubt that incest was and is an abuse of epidemic proportions and that the Holocaust really, horrifically, happened. Denial, either categorically or through a series of rhetorical shifts, becomes unbearable. The idea that the "[p]hysical residues of all events may yield potentially unlimited access to the past," or that "the whole historical record survive[s] somewhere; [and] given the right techniques, nothing would elude retrieval,"[6] assumes a tremendous attraction in this age of historical contestation and amnesia. Thus it is understandable that some historians writing about Holocaust denial have been critical of deconstructionist approaches that support, in Saul Friedlander's words, the "primacy of the rhetorical dimension . . . of the historical text" and affirm the "impossibility of establishing any direct reference to some aspects at least of the concrete *reality* that we call the Shoah."[7]

Binaristic explanation may also seem consoling. The either/or proposition is a common feature of popular and juridical discourses on catastrophic events: sexual abuse happened and recollections of it are true, or it did not happen and purported recollections should be culled out and attributed to "false memory syndrome";[8] Wilkomirski was traumatized in childhood or he was not. To this way of thinking, forgetting and mistaken memory are indicators that a lie or a fantasy without any legitimate link to the past is being perpetuated.

However, the premise of this book is that recourse to empiricist or disjunctive approaches is unwarranted and inadvisable. Empirically based realist historiography, even if it were possible, is not the most appropriate mode for certain historical representations because it cannot adequately address the vicissitudes of historical representation and memory.[9] This is not to say that we should throw out the baby of fact with the bathwater of empiricism. I concur with Friedlander's caution against deconstructionist analyses that unfasten the rhetorical dimension from any material mooring. But that particular impulse is extreme and not really characteristic of most new historical writings, which work hard to account for the relationship between fact and subjective representations. This is Michael Frisch's interest when he emphasizes that history is "structured, variable, and problematic," and it is Friedlander's as well. The historian's attention, the latter writes, should be balanced between "the simultaneous acceptance of two contradictory moves: the search for ever-closer historical linkages and the avoidance of a naive historical positivism leading to simplistic and self-assured historical narrations and closures."[10]

We have an ethical and political obligation to remember, acknowledge constantly, and deal with the aftermath of traumatic events.[11] At the same time, though, we must recognize that these events are subject to interpretation as they are experienced, reimagined, reported, written down, and visually communicated. Here lies the paradox of memory and history: there is a dire need to write histories of trauma and/or traumatic histories with regard to the relationships among experience, memory, and fantasy; but memory is friable, and, as David Thelen has argued, "The struggle for possession and interpretation of memory is rooted in the conflict and interplay among social, political, and cultural interests and values in the present."[12] The challenge Friedlander throws down is to integrate the so-called "'mythic memory' of the victims within the overall representation of the past without its becoming an 'obstacle' to 'rational historiography.'"[13]

Trauma Cinema's aim is to tackle this set of problems by looking at how selected films and videos of the last two decades establish a fresh histo-riography particularly attuned to the havoc trauma wreaks. Audiovisual media, I will argue, lend themselves to this new project because of certain intrinsic properties. Film and video texts are always already constructed through processes of selection and ordering, yet they can also reproduce, mechanically or electronically, an actual profilmic or provideographic event (occurring in front of the camera). In other words, audiovisual media figure in their very makeup the productive dilemma of those of us who would locate historical understanding at the intersection of subjective and physi-cal properties. This quality of film and video media very likely accounts in large part for the continuing attraction of Hollywood's historical epics and the History Channel's parade of events and personages. Audiovisual texts are also sufficiently plastic to render the shifting colors and shapes of human experience as it manifests internally, in people's minds, and exter-nally, in things that happen and are perceived by witnesses and participants.

What I wish to explore, therefore, is the ability of certain films and videos to externalize, publicize, and historicize traumatic material that would other-wise remain at the level of internal, individual psychology. Since the most productive aesthetic histories are also culturally specific, I will concentrate on recent films and videos made in the United States (and, in one case, Canada). This, then, is a book about a vanguard group of films and videos that adopt catastrophe as their subject and formations of trauma as their aesthetic.

Aiming to plumb the re-presentation of terribly disquieting things, I have chosen to focus on films and videos about incest and the Holocaust. Incest and the Holocaust are topics that have also been featured together in con-temporary psychological literature on trauma and memory, and I will draw on various formulations from that source as an analytical framework for this film and video study. Of particular interest are psychological explanations of how truth abides in the relationship between real events and their cor-responding mental imagery and how these mental images include cases where a gap opens up between memory and actuality. Psychological theo-ries provide insight into the amnesias, fantasies, and mistakes in memory that I believe must be taken into account, along with corroborated evi-dence, if we are to understand how historical meaning is made. Thus, a joint consideration of "trauma cinema" and psychological theorizing has the potential to radically reconstruct the roadblocks of positivism and binarism at the intersection of catastrophe, memory, and historical representation.

Cases of incest surely differ from cases of wartime trauma in their respec-tive histories, specification, and sociopolitical import. This is why incest and the Holocaust would seem incompatible subjects for a single book. Whereas incest is generally taken to be familial and private, the Holocaust was sociopolitical and public; whereas the most common form of incest depends on gender-allocated power relations, the Final Solution sought to eradicate people of both genders for the goal of racial genocide; and whereas incest is pan-national and panhistorical, the Holocaust was nationally and historically specific. One could not have a Historians' Debate on incest, for incest can and does take place anywhere, anytime. The Holocaust, on the other hand, whether interpreted as a singular event or as one that goes to the limit but does not set the limit of the atrocities of which humanity is capable, provokes a history that must still center on events and operations specific to a certain time and place.[14]

However, to say that two manifestations are different does not mean that they are incomparable. First, the division between personal and public history is artificial at best. Incest is by definition intrafamilial, but its power relations and discursive character are those of society at large. As Shoshana Felman explains, "[T]oward the end of the millennium [feminists have realized that] the renewed manifestations of domestic violence and of deceptive intimate brutality and private horror are in fact collective traumas."[15] Conversely, the public history of the Holocaust is peopled by individuals whose family life and life itself the Nazis sought to extinguish. Second, both incest and the Holocaust have been discussed as events that lack witnesses— in the case of the Holocaust because millions were killed and in the case of incest because it occurs behind closed doors. In neither context is this literally true. We do know that gas chamber exterminations were carried out so as to reduce the number of outside witnesses and that there were no inside survivors; moreover, there exists only one small snippet of film showing actual killing practice.[16] However, Sonderkommandos whose job it was to retrieve corpses from the gas chambers have lived to recount what they witnessed, and in any case there is profuse documentary evidence of the machinations of Hitler's ordered genocide. So too, while much of the organic evidence of incest is washed away, physical scars—as well as the psychological ones—remain. And, as we will see in the case of *Just, Melvin* (James Ronald Whitney, 2000), siblings and others as well as survivors still struggle to come forward with their stories. Nevertheless, incest and the Holocaust are two catastrophic happenings that depend/depended on drastic secrecy and antitestimonial measures. They are both events without witnesses in the sense that Dori Laub and Shoshana Felman convey when they write of the annihilation of witnessing.[17]

Both incest and the Holocaust have been subject to furious denial by perpetrators and other individuals and by highly organized groups such as the False Memory Syndrome Foundation and the Committee for Historical Review. Incest and the Holocaust are vulnerable to this kind of concerted denial because of their unfathomability, their unjustifiability, and the threat they pose to the politics of patriarchy and anti-Semitism respectively. Over and over, survivors of the Holocaust attest that they were warned of what was happening in Poland but could not believe it at the time, could not believe it later as it was happening to them, and still to this day cannot believe what they, at the same time, know to have occurred. For Holocaust deniers this is a felicitous twist, for their arguments denying the Holocaust and therefore the legitimacy of Israel as a Jewish state capitalize on the discrepancies of faded memory. In the case of incest, although post-traumatic stress disorder, amnesia, and dissociation represent some of the mind's strategies for comprehending the incomprehensible, incest deniers have taken advantage of inconsistencies to discredit survivor testimony.

I am particularly interested in incest and the Holocaust because the filmic output they both continue to inspire often foregrounds issues of historiography and intergenerational friction. Although the Holocaust occurred more than fifty years ago, new films and videos continue to appear and garner worldwide attention. For example, *Into the Arms of Strangers: Stories of the Kindertransport* (Mark Jonathan Harris, 2000), *The Last Days* (James Moll, 1998), *The Long Way Home* (Mark Jonathan Harris, 1997), and *Anne Frank Remembered* (Jon Blair, 1995) have all won Oscars for Best Documentary Feature since 1995. And though incest is neither temporally nor culturally specific, it is noteworthy that the current output of films on the subject is increasing and that a significant number of these works opt for a retrospective structure in which people's memories loom large. As I write this, *Capturing the Friedmans* (Andrew Jarecki, 2003), a new documentary about pedophilia and incestuous abuse, is being given a theatrical run. Thus we can say that in this subject area too, the processes through which we come to know traumatic events of the past are being probed in the present.

A book about films and videos about incest *and* the Holocaust is one way to bring out the conceptual affinities of the two subjects. This cross-talk is necessary for a thorough understanding of the epistemology of traumatic representation. Looking at texts and discourses on incest in reference to historiographic questions of evidence, argumentation, and representation while looking at Holocaust representations in reference to psychological theories of personal memory can trigger insights into the various connections between traumatic memories and catastrophic histories. Incest and the Holocaust are two wave forms that resonate intermittently as they advance across textual media, including history, film, and the internal sounds and images of memory. The subject of this book is how these and, by implication, other traumatic events are remembered awkwardly—"disremembered," I will say—by people who live through them or experience them vicariously and, crucially, by the films and videos that result.

PART I

The Traumatic Paradox

ONE

Catastrophe, Representation, and the Vicissitudes of Memory

TRAUMA (PSYCHICAL): An event in the subject's life defined by its intensity, by the subject's incapacity to respond adequately to it, and by the upheaval and long-lasting effects that it brings about in the psychical organization.

JEAN LAPLANCHE AND J.-B. PONTALIS,
The Language of Psycho-Analysis

POSTTRAUMATIC STRESS DISORDER (PTSD); DIAGNOSTIC FEATURES: Traumatic events that are experienced directly include, but are not limited to, military combat, violent personal assault (sexual assault, physical attack, robbery, mugging), being kidnapped, being taken hostage, terrorist attack, torture, incarceration as a prisoner of war or in a concentration camp, natural or manmade disasters, severe automobile accidents, or being diagnosed with a life-threatening illness. For children, sexually traumatic events may include developmentally inappropriate sexual experiences without threatened or actual violence or injury. Witnessed events include, but are not limited to, observing the serious injury or unnatural death of another person due to violent assault, accident, war, or disaster or unexpectedly witnessing a dead body or body parts.

AMERICAN PSYCHIATRIC ASSOCIATION,
Diagnostic and Statistical Manual of Mental Disorders (DSM-IV)

"Memory for traumatic events can be extremely veridical," asserts Elizabeth Waites.[1] In fact, memories for traumatic events are known for being *more* veridical than memories for everyday events when it comes to the "gist" of memory.[2] But it is also true that real catastrophes can disturb memory processing. Whereas popular and legal venues tend to take an "it happened or it didn't" approach that rejects reports of traumatic experiences containing mistakes or amnesiac elements, contemporary psychological theories show that such memory features are a common consequence of traumatic experience itself. Forgetting and mistakes in memory may actually stand, therefore, as testament to the genuine nature of the event a person is trying to recall. This is the inherent contradiction of traumatic memory—what I have termed the "traumatic paradox": traumatic events can and do produce the very amnesias and mistakes in memory that are generally considered to undermine the legitimacy of a retrospective report about a remembered incident.[3]

Contemporary psychological theories of trauma and memory illuminate the subject in all its complexity and suggest the limitations of other approaches to traumatic memory that neglect its complications as a means of learning and assessing information about the past. One of the goals of this chapter is to explore what psychological literature can contribute to current research in the areas of new history and humanities-based trauma studies. Although there has been significant cross-fertilization between critical theories of trauma and critical theories of history, for institutional as well as intellectual reasons the literature of contemporary psychology has not been brought into the discussion in any significant way. Here I take the position that contemporary psychological theories of trauma and memory have much to offer historiographers, including theorists and audiences of films about the past.

A second goal of this chapter is to demonstrate that certain films and videos express their own vernacular attitudes toward the vicissitudes of memory that relate synergistically to those developed through the contemporary psychology of trauma and memory. Reading back and forth between psychology and cinema, this chapter will explore the intricate patterns that compose our conscious and unconscious means for remembering and representing catastrophic events.

TRAUMA AND MEMORY

A large portion of *Testimony: Crises of Witnessing in Literature, Psychoanalysis, and History,* by the literary critic Shoshana Felman and the clinical psychiatrist Dr. Dori Laub, is concerned with the mechanisms through which eyewitnesses to real historical events entertain memories and deliver testimonies that are divergent often to the point of incommensurability. Instead of dwelling on factual errors embedded in the memory texts, as is the convention in popular and professional historiography, Felman and Laub explore how a fallible memory may speak to historical truth. Drawing on Laub's experience with oral testimony and the Holocaust, *Testimony* proffers the case of a woman in her late sixties who testified to researchers from the Video Archive for Holocaust Testimonies at Yale that she had seen four chimneys explode as a result of actions during the Auschwitz uprising. "The flames shot into the sky," she recounted. "People were running. It was unbelievable."[4] Apparently, it *was* unbelievable. At a subsequent meeting of historians watching the videotape of this testimony, the accuracy of the woman's account was questioned. In reality only one chimney and not all four had been destroyed. Thus, as Laub explains, the historians discredited the woman's account: "Since the memory of the testifying woman turned out to be, in this way, fallible, one could not accept—nor give credence to— her whole account of the events." But Laub disagreed:

> She was testifying not simply to empirical historical facts, but to the very secret of survival and to resistance to extermination. . . . She saw four chimneys blowing up in Auschwitz: she saw, in other words, the unimaginable. . . . And she came to testify to the unbelievability, precisely, of what she had eyewitnessed—this bursting open of the frame of Auschwitz. . . . Because the testifier did not know the number of the chimneys that blew up . . . , the historians said that she knew nothing. I thought that she knew more, since she knew about the breakage of the frame, that her very testimony was now reenacting.[5]

Laub's unconventional point is that the register of reality testified to here is not just empirical but abstract. Ignorant of the exaggeration of the number of chimneys, we would read the woman's memory as simple reportage. Knowing the facts, we might be tempted to dismiss the woman's evidence. But by recognizing the pseudomemory for what it is, we come to understand the event as a breaking open of the frame. In other words, the historical payoff comes from our knowing the difference between the veridical memory (one chimney did blow up; there was effective resistance at Auschwitz) and the pseudomemory (the other three chimneys did not blow up; the woman's memory exaggerates; hyperbole best expresses that resistance at Auschwitz was resistance against all odds). Although pseudomemories also testify, we know more about memory function when we have additional information about a memory's basis in real occurrence. It is partly our recognition that a memory is not wholly veridical that enables us to read the historical meaning that it nevertheless possesses.

In developing comparable findings, feminist memory researchers are preeminent, for they have a motivation born of conflict. At the same time that they seek to redress the crime of childhood sexual abuse through social and legal activism and appropriate therapeutic procedures that rely on women's testimony about past events, they must also stem the antifeminist backlash against the assumption held by some feminists that all ostensible memories are equally valid. The challenge is to account both for cases where the memories reflect what really happened and cases where it does seem that women's memories have departed from literal truth. Seriously mistaken memories—internally produced fantasies—of satanic ritual abuse, alien abduction, or incest, for that matter—are threatening because they may be as powerful as genuine memories (which they mimic) in the psychic life of an individual. But nothing will be learned if internally generated memory formations are either dismissed out of hand or taken at face value. Multiple types of mental constructions must be studied—and studied, furthermore, in the context of their respective relationships, however attenuated, to real past events. Feminist clinicians and theorists are compelled, in short, by the truths that abide in fantasy constructions and, conversely, by the fantasies that abide in veridical constructions. To proceed as if truth and fantasy could be cleanly separated is to miss crucial aspects of both.

The case of Eileen Franklin Lipsker and her father, George Franklin, is illustrative. On November 30, 1990, a jury found George Franklin guilty in the first degree of the murder of eight-year-old Susan Nason. According to the jury's finding and to Lenore Terr's account in *Unchained Memories,* Eileen had been present and had witnessed the crime, which began with Susan's rape.[6] Dr. Terr, an expert witness for the prosecution, describes in her book how Lipsker repressed the memory of her father's actions only to recall them twenty years later, the recall triggered by the tilt of her own daughter's head and her daughter's similar appearance to that of the murdered girl. George Franklin was convicted in spite of expert testimony for the defense by the memory researcher and False Memory Syndrome Foundation board member Dr. Elizabeth Loftus, who argued strenuously against the possibility of repressed memory. Lipsker could not have *lost* such a memory, Loftus maintained, so it must not have been a true memory at all. She also used the content of the memories to undermine their validity. Eileen Franklin Lipsker's memories were mistaken in several details. The murdered girl did not wear a sweater or jacket, she was not buried where she was killed, and she was not covered with a mattress from the murderer's van. This, for Loftus, though remarkably not for that particular jury, was additional evidence that the memories were false. Defense attorneys also argued consistently against the validity of recovered memories, saying that Eileen Franklin Lipsker's memory in particular was "an unstable machine that generates wildly contradictory images."[7]

But Lenore Terr counters that real (exogenous) traumas "will often be accompanied by symptoms of post-traumatic stress, which itself is often accompanied by the disruption and dissociation of memory."[8] Furthermore, biological symptoms can "bear witness to the actualities of traumatic events" for which a person has no active memory.[9] According to Terr, Eileen Franklin Lipsker developed the habit of "pulling out the hair on one side of her head, creating a big, bleeding bald spot near the crown" after watching her father crush the skull of her best friend with a rock.[10] And indeed, that these symptoms predated Lipsker's conscious recovery of the memory itself would seem to testify to the validity of that memory. According to Terr, children especially learn to deal with repeated trauma by dissociating (splitting) or repressing the events during and after their occurrence. This makes it possible to understand how Eileen Franklin Lipsker, while habitually pulling the hair from her head, forgot on a conscious level the real rape and killing she had witnessed.

How can we cope with the difficulty—the traumatic paradox—that while a traumatic experience can produce either veracious memories or a trail of symptoms connecting an event with its psychic manifestation, it can also, especially when repeated over time, as in the case of incest, trigger fantasies, repression, misperceptions, and interpretations created by the real events but not realistically representative of them?[11] The fantasy/reality duality is at the crux of the issue in that what must be decided is the relationship, or the array of possibilities for the relationship, between mental imagery as an independent creation of the mind and the real-world events that contribute memory's color palate, its graphic qualities, and its repertoire of characters and narratives.

Students of psychoanalysis generally agree that the discipline—through the notion of fantasy—was created when Freud stopped believing that the etiology of hysteria lay in "premature sexual experience," or when he began to question the reality of the stories he was hearing from his women patients about abusive and often incestuous childhood sexual relations with adult males.[12] Psychoanalysis began when Freud retracted the theory he had propounded in "The Aetiology of Hysteria" (1896) that "at the bottom of every case of hysteria there are one or more cases of premature sexual experience, occurrences which belong to the earliest years of childhood,"[13] in favor of a theory of fantasy. Accounts of childhood sexual assault are based on the girl's own sexual desire and fantasies of its satisfaction, Freud purported. "I was at last obliged to recognize that these scenes of seduction had never taken place, and that they were only fantasies which my patients had made up."[14]

But if there is agreement that that was the sequence of events during this key moment in the intellectual life of psychoanalysis, there is substantially less agreement as to whether the story ends there. Individual trauma specialists vary in their readings of the finality of Freud's turn and in their resulting sense of Freudian heritage. As Diane Waldman and I have pointed out elsewhere, some feminist scholars, particularly Florence Rush and later Jeffrey Masson, "consider psychoanalysis anathema to feminism" precisely because of its putative denial of women's accounts of childhood sexual assault.[15] In the words of the psychiatrist and author Dr. Judith Herman, perhaps the most widely cited feminist theorist of psychological trauma, "[T]he dominant psychological theory of the next century was founded in the denial of women's reality."[16] She thus turns away from Freud and toward the legacy of Pierre Janet and his theory that, through "dissociation," the traumatic memories of his hysteria patients were "preserved in an abnormal state, set apart from ordinary consciousness."[17]

It is important to realize, however, that Herman does acknowledge that not all traumatic memories are true to real events. She points out that traumatic memories feature bodily and visual sensation over "verbal narrative and context,"[18] and she provides moving case histories to demonstrate how memories that are unconsciously reenacted often present themselves in disguised form. But Herman does generally reserve the term *fantasy* for wishes directed to hoped-for future actions: the "revenge fantasy" or the fantasy that the perpetrator may become contrite. Her theoretical framework for the "abnormal" traumatic memories is not that of Freudian fantasy but that of Janetian dissociation.

Other feminist scholars, while agreeing with their compatriots that to deny or ignore real childhood sexual assault would be reprehensible, contend nevertheless that Freud's position was not a complete denial and that the acknowledgment of fantasy as a concept need not preclude the realization that sexual assault on children does occur. Influenced greatly by the perspective of Juliet Mitchell and Jacqueline Rose,[19] Diane Waldman and I have insisted that Freud "continued to seek a *relationship* between actual child abuse and unconscious Oedipal fantasies and desires." We argued that Freud's work "is all the more interesting for its refusal to resolve the question by dismissing either the social reality of rape or the importance of fantasy construction—for its simultaneous insistence on both possibilities."[20]

Jean Laplanche and J.-B. Pontalis's definition of Freudian fantasy supports this reading of fantasy's variability. According to these researchers, fantasy (or phantasy) is "[an] imaginary scene in which the subject is a protagonist, representing the fulfillment of a wish (in the last analysis, an unconscious wish) in a manner that is distorted to a greater or lesser extent by the defensive processes. Phantasy has a number of different modes: conscious phantasies or daydreams, unconscious phantasies like those uncovered by analysis as the structures underlying a manifest content, and primal phantasies."[21] An "imaginary scene," yes, but where does it come from—is it internally or externally derived? That is a main question explored in the definition's commentary, where Laplanche and Pontalis do justice to the term's complexity on this count. In certain of Freud's writings, they explain, a distinction is preserved between "imagination and reality (perception)." Phantasy is a "purely illusory production which cannot be sustained when it is confronted with a correct apprehension of reality." Yet, the authors emphasize, Freud sought to retain a special role for "psychic reality," distinguishing it from other psychical phenomena on the basis, precisely, of its relation to the "truly 'real.'" He refused to be restricted, they argue, to a choice between these approaches. Fantasy is both "a distorted derivative of the memory of actual fortuitous events" and "an imaginary expression designed to conceal the reality of the instinctual dynamic."[22] In the first case, *fantasy* refers, in other words, to a nonveridical construction that is nevertheless "propped on" a real event.[23] To be sure, the real event is "fortuitous," meaning that it is not the origin of the fantasy but rather the grain of sand around which the pearl of fantasy is deposited, but it plays a role nonetheless.

Many critical theorists of trauma assert the significance of mental processes of fantasy over that of real events in the etiology of traumatic memory. As Katharine Hodgkin and Susannah Radstone explain, "[E]mphasis on the traumatic event as origin is misleading; what is absent from this teleological narrative, in effect, is precisely the way the mind makes its own meanings."[24] While I agree with the limitations of originary thinking as identified by Hodgkin and Radstone, I would nevertheless assert the need to guard against overcompensation. Perhaps the difference is one of emphasis, but my point is that fantasy and reality are inextricably—if mysteriously—bonded. Following my reading of Freud's theory, I posit that fantasy constructions, while assuredly internal phenomena, may indeed be responsive to the pressure of real events.

Illustrating the oblique connections between fantasies and lived reality, Jacqueline Rose's psychoanalytic orientation brings her to the realization that a child who has been abused in reality may have desired the father without actually wanting sexual relations to take place. The problem, explains Rose, is that neither social work nor the courts have a language capable of distinguishing between a desire and a want. But if the two are collapsed, then the reality of rape is vacated in the presence of desire—in the minds of the judges and perpetrators who read the sex as being desired by the girl and therefore as being consensual.[25]

Elizabeth Waites, Susan Reviere, Janice Haaken, and Lenore Terr are feminist theorists of the psychology of trauma attentive to the psychological harm wrought by instances of childhood sexual assault. Nevertheless, they are more willing than Judith Herman to apply themselves to the ambiguities of Freudian psychoanalysis with regard to fantasy structures and to cull out useful concepts.[26] Waites and Reviere distance themselves from those who claim that Freud denied the existence of sexual abuse. What he denied, Waites specifies, was the "etiological significance of sexual abuse in the development of neurosis."[27] Thus, although she is troubled by even that denial for its presentation of fantasy *as an autonomously internal phenomenon* disconnected from real abuse, Waites retains Freud's more complex notion of fantasy. Trauma, she theorizes, impoverishes fantasy life by generating an endless repetition of flashbacks that almost mechanically reproduce the remembered trauma, and it contributes to fantasy life by helping to generate elaborate structures that depart from literal transcriptions of past events.[28]

Haaken is the most explicit of these four feminist trauma specialists in identifying trauma theory's debt to classical psychoanalysis and, in particular, to the concept of fantasy. Freudian ideas, she believes, are a necessary corrective to the "trauma paradigm."[29] The "trauma/dissociation model" of the 1980s sought to restore attention to the real tragedies its adherents saw as being sidelined by Freud's abandonment of the seduction theory and prioritization of intrapsychic conflict. "By recognizing the unique suffering of the survivors of politically organized torture and of violence, including family violence and sexual abuse, [the trauma paradigm restores to] psychoanalysis . . . the social-reformist dimension of its legacy, one that was central to its early vitality as an intellectual movement." Haaken acknowledges the progressiveness of this model in "'break[ing] the silence' around professional collusion in such villainy" (63). But the critique she offers of the trauma paradigm is that it neglects the extent to which "the mind is an active agent in the defensive transformation of events" (68). What of the mind's imaginative elaborations of reality; the projection of internal conflicts onto the external world; sexual desire, including desire for an aggressor; and "transformative remembering"? These are the essence of Freudian psychoanalysis, she argues, and must not be dropped as unfortunate later developments.

Furthermore, if trauma's definition is fully encompassed by the notion that it is the mind's pathological response to an external shock, then the radical possibilities of the psychoanalytic model are obviated. For in that case trauma will be seen as an abnormal condition of the mind rather than as a figuration of the possibilities and limits of human fantasy and memory. Haaken is critical, therefore, of Herman's *Trauma and Recovery* on the grounds that it "constructs memory as a literal representation of past events" and in so doing "close[s] off" any recognition of the "mingling of disturbing events and their fantasy elaborations" (93). In other words, Haaken sees Herman as a literalist—all mental scenes that are judged true by their "envisioners" (here we need a neologism that is neutral as to whether the scenes reproduce real past events) are "flashbacks" and not inventions. Both this "literalist approach" to traumatic memory ("believing women") and the "social constructivist approach" (not minding women's avowals; what matters is psychic reality) are rejected by Haaken in favor of a "negotiated space for reconciling polarized claims" (8). She arrives, therefore, at a radically antibinarist formulation of incest memory: "In the realm of the symbolic, incest emerges as an insurgent form of female storytelling based on actual, historical trauma. But the very reality of incest, and rumors of incest, creates a generative space for metaphorical truths, for the vivifying of female boundary violations and bodily located threats to well-being" (13). Indeed, in a climate of antifeminist backlash including the denial of women's claims of childhood sexual assault, it is courageous for feminists to insist, as do Waites, Terr, Haaken, and Reviere, that trauma symptoms can encompass symbolic elaboration—the creation of scenes that pertain to actual trauma but do not correspond to it literally. It is crucially important to say, as does Haaken, that incest "creates a generative space for metaphorical truths."

The *Diagnostic and Statistical Manual of Mental Disorders* does not venture such ideas. The entry on post-traumatic stress disorder (the fullest account of the effects of trauma contained in *DSM-IV*) enumerates a set of diagnostic criteria including dreams, hallucinations, dissociative flashback episodes, intrusive recollections, and reenactments that result from the experience of trauma. However, one gathers that these mental constructions are thought to be veridical, since they are referred to as "recollections of the event," as "recurrent distressing dreams during which the event is replayed," or as being "triggered" by "events that resemble or symbolize an aspect of the traumatic event (e.g., . . . cold snowy weather or uniformed guards for survivors of death camps in cold climates)."[30] The preeminent reference work on mental disorders stops short of a fuller elaboration on the content of such mental constructions. It supposes no correspondence other than the most direct and simple between such constructions and the real traumatic events that occurred. It is left, then, to feminist psychological literature on trauma, and to the work of certain other pioneering memory researchers discussed below, to elaborate the features of the traumatic mindscape in all its complexities.

Imagine memory ranged along a continuum, with extremely veridical memories to the right, false memories to the left, and fantasies propped on reality but not perfectly reflective of it in the center.[31] People would surely be more comfortable if memories on the right were easily distinguishable from memories on the left and could be seen as completely separate, or if it were clear which memories belonged on the right and which on the left. But this is not the case. As the memory researcher John Kihlstrom writes, "[I]n the absence of independent corroboration no criteri[a] appear to distinguish reliably [among] accurate recollections and fabrications and confabulations."[32]

The furious professional and public debates of Freud's time reemerged in the 1980s and 1990s, with false/recovered memory as the most embattled site of the new "memory wars."[33] Popular media attention to the "problem" of "false memory" became intense in 1993, with newspapers and magazines reporting story after story of families sundered by a daughter's "false" accusations against her father, or of families struggling to come together again after a daughter's retraction of incest charges. The professional journal *Family Therapy Networker* reported that by 1994 over three hundred magazine and newspaper articles on "false memory" had appeared.[34] Numerous ads were sponsored by the False Memory Syndrome Foundation, an organization of parents and supportive professionals formed to combat the "growing wave of accusations of incest or sexual abuse brought on by adults who recovered 'memories' of events that families and people involved in the memories claim *just could not have happened.*"[35] Scientific studies denying the validity of repressed memory were written and reviewed, the most prominent being *The Myth of Repressed Memory: False Memories and Allegations of Sexual Abuse,* by Elizabeth Loftus and Katherine Ketcham, and *Making Monsters,* by Richard Ofshe and Ethan Watters.[36] Denunciations of the therapeutic "incest industry" abounded, attributing to feminist therapists financial and personal motives for planting incest memories in the minds of daughters whom the parents regarded as deluded victims of the therapists' manipulations. The *Frontline* documentary *Divided Memories* (Ofra Bikel, 1995), while ostensibly balanced in its investigation, "makes its point" (as one reviewer put it) against the credibility of recovered memory by telling the stories of distraught parents in the context of an investigation of fringe therapists who regard past life regression and recovered memory in the same light.[37] While these representative and mainstream pieces stopped short of denying the existence of actual incest in epidemic proportions, all were far less concerned with that criminal reality than with the mission to discredit what the most serious and scientifically legitimate among them would likely acknowledge to be the minority of cases in which the incest exists only in fantasy form.[38] As Judith Herman has written, "[R]epression, dissociation, and denial are phenomena of social as well as individual consciousness."[39]

On one side are those who believe, with Elizabeth Loftus, that memories cannot be lost and found and that "recovered" memories are therefore "false" memories created by ungrateful daughters or induced by overly zealous feminist therapists. Incest daughters and their therapists are embarked on a modern-day witchhunt, alleges the rhetoric of the well-entrenched False Memory Syndrome Foundation. On the other side are those who consider such attacks on adult survivors, their therapists, and the validity of their memories to be part of a misogynist backlash against perceived feminist threats to the patriarchal domination of women and girls. Abuse memories are either objectively true or true for all practical purposes, this side attests; "false memory syndrome" was invented to divert attention away from the continued prevalence of incest throughout all socioeconomic levels.

I contend that we must try to bear the vicissitudes of memory that find their expression along the continuum.[40] Fantasy constructions in memory are not, to adapt Saul Friedlander's words, an "obstacle to rational historiography"[41] but part and parcel of its character. And some contemporary research on memory, again especially psychoanalytically informed research, is explicitly illuminating with regard to the variability of memory. For example, John Kihlstrom, David G. Payne, and Jason M. Blackwell, along with feminist researchers including Terr, Waites, Haaken, and Reviere, have developed theories of memory that foreground its inherently interpretative or "reconstructive" nature: As Payne and Blackwell put it, "[M]emory errors are not bothersome anomalies to be explained away or minimized [or used to discredit testimony, I would add], but rather they reflect the normal processes by which we interpret the world around us."[42] These researchers propose that memory be thought of not in terms of the storage and retrieval of a discrete quantity of information but rather in terms of correspondence—and loss of correspondence—between recollections and actual past events.

Like Elizabeth Loftus, the psychologist Michael Nash upholds laboratory research results showing that people are quite capable of entertaining the illusion that they recall events that did not actually happen. But unlike Loftus, who has a tendency to portray all recovered memories as false,[43] Nash's research encompasses the wider implications of the "malleability of human memory and the fallibility of self-report."[44] According to Nash:

> Two broad types of mnemonic errors are possible when adult psychotherapy patients reflect on whether or not they were traumatized as children. They may believe they were not traumatized when in fact they were (false negative), or they may believe they were traumatized when in fact they were not (false positive). . . . [I]t is exceedingly important to realize that the problem of false positives and the problem of false negatives are distinct. . . . If patients sometimes report a traumatic event when it did not happen (a false positive), we are not required to reject the possibility that patients may fail to remember such an event when it *did* occur (a false negative).[45]

For one thing, the presence of the word *sometimes* in the passage "[I]f patients sometimes report a traumatic event when it did not happen . . ." implies that, for the most part, reports of traumatic events are reliable. This would make it wrong to dismiss all claims of recovered memory on the basis of the presence of some false ones. Moreover, by bringing up the possibility of the "false negative"—forgetting a trauma that really did happen— Nash shows that false positives fail to exhaust all possibilities for slips of memory. For example, an article published in the *Journal of Traumatic Stress* outlines a study in which 129 women with documented histories of child sexual abuse that occurred between the ages of 10 months and 12 years were interviewed. Of those, 38 percent had forgotten the abuse. Of the remaining women who remembered, 16 percent reported that they had for a period of time forgotten but subsequently recovered their memories.[46] Thus, during that time a "false negative" would have been recorded for those women.

These are the sort of distinctions for which Elaine Showalter in *Hystories: Hysterical Epidemics and Modern Media* fails to account. There she argues that "as we approach [the] millennium, the epidemics of hysterical disorders, imaginary illnesses, and hypnotically induced pseudomemories that have flooded the media seem to be reaching a high-water mark."[47] She includes a chapter on recovered memory among chapters on alien abduction, chronic fatigue syndrome, and satanic ritual abuse. This line-up has led some feminists to take issue with what they see as Showalter's irresponsible discounting of the crime of sexual assault on children, especially girls. But since Showalter says very clearly that childhood sexual assault is a crime that cannot be tolerated *where it is deemed to have occurred,* my own objection lies elsewhere.

What I along with others find troubling about the logic of the book is the casual interspersal of different phenomena grouped by topic and the absence of any effort to distinguish among them, or among their modalities of memory.[48] On the principle of similarity, Showalter's book places chapters on supposedly remembered phenomena for which there is absolutely no scientifically or independently confirmed evidence (alien abduction, satanic ritual abuse) alongside the chapter on recovered memory, which has been shown empirically to exist in some cases. But Showalter disregards such clinical research to concentrate on the plight of alleged perpetrators of sexual abuse of children. She writes, "If 5000 people—or five people, or one—are unjustly accused, that is important. It cannot be factored in as an allowable margin of error."[49] But what of the cases of genuine incest memory discounted because some false memories are just that? Is that an "allowable margin of error"? And what of the "margin of error" that results from conflating recovered memories with putative memories of alien abduction? Is that allowable? Moreover, what of memories that are false in their specific content but still allude to a different underlying trauma? Louise Armstrong, in *Rocking the Cradle of Sexual Abuse,* suggests that it may be more psychically comfortable, given the power relations of U.S. patriarchy, for a woman to invent a whole satanic cult than to accuse her own father.[50] Although Showalter approvingly mentions Armstrong's harsh criticism of the media circus around woman's victimhood, she neglects Armstrong's unequivocal opinion that repressed memory exists and her description of the social unpalatability of incest avowal. Showalter also neglects psychological literature that points to sexual abuse as the underlying trauma beneath screen memories of alien abduction and satanic ritual abuse.[51]

In my estimation, Showalter's mistake, which I believe to be profound, is that she does not consider the extreme variability of memory. In dismissing as false all the "hystories" in which memory is asserted and plays a part, she takes the "memory" out of recovered memory, replacing it in these blanket cases with something akin to "invention." It is neither correct nor adequate to link these scenarios on the basis of the gross supposed analogy that they are all cases of hysterical invention. Showalter's book teeters, therefore, on the left-hand edge of our continuum running between false memory and veridical memory.

In spite of the difficulties of holding in one's mind fine distinctions and seemingly contradictory premises, that is precisely what we must do to understand traumatic memory: abuse *and* confabulation happen; forgetting *and* making up are characteristics of trauma; ritual abuse, alien abduction, and recovered memory all have elements of fantasy, but these elements are not evenly distributed, nor are they autonomous of exogenous reality. Traumatic memories blur into one another on the continuum, and/or they have to be relocated, and/or they contain features that pertain to disparate places on the continuum, and/or we just can't tell where some of them belong. Traumatic memories must be unpacked and arrayed where they may be examined and where their scents of truth and artifice may be picked up. They will not be laundered, folded, and put away.

DISREMEMBERING

Wildly contradictory images and pseudomemories; memory friable, fallible, and frail; the variability of fantasy construction, and the memory continuum: How can we speak of these in all their complexity without getting tangled up in language and without reverting to the true memory/false memory binarism that is convenient but hopelessly specious? *Memory* is commonly understood to refer to a kind of realistic registration of past events, as if the mind were a passive photochemical surface. But *false memory* implies an impermeable wall between events and their mental representations. *Pseudomemory,* for its part, suggests that departures from veridicality are a special case rather than an inherent characteristic of traumatic memory. How can we conceptualize mental images and sounds that bear a relationship to past events, but a relationship that is oblique and not represented through simple imagistic transcription?

I propose that we continue to cultivate the connection between psychological and popular debates on memory and humanities-based cultural theory and criticism. And since I am less an interloper in the latter realm than in the former, I will adapt a term to be used here. The process described by psychological literature as that of conjuring mental images and sounds related to past events but altered in certain respects shall be termed "disremembering." Disremembering is not the same as not remembering. It is remembering with a difference. Amnesia could therefore be included under this rubric as a phenomenon that may describe an active process of repression of the memory of events rather than a nonpresence of memory. Furthermore, disremembering should be understood as a common feature of traumatic memory rather than as an anomaly.

The inspiration for use of the term *disremembering* comes from two sources: Toni Morrison's novel *Beloved* and the work of the cultural theorist José Muñoz. Morrison introduces the term in an offhand manner. The book's protagonist, Sethe, puts an occasional question to her mysterious houseguest, the corporeal ghost Beloved. "You disremember everything? I never knew my mother neither, but I saw her a couple of times. Did you never see yours?"[52] To suggest that one "disremembers everything" is more than a simple, evocative way to allude to forgetting. Beloved is both the manifestation of Sethe's two-year-old daughter whom she was forced to put to death eighteen years before and Sethe's African mother from whom she was torn. Thus, for literary critic Deborah Horvitz, Morrison's word evokes "the women whose stories are lost . . . 'disremembered,' meaning not only that they are forgotten, but also that they are dismembered, cut up and off, and not re-membered."[53] The term is linked with another term, *rememory,* that is used more frequently in the novel. Sethe explains that even if something is gone, a picture of it can stay, both in a person's memory and "out there, in the world."[54] "To 'rememory,'" interprets Caroline Rody, "is to use one's imaginative power to realize a latent, abiding connection to the past. 'Rememory' thus functions in Morrison's 'history' as a trope for the problem of reimagining one's heritage."[55] The two concepts are slightly mismatched twins. If rememory is a means of maintaining a picture of something that is absent, then disremembering may be a means of disassembling a picture of an absence. At the end of *Beloved*, the term returns to render the transubstantiation of a nonpresence: "Everybody knew what she was called, but nobody anywhere knew her name. Disremembered and unaccounted for, she cannot be lost because no one is looking for her. . . . By and by all trace is gone, and what is forgotten is not only the footprints but the water too and what it is down there. The rest is weather. Not the breath of the disremembered and unaccounted for, but wind in the eaves, or spring ice thawing too quickly."[56] A being is not gone after all but turned into the wisps of an ectoplasmic landscape: "the rest is weather." Through disremembering, "Morrison makes absence exquisitely tangible."[57]

If this "exquisite tangibility" is crucial for an understanding of the true complexity of memory and forgetting, so too is Muñoz's creation of a political context for a related term. Muñoz defines *disidentification* through his description of a performance piece by Cuban and Puerto Rican American artist Marga Gomez. During her performance, Gomez expresses her childhood attraction to the images of lesbian panelists who appeared on the David Susskind show, their identities masked by raincoats, dark glasses, and wigs. Muñoz explains that Gomez sees herself as having been both interpellated as a lesbian and repelled by the stereotypical images of the "lady homosexuals" as Susskind put it. Gomez's own performance is a restaging of a prior, troubling performance that is nonetheless key to her identity. As Muñoz explains, Gomez "performs her disidentificatory desire for this once toxic representation." Her "public performance of memory is a powerful disidentification with the history of lesbian stereotyping in the public sphere."[58] The elements that resonate with my discussion are reperformance, memory, counteractive desire, and toxicity. As discussed above, when one is traumatized, repeated images may present themselves as unbidden, unpleasant memories. But at the same time that such images may feel involuntarily imposed, they may engage a desire to remember more. The subject may want to enter therapy, be hypnotized, reflect continuously, or make a video.

The real events to which the reperformance refers are often elusive. Muñoz reveals that he, like Gomez, remembers being "mesmerized" in childhood by "talk-show deviants." He gives the example of hearing a televised Truman Capote make his mean-spirited comment that Jack Kerouac's work consisted of "typing," not "writing." But when Muñoz went back to check facts while preparing his book, he realized that Capote had made his remark on a show that aired initially eight years before Muñoz's birth. Muñoz speculates that he may have seen a rebroadcast or heard or read about the cutting comment later in life. In any case, he terms this mental impression of Capote on television a "disidentificatory memory" with "revisionary aspects."[59] It might also be an instance of disremembering. There is a genuine reference point to Muñoz's would-be memory, but the mental image he possesses elides the information that the show was a rerun (which he may not have known at the time) or that the would-be memory was constructed from conversation or printed words. The dismemory is fragmented and cut off.

As both Morrison's story of slavery and Muñoz's examples of gay subjectivity suggest, disremembering is not a whimsical practice but a survival strategy for minoritarian subjects. Disremembering can become urgent when events are personally unfathomable or socially unacceptable. Disremembering incest or the Holocaust is a survival strategy par excellence.

TRAUMA CINEMA

Films do not exactly "theorize" memory processes, but alongside psychological writing on trauma and memory (and alongside the mass-mediated public debates on the history of various catastrophes), the years from the 1980s to the present have seen the development of a theoretically informed "trauma cinema." By *trauma cinema* I mean a group of films that deal with a world-shattering event or events, whether public or personal. Furthermore, I define trauma films and videos as those that deal with traumatic events in a nonrealist mode characterized by disturbance and fragmentation of the films' narrative and stylistic regimes. Trauma films depart from "Hollywood classical realism," a highly evolved editorial, compositional, and narratological *illusionist* system (in spite of its name) that facilitates the identification of spectators with characters and purports to show the world as it is.[60] Trauma films, in contradistinction to this classical regime, "dismember" by drawing on innovative strategies for representing reality obliquely, by looking to mental processes for inspiration, and by incorporating self-reflexive devices to call attention to the friability of the scaffolding for audiovisual historiography.

The catalog of film topics encompassed by trauma cinema finds its best description—not coincidentally—in the list of diagnostic features for post-traumatic stress disorder that begins this chapter. Hayden White has made a similar list that samples what he calls the "holocaustal" event: "the two World Wars, the Great Depression, a growth in world population hitherto unimaginable, poverty and hunger on a scale never before experienced, pollution of the ecosphere by nuclear explosions . . . programs of genocide undertaken by societies utilizing scientific technology and rationalized procedures of government."[61]

One thinks, therefore, of certain well-known Vietnam- or World War II–themed films, including Francis Ford Coppola's pioneering *Apocalypse Now* (1979), Oliver Stone's *Platoon* (1986), and the opening of Steven Spielberg's *Saving Private Ryan* (1998), in which fragmented editing and the use of extreme camera angles create in viewers a sense of disorientation and moral ambiguity designed to echo the experience of combat trauma.[62] One thinks of *JFK* (Oliver Stone, 1991) (which White explicitly mentions) and *Thunderheart* (Michael Apted, 1992), in which catastrophic past events (the Kennedy assassination and the Wounded Knee Massacre respectively) intrude on linear narrative and disturb realist representation. One might also reflect on documentary films, including *The Thin Blue Line* and *Mr. Death* (Errol Morris, 1988, 1999), that are explicitly about how the past is difficult but perhaps not impossible to know and that use reenactment and extreme stylization to press this epistemological concern. Moreover, trauma cinema is an international and transnational phenomenon. Numerous entries exist, ranging from the striking early example of Alain Resnais's *Hiroshima, Mon Amour* (1959), a French-Japanese co-production combining documentary and fictional elements in an emotional meditation on memory for acts of war, through Milcho Manchevski's *Before the Rain* (1994), an English-French-Macedonian co-production that is a historical fiction, told achronologically, about a photojournalist who witnesses wartime violence in Bosnia and Macedonia. These films are linked as troubled retrospections on matters of cataclysmic history.

I would not give as much credence to Hayden White's claim that such holocaustal events of the twentieth century are "hitherto unimaginable" and fundamentally different in nature and size from disasters of prior centuries—that the "historical event" has undergone a "radical transformation"—if not for his concomitant claim that what has also changed is the "notion of the 'story.'" There has been a "revolution in representational practices known as cultural 'modernism' and the technologies of representation made possible by the electronics revolution."[63] Representational practices are a crucial factor, White argues, along with the "scope, scale, and depth" of events and our "dismantling of the concept of the event as an object of a specifically scientific kind of knowledge," in a new and more public historiography. "Post-industrial 'accidents'" such as the Challenger disaster (and now the explosion of the shuttle Columbia), Chernobyl, or the collision of three high-tech jets in an air show over Ramstein, Germany, are made even more "incomprehensible" by the sheer amount of photographic video coverage and by its increasing manipulability. "Modern electronic media," White writes, . . . "'explode' events before the eyes of viewers."[64] It is not that the events of which White speaks are unreal or unrepresentable. What they are, rather, is unrepresentable *in the realist mode*.[65]

The constituents of trauma cinema are found in many genres, modes, and national cinemas. In fact, trauma cinema "explodes" these categories in favor of an identity "possessed by the past"[66] and characterized by a fragmented style striated by fantasy constructions. How, then, to study this large and ever-expanding body of films?

Here I have elected to go to the vanguard of this new representational form described variously as traumatic or holocaustal. Contemporary experimental documentary practice, especially feminist and/or autobiographical, is in that vanguard. Stone, Apted, and Morris may not be leafing through the catalogs of alternative film and video distributors such as Women Make Movies or Video Data Bank (though I recommend their doing so), but they are not alone in their experimentation. For "probing the limits" of the filmic—and videographic—representation of traumatic past events has been for several decades a fully articulated project of feminist experimental autobiographical documentary theory and practice.

Daughter Rite (Michelle Citron, 1979), *Confessions of a Chameleon* and *First Person Plural* (Lynn Hershman, 1986, 1989), *Attic Secrets* (Heidi Bollock, 1998), *Family Gathering* (Lise Yasui, 1988), *History and Memory* (Rea Tajiri, 1991), and *Tak for Alt* (Laura Bialis, Broderick Fox, and Sarah Levy, 1999) are exemplary works, dealing respectively with incest, Japanese internment, and the Holocaust, that represent a growing list of (auto)biographical documentaries seeking appropriate expression for catastrophic events in the possibilities of nonclassical, basically nonfiction cinematic language. Such works broach their topics and breach the standards of journalistic documentary filmmaking by incorporating fictional and personal elements. And in that breach they discover new truths about the correlation between the objective mode of documentary production and mainstream history and about the potential of experimental documentary for historical understanding. For example, Rea Tajiri's *History and Memory* explores Japanese and Japanese American internment in the United States during World War II by combining official documents, unofficial documents (the relics, musings, and photographs of her own family members), and invented elements (a repeated sequence in which Tajiri plays her own mother performing an abstracted gesture the mother may never have performed). The resulting piece is counternarrative, counterhistorical, and all the more "true" for its deliberate inclusion of acknowledged fictionalizing and forgetting in a new historical record.

Writing about "postmodern documentaries" in her groundbreaking article "Mirrors without Memories: Truth, History, and the New Documentary," Linda Williams characterizes how these films refuse the realist mode while insisting that the events they depict are posed against a "horizon of truth": "What interests me particularly is the way a special few of these documentaries handle the problem of figuring traumatic historical truths inaccessible to representation by any simple or single 'mirror with a memory,' and how this mirror nevertheless operates in complicated and indirect refractions."[67] Historian Robert Rosenstone has also observed new historiographic possibilities in the audiovisual media: "[W]hile professional historians continue, with but a few exceptions, to write in a highly traditional manner, some little-known filmmakers and videographers have begun to create a kind of history that we can truly label post-modern, producing works that provide a distinctly new relationship to and a new way of making meaning of the traces of the past."[68]

In the idiom of documentary aesthetics, postmodern films and videos, and especially but not exclusively women's experimental autobiographies, tend to adopt a historiographic language analogous to what Saul Friedlander advocates for historical writing. That is, either overtly or implicitly these documentaries are built around an enunciative presence, comparable to Friedlander's "commentary," that "disrupt[s] the facile linear progression of the narration, introduce[s] alternate interpretations, question(s) any partial conclusion, [and] withstand[s] the need for closure."[69] Under this organization, the words and experience of any one interview subject or protagonist are qualified and correlated with other evidence and commentary presented in the film. They are "triangulated," as an anthropologist might say, with written documents and historical interpretation so that their partial truths and partial misperceptions may emerge in the place of a reductive true/false regime. For example, in *The Ties That Bind* (Su Friedrich, 1984), handwritten titles spell out phrases such as "so you did know" on a black background, thereby interrupting and qualifying a woman's contemporary oral testimony that as a young woman in Germany she did not know about the genocidal mission of the concentration camps. Structurally, these films and videos are each compiled of different types of footage, including archival, interview, and amateur footage, titles used as commentary, found fictional footage, and stylized reenactment. In keeping with Friedlander's description of traumatic history, these films and videos "introduce splintered or constantly recurring refractions of a traumatic past by using any number of different vantage points." [70]

Why are women's autobiographical documentaries a particular site of these "splintered" and "constantly recurring refractions"? Perhaps it is because, while women continue to be disenfranchised with regard to patriarchal politics, society, and culture (the minority of women senators, the existence of battered women and rape survivors, the minority of women feature film directors), our disenfranchisement is not complete. The women's movement and women's and feminist studies in the academy have provided a voluminous literature critical of oppressive patriarchal institutions, including language systems, and inventive when it comes to alternatives. Autobiography has fueled this turn. As Laura Marcus has written, "Autobiography has been a topic of central interest for literary and cultural theory in the past few decades, enlivened and in many cases transformed by feminist, working-class and black criticism and historiography. Autobiography was a central case for feminist criticism in the 1980s, exposing processes of exclusion and marginalisation in the construction of literary canons." [71] From this position of women's "otherness," the theory and practice of women's autobiographical writing emphasize the constructedness of the unified "self" upon which traditional male autobiographical writing is based. Women autobiographers and feminist theorists of autobiography are more likely to explore, instead of keeping at bay, what Lacan has shown to be the "primordial division of the speaking subject." [72] Feminist theories of literary autobiography also emphasize the artificiality of any firm division between public and private selves. [73] All these conceptual points are made in autobiographical writing itself, especially women's autobiography, by "an enlivening instability in both text and context." [74]

I propose, therefore, that we read the memory continuum in relation to what we might conceive of as a cinema continuum that reflects, in its entries, the provocative instabilities of trauma cinema. The two continua should be, not mapped in one-to-one correspondence, but read back and forth so that theories of memory and theories of film language may signal one another across a topography of truth and representation.

Imagine trauma cinema ranged across a continuum, with the most veridical forms of documentary to the right and fiction films in which there are invented characters and stories to the left. (Wholly imagined genres such as science fiction would range beyond the left-hand edge of this study.) Rightward we find those documentary devices making the strongest overt claims to authenticity: news-style direct-address interviews with experts or other "witnesses to history"; archival footage or photographs of historically important events; shots of primary historical artifacts (visas, ships logs, etc.), direct cinema material, or the documentation of events as they unfold spontaneously (for example, the George Holliday tape of the Rodney King beating); and reels of home movie footage. These elements are generally presented so as to maximize documentary's realist project. Then, as we move left (but not all the way left) we find reenactments by actors of real or past events; the use of staged events that would not be occurring if not for the purpose of being filmed (these are often deemed acceptable in documentary practice, as in the case of returning a Holocaust survivor to Auschwitz in order to film the experience, but are sometimes deemed to be outside the documentary rubric, as in the case of a game show where participants are real people and the outcome is unknown but a set-up scenario is being followed); the use of drawings, paintings, or even paper cutouts (as in Jan Oxenberg's *Thank You and Good Night,* 1991) to provide commentary on past events; abstract sequences where moving camera shots and rapid editing combine with patterns of color and volume to evoke internal states; and the representation of dreams, hallucinations, stories, and fantasies.

The middle area is of great interest here, and the more closely one studies documentary and fictional modes, the more it becomes obvious that "pure documentary" and "pure fiction" are heuristic categories. For example, the cinema verité (cinema truth) form was pioneered in the United States by Robert Drew, who stressed the dramatic or "story" element of even "fly-on-the-wall" documentaries.[75] And Vivian Sobchack, who writes mostly about fiction films, has emphasized the traces of the real they do contain. The (actual) death of the rabbit in the poaching scene in Jean Renoir's *Rules of the Game* (1939) becomes Sobchack's example of a momentary instance when our attention is drawn to fiction film's thoroughgoing correspondence to the real world.[76] Characters are embodied by real people (actors) after all, and fiction films are usually set within a recognizable reality of workplace and family patterns, even when they are not explicitly historical.

Michael Renov has adopted the term *fictive* to describe the many elements of "creative intervention" that inform nonfiction film: "Among these fictive ingredients we may include the construction of character (with Nanook as the first example) emerging through recourse to ideal and imagined categories of hero or genius, the use of poetic language, narration, or musical accompaniment to heighten emotional impact or the creation of suspense via the agency of embedded narratives (e.g., tales told by interview subjects) or various dramatic arcs (here, the 'crisis structure' comes to mind). . . . With regard to the complex relations between fiction and documentary, it might be said that the two domains *inhabit* one another."[77]

Bill Nichols's *Representing Reality,* appearing in 1991 after a long hiatus in the publication of single-author books about documentary, contains a second part entitled "Documentary: A *Fiction* (Un)Like Any Other" (emphasis mine). There, and in the book as a whole, Nichols grapples with the problem of how to account for the "closely intertwined relationships between documentary and fiction" without vacating the verities that do inhere in the documentary form.[78]

Here we will concentrate on documentary films that, in their chosen strategies of representation, refuse to be shoved to the right-hand side of the continuum but refuse as well any suggestion that they are not, therefore, aimed at certain human truths that are non-negotiable. In other words, trauma documentaries warp the continuum by combining alternative strategies with those conventions that have established documentary as a nonfiction mode. They signal the abjection of supposedly objective forms of filmmaking in the process of disremembering history.

Reading back and forth between memory discourses and trauma cinema can make resonant the representational strategies deployed. For example, a scholar of history and memory told me she was offended by the use of reenactment in the film biography *Tak for Alt,* about Holocaust survivor Judy Meisel (discussed further in chapter 5). In the contested sequences, actors replay fragments of childhood scenes that Meisel remembers and recounts: we see brief snippets of Judy's mother's hands kneading and braiding challah dough and lighting the Sabbath candles. If filmmakers are allowed to combine genuine and fictive footage, the scholar argued, won't that make us vulnerable to charges that all Holocaust footage is manipulated?

I believe the risk is worth taking, and I appreciate the film's particular use of reenactment. For one thing, there is no attempt to pass off the reenacted sequences as genuinely documentary. In the context of the life being

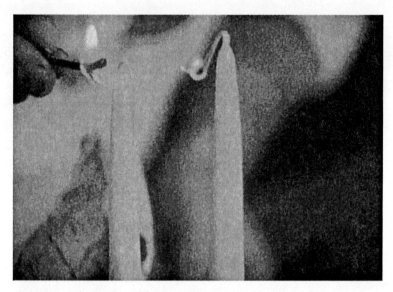

Figure 1. Lighting the Sabbath candles, reenacted; *Tak for Alt*.

narrated, we realize that even if there had been home movies taken of everyday scenes in Jewish family life, the footage probably would not be extant today.[79] Thus, the images evoke Judy's happy childhood before deportation while at the same time standing as an obvious substitute for all that has been lost. We "know more," as Dori Laub might say, because we know what can no longer be represented except through flights of imagination. In the challah sequence, *Tak for Alt* disremembers what Judy identifies as veridical memory. I think we need more, not fewer, Holocaust documentaries that incorporate reenactment, staging, and other fictive strategies through which the Holocaust may be remembered and disremembered.

Because reenactment footage is to a greater or lesser extent "inauthentic," it must be located somewhere in the middle of the trauma cinema continuum. The challah sequences are complicated and illustrate the unevenness of the parallel memory and cinema continua because while Judy's memory supplies images of the actual people from her past, the film must resort to the use of actors. The latter is a film "fantasy" propped on reality: we have no existing image of Judy's mother's hands, but we have every reason to believe that the woman did bake challah in the years before she went to her death in the gas chamber at the Stutthoff concentration camp.

But even if she had not baked challah (if the sequence were not only inauthentic but false), I might still defend the use of such a fiction—if it were clearly presented as such—for its evocation of Jewish ritual. For it would be a fantasy pertaining to other cases, if not to her own, and pertaining as well to an imaginative community that such an hypothetical film might help to constitute. Conversely, if the footage were genuine home movie footage, I would emphasize that fantasy elements still do inform the film's truth value. As it is, the choice to show hands with challah and the placement of that sequence in relation to other sequences in the film allude to an active (if unconscious) process of memory and/or film work at a distance of space and time from the past events to which the images relate.

The use of reenacted footage does not produce meaning identical to the use of archival footage. The difference makes a difference. But the point is not to sort out the legitimate representation from the illegitimate one but to read, in individual cases *and* in the differential, the workings of history, memory, and fantasy.

This book, therefore, will conduct close textual analyses of selected trauma films, analyzed in their film historical context and by way of concepts gleaned from contemporary memory theories. Since father-daughter incest (the most threatening category of childhood sexual abuse) has provoked the richest theoretical lode in psychological literature, the most contentious public discourse, and the grounds for a significant area of filmic representation, the next three chapters (Part II) will be devoted to Hollywood films, television movies, and experimental documentaries on that theme. The final two chapters (Part III) will expand the implications of fantasy-friendly conceptions of truth by studying new documentary works on the subject of the Holocaust.

The choice to turn from the family trauma films of Part II to the public historical documentaries of Part III is political. By adopting this configuration, I hope to show that the two categories are not completely unlike one another in their application of truthful and fantasied constructions. Public history owes a debt to personal memory, and personal memory is embedded within a social context. Of course, as I have acknowledged in the preface, the situations of children being abused in their homes, children and parents being wrested from their homes and confined to camps, and whole Jewish populations being the intended target of the Nazis' Final Solution have their respective and meaningful historical specificity. But we have much to gain from the joint consideration of incest and Holocaust remembrance. The first enunciations in the 1980s of the similar effects of the victimization of girls in their homes and of the traumatization of soldiers on the battlefield brought real advances in the literature on traumatic memory as psychiatrists and psychologists pooled their resources. I expect that the public attacks beginning in the mid-1990s on women's recovered memories will have a silver lining in the form of more studies of the fantasy elements that inhere not only in memories held by childhood sexual abuse survivors but in those held by wartime survivors as well. For example, the common wisdom that soldiers' accounts of wartime experiences are unproblematically veridical[80] is changing. Of course, he was the perpetrator and not the victim, but former senator Bob Kerrey's account of a commando raid on an isolated hamlet in Vietnam's Mekong Delta in which thirteen unarmed women and children were killed has been called into question. Alternative accounts, including that of a fellow commando and that of a Vietnamese woman witness, differ markedly from Kerrey's. These latter individuals characterize the raid as an atrocity of criminal proportions. Kerrey, nearly at a loss to explain the difference, offers the following: "Please understand," he entreats, "that my memory of this event is clouded by the fog of the evening, age and desire." "It's entirely possible that I'm blacking a lot of it out"—and adding to the scene, I would hazard.[81] A film about the subject would work best if it adopted a trauma aesthetic. In any case, by moving between film and video representations of incest and representations of the Holocaust, I hope to illuminate what trauma cinema, in its fragmented nonlinearity, has to teach us about the connections between history and memory.

Chapter 2 will provide a history of the representation—and, significantly, the elision—of the incest theme in classical Hollywood cinema. Incest, however, was not vaporized but dissociated. It may be gone from finished versions of the films *Kings Row* (Sam Wood, 1942) and *Freud* (John Huston, 1962), but it abides in the extratextual elements of these films, which include a best-selling novel, a movie trailer, numerous script versions, Freudian case histories, and correspondence between psychiatrists and motion picture personnel.

In the 1980s and 1990s feminist writing and activism influenced television programming to take up the hidden topic of incest. But chapter 3's close analysis of the TV movies *Sybil* (Daniel Petrie, 1976), *Shattered Trust: The Shari Karney Story* (Bill Corcoran, 1993), and *Liar, Liar* (Jorge Montesi, 1992), as well as the *Frontline* television documentary *Divided Memories*, argues that these texts retain the true/false dichotomy that brought historiography to its impasse. The impasse is surmounted in the vanguard autobiographical documentaries *Daughter Rite*, the *Electronic Diary* series (Lynn

Hershman, 1984–96), *Some Nudity Required* (Odette Springer, 1998), and *Just, Melvin* (James Ronald Whitney, 2000), examined in chapter 4. Courageously, these films unimpeachably and impeachably testify to the necessary imbrication of truth and fantasy in traumatic historiography.

The premise of Part III is that the personal is the public historical. Chapter 5 compares the Oscar-winning documentary *The Last Days* (James Moll, 1998), structured around the testimonies of five Hungarian Holocaust survivors, to its experimental counterparts *Shoah* (Claude Lanzmann, 1985), *The March* (Abraham Ravett, 1999), and *Tak for Alt.* The chapter argues the particular worth of (auto)biographical works such as these latter ones that breach the strict positivist conventions of Holocaust documentaries in the attempt to get at the deeper truths of trauma and memory. Chapter 6 reconsiders the Holocaust and Holocaust representation from a generational remove. Although survivors are still featured in *Everything's for You* (Abraham Ravett, 1989) and *Second Generation Video* (Joshua Hirsch, 1995), these films, and the Errol Morris documentary *Mr. Death,* emphasize the difficulties peculiar to second-generation disremembering rather than what the survivors themselves faced and are left with.

This, then, is a book about strange bedfellows. It seeks to work through continuing resistance to thinking about certain terms in relation to one another, namely, contemporary psychology and cinema, feminism and historiography, experimental filmmaking and commercial features, documentary and fiction film, personal history and public history, and familial and war-related trauma. If we are to understand how retrospective representational forms meditate on catastrophe, we must grapple with the magnetic push-pull of these forceful terms.

PART II

Personal Memory: The Case of Incest

TWO

The Excision of Incest from Classical Hollywood Cinema

Kings Row and Freud

In this book, spiced with harlots, idiots, nymphomaniacs and homosexuals, there are three fathers who become sexually enamored of
their daughters; . . . a sadistic doctor who performs unnecessary operations for the gloating pleasure of seeing his patients suffer to
the human breaking point, and a whole horde of halfwitted, sensual
creatures preoccupied with sex.

> *Daily News,* June 7, 1940; from a review
> of the best-selling novel *Kings Row,* by Henry Bellamann

It is difficult to imagine how a novel described this way could be adapted
to the screen to meet the standards of the Hollywood motion picture Production Code then in force.[1] Yet the film *Kings Row* (Sam Wood) did appear in 1942—in a version from which any overt mention of the incestuous
relationships so prominent in the novel had been carefully excised.[2]

Likewise, incest was excised from the finished version of the John Huston
film *Freud* (1962).[3] In the original Jean-Paul Sartre script dated 1959,[4] in the
first draft screenplay by Charles Kaufman and Wolfgang Reinhardt dated
April 26, 1961, in the final screenplay dated August 9, 1961,[5] and reportedly
in the previewed version of the film itself,[6] there exists a character, Magda,
who relates an incestuous sexual experience that is never relegated either to
lie or to fantasy. Indeed, her claims are confirmed by the demeanor of her
father, in whose presence she tells of the sexual abuse, and by the abreac-
tion of her hysterical symptoms that results from her revelation.

But Magda's case is the odd one out in a collection of cases that purport to disprove the reality of incestuous abuse and establish the existence of childhood sexual desire as a fantasy construction. As the character Freud states "emphatically" to the character Dr. Joseph Breuer, "The case of Magda was an exception, a hideous freak. All the other patients who recalled an aggression by an adult gave expression to a fantasy. . . . [T]hey 'dreamed it up' as we say."[7] Moreover, in the final film version, the character of Magda has been superseded by the character of Cecily (Susannah York), who is generally taken to be a composite of Anna O. and other subjects whose case histories became *Studies on Hysteria*.[8] With Cecily, the suggestion of incest is broached only to be revoked.

These changes were deliberate, made to conform to the standards of the day, and at the urging of Production Code Administration (PCA) personnel. In a memo on the *Freud* script, Geoffrey M. Shurlock, head of the PCA at the time, wrote that they might have to withhold a Code Seal for the film "because of this highly clinical nature of this script, dealing as it does with all sorts of incestuous relations and other sexual aberrations."[9]

That *Freud* is also a biopic adds further interest to this investigation of the fate of movie incest, for the abandonment of the incest theme by film fictions resonates unmistakably with another abandonment: that of the so-called seduction theory (attributing the etiology of hysteria to incestuous childhood molestation) in what I characterized in chapter 1 as a conservative version of the intellectual history of psychoanalysis. Belief in the reality of childhood molestation supposedly had to be left behind to enable a theory of fantasy. Incest posed a difficulty to the operations of scenarization and censorship in Freud, the theory, as well as *Freud*, the movie.

But in neither case was abandonment complete. Such overturnings or excisions are radical surgeries. They leave behind at the site of the incision a kind of textual scarring and phantom presence. My analysis proceeds, then, from the position that a textual excision can serve as what Ned Lukacher has termed a "repressive ruse"—a strategy to give covert expression to a deeply troubling subject.[10] Watching *Kings Row*, we do receive intimations of incest, which in *Freud* (the later of the two films) are even more overt.

Moreover, there is always the possibility of a resurgence of the complaint of incest. The absence of childhood sexual assault from Hollywood films is striking. But so is its entangled presence, seen in the subsidiary materials surrounding the films: a source novel, reviews, numerous script versions, a movie trailer, censorship documents, and psychoanalytic writings on the subject. In this expanded corpus one may indeed discern the presence of childhood sexual assault.

This chapter, then, presents *Kings Row* and *Freud* as case studies of postwar Hollywood representation/prohibition of incest. Later, made-for-TV movies would breach the taboo against communicating about incest (chapter 3), as would experimental documentaries (chapter 4). But *Kings Row* and *Freud* represent very well how the topic of incest was once treated.

WHAT IS THERE WHERE INCEST MIGHT HAVE BEEN?

With the banishment of the explicit incest theme, the film version of *Kings Row* stands as an exceptionally good example of how classical Hollywood films found constructive means to represent what could not be (represented).[11] The story, set in a midwestern town, revolves around two families, each composed of a doctor, his wife, and an only daughter. Not much is known about Dr. Tower (Claude Rains), who is relatively new to the town when the story begins. He is considered brilliant but is no longer practicing. His wife is confined to the house for unexplained reasons, and near the beginning of the story he pulls his daughter Cassandra out of school and confines *her* to the house. In the course of the story, the wife dies, and, near its middle, Dr. Tower kills his now grown and stunningly beautiful daughter (played by Betty Fields) and commits suicide. Acting as a surrogate father, Dr. Tower bequeaths his estate to a young man, Parris Mitchell (Robert Cummings), the protagonist of our story. Parris had been studying medicine with Dr. Tower in preparation for going to Vienna to study psychiatry, and he had been involved in a secret affair with Cassandra, an affair supposedly known only to Parris's best friend, Drake McHugh (Ronald Reagan).

Dr. Tower is a brilliant physician, a passionate but highly controlled man—until he murders his daughter, that is. Where does this murderousness come from, wonders Parris? Luckily Dr. Tower has left a diary that Parris finds, reads, and relates to Drake McHugh. In the novel, the revelation is that Dr. Tower perpetrated incest on his daughter Cassie.

PARRIS: I have to tell you first it looks like he'd been going kind of crazy for a long time. . . . Well, not the usual kind of crazy. He was so proud of his intelligence that he began to think he was better than anybody else, and beyond any kind of law that—you know—that keeps us all kind of in place.

DRAKE: Just crazy—plain crazy, if that's so, Parris.

PARRIS: No, not just *plain* crazy. . . . Drake, do you know what incest is?

DRAKE: You mean father and daughter. Was Dr. Tower—?

PARRIS: (*Nodding.*) Incest was at the bottom of this last phase of the whole business.[12]

The film version, however, presents more attenuated relationships all the way around by erasing the novel's portrayal of incest and of the more obvious sexual rivalry between Dr. Tower and Parris over Cassandra. In the film version, the explanation for Dr. Tower's actions is the madness of his wife and, increasingly, that of his daughter. As Parris reads in Dr. Tower's journal, "Today, I noticed the first sign in Cassie . . . Dementia Praecox." Dr. Tower's homicide, or so the filmic explanation goes, was a kind of mercy killing carried out for Cassie herself and for Parris. Dr. Tower had known of the affair and had killed his daughter to protect Parris from the kind of stunted and secluded life he himself had been forced to lead due to the insanity of his wife.

Where there was incest now there is denial, smoldering rage, and murderousness. The novel's father-as-incest-perpetrator is transformed by the film into a father with the necessary personal restraint to protect others against the seductiveness of his daughter, an appeal he clearly recognizes but presumably does not feel. On behalf of the father, the film perpetrates a denial: that of the *father's* active seduction of his daughter.

How, then, can we come to grips with the father's violence? There is another doctor in the town of Kings Row: Dr. Gordon (Charles Coburn), the father of Louise (Nancy Coleman). He is also enraged by his daughter and, in particular, by his daughter's account of his own past actions. It is this second father-daughter pair, I will argue, that represents in symbolic fashion the implicit sexuality of some father-daughter relationships and represents as well the way in which the traumatic past becomes legible in violent actions in the present.

In her book *Flashbacks in Film*, Maureen Turim defines the flashback as "a privileged moment in unfolding that juxtaposes different moments of temporal reference. A juncture is wrought between present and past and two concepts are implied in this juncture: memory and history."[13] *Kings Row* does not use flashbacks per se, but it does include sequences introducing Parris, Drake, Cassie, and Louise as children in addition to the main action of the film, which portrays—across a temporal ellipsis—these characters as adults.

Once an adult, our protagonist, Parris Mitchell, is given the dilemma of having to evaluate contradictory claims to memory and historical truth in order to decide how to proceed in the present. At the enunciative level, the film places the past at stake for the present and yet withholds any enabling return to the past such as would be represented in a flashback. But the very absence of the flashback, in conjunction with frequent allusions to the past, actually enhances the privileging of memory and history in *Kings Row*.

In the portion of the childhood sequences concerning Dr. Gordon, young Parris and his friend Drake McHugh come upon another boy crying on the sidewalk in front of his house. The boy tearfully relates that Dr. Gordon is inside operating on his father without anesthetic, ostensibly because the man's bad heart will not hold up to anesthetic procedures. Horrible screams emanate from the house, and the boy runs up the steps to pound futilely on the closed and locked door. We, like the boys, are aware of a catastrophic event but barred from an eyewitness view. Furthermore, the nearly decade-long ellipsis withholds the outcome of the event, which is revealed later: the boy's father died in agony.

But eyewitness evidence and corroboration, just what we have been denied, will become crucial to determinations of character credibility when an accident occurs. Drake McHugh, the object of Louise Gordon's unrequited love, falls onto the train tracks and is operated on by Dr. Gordon, who amputates both of his legs. Louise learns from a man at the scene that her father has operated unnecessarily, and she surmises that he has done so out of disgust for Drake's womanizing, and more particularly because of his animosity toward Drake for courting Louise. She accuses her father of a whole career of such unnecessary and punitive operations, going back to the long-ago operation on the boy's father who screamed behind closed doors.

The problem faced by Parris as a young and pioneering psychiatrist is to weigh the validity of Louise's version of the past. Is her accusation of her father legitimate, as she attests, or is it the invention or false memory of a diseased mind, as her surgeon father attests? Should she be believed or institutionalized? Is the father a crazed and barbaric surgeon willing to trade his daughter's life for his own, or is he a decent man, victim of his daughter's deluded fantasies?

These are some of the questions brought up by the film and echoed eerily in the broader filmic and social discourses around abuse allegations. In the case of *Kings Row* there is a suggested reading. The spectator witnesses a moment in which Dr. Gordon, confronted by Louise with her knowledge of his punitive surgeries, strikes his daughter in the face. In this way, we become witnesses to the telling violence of the present, even though we are barred by a gap in time and the mise-en-scène from the operating theaters of the past. Louise's version of her father's past abuses of others is thus corroborated by his demonstrated capability of violence toward her. The significant scene is a transferential one in which the actions of the present reenact the conflicts of the past, but in a changed manner and with different people in the crucial roles. Still further indirection results from the fact that our view of the slap is blocked by the body positions of the actors. Joseph Breen, of the PCA, guided the handling of this choreography. In a letter to Jack Warner he indicated that "this action of Dr. Gordon striking Louise should be masked, [since if it is] done in a full shot it will be deleted by the censor boards."[14] One can only speculate to what extent his conscious or unconscious aim was to mitigate the indictment of this hotheaded criminal father.

But what light can the treatment of Louise shed on that of Cassie? In *Kings Row* we have two doctors' daughters whose lives are compared in the story; two daughters exposed to the rage of their fathers; two daughters whose mental states are called into question. In both cases, attributions of paternal abuse stand or fall on the basis of whether the young woman in question is judged sane or insane. Louise's case is not literally or even implicitly one of childhood sexual abuse. But sexual jealousy is nevertheless an overdetermined meaning of the father-daughter pair. Dr. Gordon didn't actually molest Louise, he just cut off the legs of the man she loved. One can understand, according to this symbolic logic, the desire of Production Code administrators to "mask" the action of Dr. Gordon striking Louise. For that action, masked though it may be, is the mark not only of past abuses that cannot be represented but also of sexual jealousy that is suggested but simultaneously denied in the case of Louise as in that of Cassandra.

But what of Cassandra Tower's perspective? Another myth suggests itself. The entry for Cassandra in a mythology reference book published contemporaneously with the novel *Kings Row* tells us that "Cassandra, one of Priam's daughters, was a prophetess. Apollo had loved her and given her the power to foretell the future. Later he turned against her because she refused his love, and although he could not take back his gift . . . he made it of no account: no one ever believed her. . . . It was her fate always to know the disaster that was coming and be unable to avert it."[15]

When the Greeks sacked Troy, they tore Cassandra from the altar of

Athena's temple and gave her to Agamemnon, for she was "very beautiful, but very strange-looking . . . the flower of all captive women." But when she was about to enter the house of the son of Atreus she looked around "wildly" and cried out, "I hear children crying. . . . Crying for wounds that bleed. A father feasted—and the flesh [was] his children." And as the mythological reference continues, "Cassandra cried out that on that very day two more deaths would be added to the list, one her own."[16]

The characterization of Cassandra Tower in *Kings Row* (both film and novel) follows this mythical model rather closely. She is a "captive woman," "very beautiful but very strange." She is confined to her home, a home in which a father could be said to "feast" on a child and in which that child is finally murdered. Most interesting is the role of the character Cassandra Tower vis-à-vis the enunciative process of the film as laid out in the opening sequence; for while Parris enacts history, Cassandra predicts its shape.

The film's opening suggests Cassandra's embarcation on a knowing but fateful journey that proceeds against the flow of the film's alternate work to deny her sexual exploitation. As the opening titles end, a horse-drawn wagon surges across the frame, obscuring a sign that, when revealed a moment later, protests rather a lot: "Kings Row, 1890, A good town, a good clean town, a good clean town to live in, and a good place to raise your children." Soon Cassie Tower appears with Parris Mitchell behind, filing out of the schoolhouse. The film's first dissolve brings us to her: Cassie posed seductively by a tree in long shot and close-up and long shot again as Parris jumps down into the frame. The mise-en-scène and editing conspire to let Cassie lead and Parris follow as they arrive at Parris's pond for an intimate splash. Cassie asks Parris to unfasten the back of her dress, acknowledges that "girls have to go in gradual," and states that her papa will take a switch to her if he finds out: a risked whipping that may read retrospectively as an early example of presumed sexual jealousy.

These connotations are emphasized in the scene in which a crying Cassie, under the tree at the edge of Parris's property for the last time ever, tells Parris that she has been pulled out of school and issues her prediction: "Maybe I can't ever go anywhere. Maybe I'll just have to stay home like Mama does all the time." In fact, Cassie's words do predict the way in which she will be used "like mama," and they condense the Cassandra myth, putting together the dangers of the home, the cries of children, sexual captivity, and death. Of course, the excision of father-daughter incest from the literal film plot renders the full import of Cassandra Tower's predictions unrecognizable to her fictional contemporaries, to those cinema goers who had not read the novel, and to those who refuse to read between the images. But her predictions may remain legible, as we have seen, to the readers of the Cassandra myth and those open to the parallels the film implicitly draws between the two doctors' families.

I have indicated that a temporal ellipsis exists between past and present or between scenes of childhood and scenes of adulthood. What we see in the two halves of this divide are, first, the receding feet of Parris Mitchell as he ascends the few steps up and over the fence toward home and, second, across a dissolve, the approaching feet of Parris as he comes back over the fence and walks into close-up—now a young man. The dissolve is a kind of textual scar that results from a suture. As the join between two temporally uncontiguous sequences, it alludes to what is missing. In fact, this ellipsis occurs immediately following Cassie's tearful confession, which itself follows the sequence in which Parris and Drake McHugh overhear the screams of the man being operated on. Thus the confession may be seen, on a structural level, as having propelled Parris's entry into adulthood and its attendant sexual knowledge. The film's structure thereby leaves to Parris, and the audience, the task of determining the specific nature of men's actions in the intervening years. We are aided in this determination by the knowledge that Louise's accusations against her surgeon father are borne out by characters and narrative. If we accept the parallels between the two families, we may read the actions of Cassandra's father as being more self-interested than merciful and more rather than less sexually motivated. He is the protagonist of a perpetrator's story, as constituted by the complex grammar of the film's narrative and structure.

The structuring principle of *Freud* is more substitution than elision. Near the end of the film, Freud (Montgomery Clift) prods Cecily to recall an occasion of incest from her past. Handled as a flashback accompanied by the adult Cecily's voice-over narration, the incestuous act she recounts is simultaneously depicted and denied. A dissolve to the child Cecily framed in a hand mirror opens the sequence. There follows a cut to Herr Koertner, Cecily's father, carrying his daughter to his bedroom, laying her down on his bed, and removing her shoes and socks. "Is that when he promised you the doll?" Freud inquires. "Yes. No. No, it was later in the night when I woke up and cried," responds Cecily. "Why were you crying in the middle of the night?" asks Freud. In response to this question we share young Cecily's view of her father as he emerges from the bathroom and comes toward her on the bed, looming up out of a low angle shot. "Tall like a tower," she narrates, as her father turns out the light. As the screen fades to a brief interval of black, we hear

Cecily's voice describing, "strong as a god when he embraced me." "And he promised you a doll if you wouldn't tell," finishes Freud. The cries of a child and the snippet of a preliminary image evoke the incestuous act at the same time that the blank screen—the artificial replacement for live vision—insists on its cinematic unrepresentability.

But there is more to come. Cecily appears cured, but, inexplicably, she is still attached to the doll she should logically abhor as the reminder of her molestation. In a response that seems both self-absorbed and simultaneously radical for its acknowledgment that the analyst too has a psychological makeup, Freud searches for the solution to Cecily's conundrum in his own psychosexual history. He discovers that a memory he has been holding of his own father molesting his sister during a train trip is in fact false, brought into being by his own childhood desire for his mother and jealousy of the father who "took her away." The "false" memory of the father as incest perpetrator is not depicted visually except for the boy's response: in close-up we see him scream, the sound provided by the train's whistle. The "true" memory *is* visually depicted: the child Sigi watches his mother abandon him in his hotel bedroom in order to join his father. "I invented a theory to dishonor [my father]," Freud concludes.

Thus armed with the material of his self-analysis, Freud returns to the case of Cecily, and a reconstructed version of the same supposed incest scene follows. "Shall I tell you a story?" offers Freud to the grown-up Cecily. In the "story" he tells, which is represented in another flashback, the bedroom is replaced by the parlor and a child's bed, and the (unrepresented) molestation is replaced by an accomplished and solicitous father.[17] Thus, the story that is ostensibly Cecily's is re-presented with Freud as *metteur en scène* and narrator of events at which he was not present. This shift in authorial attribution explains, retrospectively, the pensive close-up that immediately precedes Cecily's original account of the past events. The close-up is of Freud, and it is he who will preside, ultimately, over the nuances that undermine Cecily's accusation of her father. In these two sequences, then, the indexical nature of cinematic representation—what we see enacted seems so true—acts to shore up the validity of psychoanalytic reconstruction as it is presented in the film.[18]

DENIAL, RAGE, AND PINNING DOWN THE PATER

This shift from the child's (Cecily/Sigi's) perspective to the adult male's (Herr Doktor Freud's) perspective can also be seen in the real Freud's writing. In a letter to Wilhelm Fliess about a dream in which he felt "over-affectionately" toward his own daughter Mathilde (aged eleven at the time), Freud refuses to interpret the dream as evidence of the commonplace nature of fathers' incestuous wishes toward daughters. Instead he interprets the dream as the fulfillment of "my wish [which he had come to see as being unfounded] to pin down a father as the originator of neurosis and put an end to my persistent doubts."[19] Charles Bernheimer has aptly observed of this explanation that, by "interpreting his dream as a confirmation of a purely theoretical desire, [Freud] displaces his incestuous impulse into the realm of theory [and] exonerates himself from a guilty complicity in male fantasies of seduction."[20] Thus, in this case, as in the film, Freud shifts the terms of the argument, to the benefit of the father's reputation, by denying not only the occurrence of incest but also any incestuous wishes that might originate with the father.

But here we come up against an interesting contradiction. For, in his 1918 essay "From the History of an Infantile Neurosis" (the Wolf Man case), Freud advocates the need to *reaffirm* the psychologically formative power of traumatic events that actually happened. With reference to the question of whether a patient's neurosis could be based, in a deferred manner, on his having actually witnessed his parents' intercourse *a tergo,* Freud argues that it would be wrong merely to attribute the fantasy to the analyst's interpretation and to discount the reality of the patient's experience. This, he suggests, would fail to account for the gradualness of the fantasy's construction, for the construction's independence of the physician's incentive, for its role in the later synthesis of the analysis, and for the sheer ingenuity such a construction would have required of the analyst.[21] Freud also takes this opportunity to clarify that his notion "of a turning away from reality, of a substitutive satisfaction obtained in phantasy," is not the whole of his theory, which resides as well in the assertion that fantasies must be constructed from "material which has been acquired from some source or other."[22] The film *Freud,* therefore, is unlike the writings of the real Freud in its treatment of "acquired material" from Cecily's past. In the film, this material is regarded not as a productive source for substitutive fantasies but as patently false information that must be rejected and replaced.

The film's conservatism with regard to the role of real traumatic experience in the etiology of "infantile neurosis" may also be highlighted with reference to psychoanalytic findings published in the United States around the time of the film's release. The eminent psychoanalyst Phyllis Greenacre, to take a notable example, dealt explicitly with the significance of actual infantile sexual trauma in the mainstream *Journal of the American Psychoanalytic Association*.[23] Her essay "The Influence of Infantile Trauma on Genetic Patterns" begins by acknowledging the traditional view that "it is of little or no significance whether or not [a sexual trauma] has actually occurred, its only significance being determined by the nature of the accompanying fantasy."[24] But the essay proceeds with an equally considered account of the particular relevance of actual sexual trauma as encountered in Greenacre's own clinical work. "While the underlying fantasy . . . is of primary importance, . . . its later derivatives may be considerably influenced by whether or not it has been carried out in any active way."[25] In an actual traumatic experience, "the child may be confronted with a different reality than his fantasy had quite represented . . . an exaggerated, distorted, or particularly intensified form of apparent confirmation."[26] In this formulation, fantasy initially predates but can be altered by real events.

Moreover, according to Greenacre, "The denial that the actuality of a sexual event in childhood had *any* importance at all above that of the fantasy itself may be held to in proportion to the power of the wish to have it happen."[27] Under the traditional interpretation of psychoanalytic theory, the "wish to make it happen" is that of the daughter. The daughter is the seductress. But if it is true, as Greenacre states, that the denial that anything occurred masks the incestuous desire for something to occur, then the desire must be attributed as much to the fathers/analysts, who have constructed a theory to deny that desire, as to the daughters to whom desire is regularly attributed. In other words, belief that sexual seduction is only important as fantasy and not for its real ramifications may be held in proportion to the power of the father's own incestuous wish.

I am not sure whether this slippage between desiring parties is intentional or whether Greenacre saw father-daughter incest as a feminist issue. In fact, the pronoun Greenacre uses to refer to the desiring child is *he.* In any case her statement certainly suggests a more resonant reading of denial, which, if applied to the defensive protestations in *Freud,* would further implicate the father in the scheme of desire.

THE DISSOCIATION OF A TEXT

The Freudian concept of repression refers to a situation in which "the subject attempts to repel, or to confine to the unconscious, representations (thoughts, images, memories) which are bound to an instinct. Repression occurs when to satisfy an instinct—though likely to be pleasurable in itself—would incur the risk of provoking unpleasure because of other requirements."[28] Recruited into film analysis, this concept may be used to explain how ideas associated with conflict get turned back from textual consciousness. This is the case, I have attempted to show, with regard to the (non)representation of incest in *Kings Row* and *Freud*. Repressed material, however, has a way of returning in the form of "symptoms, dreams, parapraxes, etc."[29] Hence, the substitution in *Kings Row* of the daughter's dementia praecox for the father's sexual desire, the doubled doctor-daughter pairs, and the use of temporal ellipsis. And hence the substitution in *Freud* of an interval when the screen goes black for envisioned incest, and the subsequent substitution of the analyst's reconstruction for the daughter's initial claims.

But the concept of repression alone is not adequate to account for the textual multiplicity that seems to result when the incest theme is introduced into film production. What we often see is "a disturbance or alteration in the normally integrative [textual] functions." In this last phrase I quote, adding a word and shortening the sentence, not from narrative film theory but from the *Diagnostic and Statistical Manual of Mental Disorders*'s entry for "dissociative disorders."[30] Sexual trauma in Hollywood psychological films operates, I submit, as textual trauma, overtaxing the filmic mechanisms for response and producing a dissociated text.

As discussed in chapter 1, the best of contemporary psychoanalytic literature on trauma is concerned with the relationships among trauma, memory, and fantasy—with the interactive rather than the either/or relationship between the ground of real events and their manifestation as psychic fantasy and trauma. In *Trauma and Survival*, Elizabeth Waites makes this point from a historical perspective. She argues that when Freud turned away from Breuer's notion of the "hypnoid state" to emphasize his own concept of repression, he "shaped the dynamics of forgetting" but also "obscur[ed] some of the most perplexing symptoms of hysterical patients . . . [such as] phenomena associated with altered states of consciousness, particularly the oscillations in cognitive and perceptual experience and self-awareness characteristic of dissociative disorders."[31]

These latter dissociative disorders may feature amnesia, states of fugue, and multiple personality, a disorder in which the subject's personality fragments into numerous partial personalities or "alters." A major difference, then, between repression and dissociation, between what Freud analyzed and what he left behind, is that "in a repression formulation, there is only an amnesia for unacceptable impulses" whereas "in a dissociation conceptualization, there is an amnesiac barrier that prevents the interchange of different memories,"[32] *which nevertheless exist.*

Likewise, the intertexts of *Kings Row* and of *Freud,* the various script versions, memos, reviews, and other publicity materials, are not completely absent. Rather, they exist on the other side of a barrier consisting of social protocols that prevent their incorporation into the release versions of mainstream Hollywood films. These alternate versions very often "hold or buffer traumatic experiences"[33] that cannot be integrated into their filmic "host" personalities. As in the novel, so in the publicity discourses from the time of *Kings Row*'s original release, the film's theme of incest found an intertextual conduit. Far from avoiding the incest theme, the film's reviews and even its trailer consolidate the force of the theme by making it a selling point for the film. For example, a review of the film in the *St. Louis Post-Dispatch* of April 5, 1942, focuses expressly on the interdicted bits of the book: "Gone are the references to the State Asylum. . . . Themes of incest, miscegenation, adultery and the like, so freely treated by the author, Henry Bellamann, are out, definitely. . . . As for the Tower family, that was only dementia praecox." In fact, as another review suggests, the material from the novel is essential knowledge for a complete understanding of the film's subject matter. In the words of the reviewer Groverman Blake, "[I]f you have read Henry Bellaman's [sic] story as it appeared in print you may wonder if the film version . . . of the father's motive in killing his daughter seems adequate and persuasive."[34] Even the film's trailer, though it never mentions the word *incest,* is organized around the suggestion that the problem of the film, the very one the spectator should wish to see resolved, is exactly that of how to use film language to suggest "incest, miscegenation, adultery and the like" without dealing with them explicitly. In the script for the trailer, whispered voices express skepticism that a film from such a book could ever be made, and a line reads, "The story of the town that lived in the shadows . . . to hide its secret shame."[35] In this way the potential audience member is prepared for a work that goes beyond reading between the scenes; the audience member is initiated more directly into a kind of parallel reading project in which the film itself is only a part of a highly fragmented, intertextual whole.

Freud too may be examined fruitfully as such a dissociated text. In an article on the film *Freud,* Diane Waldman and I wrote of the progression from the Sartre screenplays to the released film version as a progression from the acknowledgment of real sexual seduction to its denial. In other words, we wrote of the film as a work of repression. Still, I was uncomfortable at the time with the idea of the denial as being in any way complete; the text did couch the real event, I thought, but I was at a loss to say *how*.

In retrospect I think my desire for openly represented incest was rather like the incest survivor's desire for corroboration of sexual assault memories by the perpetrator. That is, the desire for corroboration is understandable: in the words of Marie Balmary, "[T]o become conscious—in order to cure—is to rediscover the witness to what we had known alone."[36] But corroboration alone can never serve the complexities of traumatic memory because, for one thing, trauma is not only an event experienced at times consciously but also a psychic process involving memory and fantasy both.

Returning to the film *Freud* with these thoughts, I question whether the repository of traumatic memory in the *Freud* archive need be restricted to the film. Perhaps it is the multiple manifestations of the intertext that provide us with the fullest view of *Freud*'s management of the incest theme. There, in the intertext, we find Magda's sexual molestation, cut with a stroke from the film, retained still in the much negotiated and contradictory versions of the script in which all the possible reactions to sexual trauma are displayed. There, in the 1959 Sartre screenplay, we find Magda, under hypnosis, uttering "a dreadful scream" and crying out the words, "He hurt me! He frightened me! He wasn't my father any more! I'll never get married, I don't want to see that look." And we find too her father's silent tears to corroborate what the screenplay calls her "confession."[37] This is one father who does remember something unspeakable.

But even in the early, uncensored, versions of the screenplay the depiction of incest is still indirect rather than overt. Both the fact and the difficulty of that subject matter, rather than its simple representation here and omission there, come to structure the negotiations surrounding its passage into filmic form. In the Sartre script, a scream and an allusive statement stand in for the moment and substance of memory. In the screenplays dated April 14, 1961, and August 9, 1961, Magda herself is not the child depicted in the incestuous flashback. She is rather the observer of another "prototypical" child shown wrestling with her father, a child whose situation she recognizes immediately:[38]

FLASHBACK TO—EXTERIOR MOUNTAINOUS COUNTRYSIDE—DAY

MAGDA'S VOICE: He takes off his left glove, I see his bare hand. He touches the child's thigh. She is wearing white lace panties. . . .

BACK TO SCENE—INTERIOR FREUD'S OFFICE—DAY

MAGDA'S VOICE: I didn't wear them. On another day . . . very long ago, I was very little . . . The day my father took off his gloves.

Here the image from the past sidesteps the direct personal import of the charge by substituting for Magda and her father the memory of an unknown father and child. Only Magda's verbal account pertains directly to her own case: "The day my father took off his gloves." Moreover, we should keep in mind that the picture painted by the script's words ("He touches the child's thigh") might not have materialized in the finished film even if this script had been the shooting script. The scene might have been handled so as to depict Magda, the observer, rather than the father and daughter her voice-over described. The absence of the character Magda in the finished film is thus foreshadowed by the attenuation of her claims in earlier versions of the script.

The repulsive force of incest creates a textual fragmentation in the form of alternate script versions. As in psychic dissociation, where the creation of an alter or a state of fugue "prevents the interchange of different memories," so the creation of subsequent script and film versions prevents the early disturbance constituted by the incest theme.

Nevertheless, the representations of incest in the *Freud* intertexts, allusive and thinned though they are, suggest the range of possibilities for giving weight to childhood sexual molestation, a range that includes the admission of incestuous relations, the denial thereof, the admission of incest with the proviso that it was a "prototypical" event and not a specific one, and even (going back to Cecily) the suggestion that incest memories are iatrogenic—a product of the psychoanalytic scene. The intertexts, then, are the repository of traumatic memory, buffered, yes, but certainly persistent as well.

The viewer's appreciation of the dissociated theme of sexual assault is strongly affected by whether he or she has seen a trailer or read reviews and/or a source novel where one exists. It is affected too by whether he or she has had previous associations with the subject matter dealt with in the film or even, perhaps, some direct, personal experiences. The spectator's reading is affected, in other words, by his or her reception of the intertext. Of

course, the same could be said for the spectators of every film, but the distinction I would make here (and it is quantitative rather than qualitative), is that films dealing with the socially and psychically incendiary topic of sexual assault encourage contestatory or split readings that harbor simultaneously the possibilities that incest did *and* did not really occur. Classical Hollywood films, in their socially mandated need to avoid the topic of incest and economically mandated need to attract an audience, are relatively innovative when it comes to finding indirect means of representing would-be unrepresentable material. For direct representation however, one must turn to subsidiary materials from which a final film version has in one sense dissociated itself but to which it remains, in another sense, unalterably connected.

THREE

Incest on Television
and the Burden of Proof

Sybil; Shattered Trust: The Shari Karney Story;
Liar, Liar; and *Divided Memories*

Made-for-television movies from the 1970s to the present have not hesitated to portray subject matter that classical Hollywood films had shied away from. Even after the motion picture Production Code was replaced in the mid-1960s by a ratings system administered by the Motion Picture Association of America, in part allowing the treatment of subject matter that could not be shown on television, the representation of themes of incest and other forms of sexual assault in theatrically released films remained less frequent and less overt than what television offered. Always topical, and influenced from the 1970s by the women's movement, television movies became a natural forum for stories of battered women and various forms of rape, including incestuous sexual assault on children. Moreover, whereas intimations of incestuous molestation in the classical films discussed in the previous chapter are ultimately retracted by the plots' conclusions, television movies on the subject made a point to affirm the existence of childhood sexual assault.

However, there are more and less effective means of exploring traumatic subjects. In the final analysis, the television movie presentation of incest is restricted by its positivist approach. Likewise, the truth-claiming strategies of the television documentary present too few lines of resolution to render incest's web of meanings. This chapter will trace the potentialities and limitations of feminist and antifeminist sociocultural discourses about incest on and off television.

The consciousness-raising groups, academic women's studies programs, and organized—or deliberately disruptive—political, social, and cultural activities that constituted the second wave of the women's movement were carried along by a flow of feminist writing, from first-person testimonials to historical studies of previously unsung women to intricate theoretical treatises. In this context, a substantial number of fiction and nonfiction books and articles broke the silence that had been maintained about childhood sexual abuse, including incestuous assault, since Freud's retraction of the "seduction theory" and the retrenchment of the American medical establishment at the turn of the century. These books and their authors stunned audiences when they began to document and examine the problem of childhood sexual assault in the United States (and elsewhere) and found it to exist at every economic level and in every family configuration, including the avowedly traditional white middle-class nuclear family.[1] Many of the authors, researchers, and educators, along with others who recognized their own experiences in what they read and heard, sought help from psychological professionals, who developed clinical methods to treat these new clients or to treat existing clients with newly recognized complaints. The emerging incest survivor "recovery movement," although criticized by some feminist activists as self-indulgent and apolitical, has had a great impact on psychotherapeutic practices. I accept Lynn Sacco's historical thesis that "it is thoroughly consistent for feminist therapists to encourage and support the recovery movement."[2]

Definitive findings about child sexual abuse are difficult to establish due to its nature as intimate, disturbing, socially and legally prohibited, and generally underreported.[3] Nevertheless, reports and statistics prepared by agencies including the National Institute of Justice and the National Center for Juvenile Justice indicate that the problem is widespread.[4] It is also generally accepted nowadays that the vast majority (80 to 96 percent) of sexual abuse offenders are men[5] and that girl victims significantly outnumber boy victims.[6] When the particular type of child sexual abuse under consideration is incestuous abuse, complications multiply. It is hard, though not impossible, for people to acknowledge that the family may not always be a safe haven for children—and particularly that it is not a safe haven for children because patriarchal family arrangements are grievously unbalanced. In her definitive history of incest in the United States, Lynn Sacco details how the existence of incest has been disavowed over the long term up to the present day, except when its perpetrators were thought to be poor whites, nonwhites, and/or immigrants.[7] But, as Sacco's book makes abundantly clear, the difficulty of conducting studies and the variation in findings do not provide a legitimate excuse for avoiding the topic altogether. Variations notwithstanding, studies show that incestuous assault is "a problem of enormous dimension and implication for the lives of uncounted thousands of young people who carry their secret alone and in silence."[8]

The feminist researchers Judith Herman in *Father-Daughter Incest* (1981, 2000) and Diana Russell in *The Secret Trauma: Incest in the Lives of Girls and Women* (1986, 1999) take a historical look at the problem. Both scholars begin their respective books by surveying preexisting studies. These they find disturbing both because the reported numbers are frighteningly high and because they are very likely not high enough to be correct and were even deflated, in some cases, by the biases of the researchers. Herman analyzed five studies that predated her own, ranging from a 1940 study by Carney Landis to the Kinsey report of 1953 to a well-respected 1978 study by David Finkelhor.[9] In these studies, she found a fairly consistent 25 percent rate of child sexual abuse among female subjects studied and a rate of incestuous sexual abuse averaging 1 percent. Finkelhor translated this percentage to a real number, reporting that approximately one million American women had had incestuous relations with their fathers.[10] According to Herman, the study of over four thousand women by Alfred Kinsey and associates contained "the largest number of incest cases ever collected from the population at large, rather than from advertisements, clinic files, or court records." There was a "wealth of information contained in these interviews . . . buried in the files of the Institute for Sex Research," Herman affirmed.[11] However, Kinsey's interpretation of his own research findings exonerated perpetrators: "It is difficult to understand why a child, except for cultural conditioning, should be disturbed at having its genitalia touched, or disturbed at seeing the genitalia of other persons, or disturbed at even more specific sexual contacts."[12] Kinsey even suggested, in a comment that prefigured the rhetoric of the False Memory Syndrome Foundation (FMSF) by four decades, that it was men who were at risk from accusations by hysterical girls: "The child who has been raised in fear of all strangers and all physical manifestations of affection may ruin the lives of the married couple who had lived as useful and honorable citizens through half or more of a century, by giving her parents and police a distorted version of the old man's attempt to bestow grandfatherly affection upon her."[13] Due to resistance to recognizing incest, it now appears likely that the 1 percent rate of incestuous abuse was and remains too low.

Diana Russell designed her own study as a corrective to earlier ones. Her findings, based on a sample of 930 women residents of San Francisco interviewed face to face during the summer of 1978, reported a 38 percent incidence of sexual abuse, a 16 percent incidence of incestuous sexual abuse, and a 4.5 percent incidence of father-daughter sexual abuse. Other studies confirm figures comparable to those presented by Russell,[14] and it is now generally accepted that 12 to 38 percent of women were sexually abused as children, that 24 to 50 percent of these were abused by family members, and that about 50 percent of abuse by family members is perpetrated by fathers or stepfathers.

In her 1978 book *Conspiracy of Silence: The Trauma of Incest,* Sandra Butler defined incestuous assault as "any manual, oral or genital sexual contact or other explicit sexual behavior that any adult family member imposes on a child, who is unable to alter or understand the adult's behavior because of his or her powerlessness in the family and early stage of psychological development."[15] Butler emphasized that, whereas incest in general may include sexual acts between consenting adults (most often brothers and sisters) and consensual relationships among children who may be involved in play or experimentation, incestuous *assault* necessarily implies a power imbalance between the adult and the child. Butler also made the point that "the forms of incestuous assault are diverse; the acts are not only genital and the experience not always a physical one."[16] In any case, the results of the abuse, though they may be imperceptible to the outside observer, are "deep and lasting." "The most devastating result of the imposition of adult sexuality upon a child unable to determine the appropriateness of his or her response is the irretrievable loss of the child's inviolability and trust in the adults in his or her life."[17] This is not to minimize the extent of the all-too perceptible physical damage to children's bodies. Medical records have been instrumental in efforts to document the characteristics and extent of the crime, and books about childhood sexual assault contain disturbing descriptions of resulting injuries.[18] The point being made forcefully through feminist research and advocacy is that child sexual abuse was and is a social reality with devastating mental and physical effects on its victims.

This atmosphere of recognition and change was the context for cable and broadcast television stations' and networks' rush to extend and perhaps capitalize on the public rediscovery of incestuous assault with a spate of made-for-television movies, talk show sessions, and documentary films. In keeping with the testamentary spirit of the women's movement, these programs, including the pathbreaking *Sybil* (Daniel Petrie, 1976) and *Something about Amelia* (Randa Haines, 1984); followed by the television documentaries *Scared Silent: Exposing and Ending Child Abuse* (Melissa Jo Peltier, 1992) and *Scared Silent: Incest* (Melissa Jo Peltier, 1994), both hosted by Oprah Winfrey; and the television dramas *Liar, Liar* (Jorge Montesi, 1992), *Fatal Memories: The Eileen Franklin Story* (Daryl Duke, 1992), and *Shattered Trust: The Shari Karney Story* (Bill Corcoran, 1993) all took pains to support their heroines' allegations of incestuous abuse. The dramas depicted the gestural acts leading up to and/or encompassing familial sexual abuse. Moreover, what seems remarkable now, from the other side of the backlash against recovered memory that would follow closely the airing of the later dramas, is that the prebacklash movies all depicted memories of incest as true to past events. This was the case whether the memories were continuous (that is, never forgotten by their owner, as in *Liar, Liar*) or repressed and then recovered (as in *Sybil, Fatal Memories,* and *Shattered Trust*).

Television movies have been scorned for what is seen as their excessive topicality—pouncing on and sensationalizing every salacious or catastrophic turn of events. For example, one review of *Shattered Trust: The Shari Karney Story* begins by acknowledging that "network television has often come under attack for exploiting the trials of real people in order to garner ratings."[19] Another states that "television audiences in recent years have become much too acquainted with trumped-up and sensationalized movies based on real stories [such as] [t]he three Amy Fisher flicks (one apiece by ABC, CBS, and NBC) about the cheerleader . . . and the movie based on the Waco, Texas, confrontation, filmed even before the tragic end had arrived."[20] Programs about childhood sexual assault are doubly vulnerable to such attacks because they feature emotional stories of girls and women in a context critical of patriarchal family structure. They make viewers uncomfortable. How else can we account for the scorn heaped on "child molestation stories," perceived as being "done to death,"[21] while the deranged-killer-on-the-loose plot is endlessly repeated? In light of this potential for negative response, it is a testament to the relative quality of *Sybil; Something about Amelia; Liar, Liar; Fatal Memories;* and *Shattered Trust* that they garnered generally positive reviews. As one reviewer stated,

"'Shattered Trust: The Shari Karney Story' . . . brings a fierce perspective to the subject. It's as if writer Susan Nanus had picked up the pieces of an oft-told tale and reforged them in the white heat of renewed passion on a subject many people have grown weary of." [22]

Given the breadth of the problem of childhood sexual assault and the depth of the silence, television's topicality may have found one of its most worthy expressions in this particular subject matter. At one time—in the late 1980s and early 1990s—prior to the age of the personal home page and the Internet link, television was the premier medium for widely shared discourse on incestuous assault and recovery. Although this chapter will seriously critique the realist strain of television offerings on the topic, I regard this programming as fundamentally courageous and as having the potential to improve prospects for many victims and survivors of incest. *Shattered Trust* ends with Shari listening to a message recorded on her telephone answering machine thanking her for inspiring the caller to prosecute her own father. The scene models one possible action a viewer might take after watching the film. Viewing these programs today, one is struck by the way they turn classical tropes toward feminist ends. Whereas the "collapse-therapy-cure" model prevalent in the postwar "women and madness cycle" very often depicted a male therapist adjusting his woman patient to her normative gender role,[23] these films show female therapists and social workers advocating their clients' autonomy from family. And whereas women's experiences were rewritten in *Kings Row* (Sam Wood, 1942) and *Freud* (John Huston, 1962), here on television they are validated and come into their own: psychotherapy and the memories elicited through it are portrayed as a path to self-awareness and empowerment, and the narratives are often presented from the perspective of the survivor.

The burden of proof was upon these movies, and they lived up to the challenge of exposing a disturbing social reality. It is not surprising, therefore, that they are all structured like a legal brief (in fact, *Liar, Liar* and *Shattered Trust* are courtroom dramas) or like a well-wrought piece of historical scholarship. In each of these telefilms, evidence is presented to dispel any doubt that incestuous assault was perpetrated and endured by the respective characters in the story. *Sybil,* based on a true story,[24] depicts the therapy of a patient (played by Sally Field) suffering from multiple personality disorder resulting from childhood sexual abuse.[25] During the treatment, the psychiatrist, Dr. Cornelia Wilbur (in real life a credited consultant on the film whose screen role was played by Joanne Woodward), journeys to her patient's childhood home to search for evidence to corroborate the memories of Sybil's alternate personalities (her personality "alters"). From its place in the barn loft, she brings to light a grain storage bin that bears on its inner sides the purple crayon scribbles that Sybil had talked about having made as a child while confined for punishment inside the box. While Dr. Wilbur is in Willow Corners, Wisconsin, she also tracks down Sybil's childhood physician. Although at first he indicates that he noticed nothing out of the ordinary in Sybil's childhood, an examination of the medical chart that he himself compiled at the time reveals a history including "torn ligament, right shoulder; fractured clavicle; palm of right hand burned on stove; fractured larynx; bean stuck up nose;" and "scarification of the inner walls [of the vagina] . . . obstruction of certain tissues." "I don't believe she can ever become a mother," he concludes. This is a history that, in the film's present, if not in the 1950s when Sybil was a child, would certainly alert medical personnel to the possibility of abuse. In fact, the doctor covertly acknowledges that he suspected something of the sort at the time but let it go unattended. "How do I find absolution?" he asks Dr. Wilbur in despair. This testimony, along with the layout and artifacts of Sybil's childhood home—all there exactly as she reported—serve to guarantee the truth of the memories Sybil finally wrests from her alters.

As courtroom dramas, *Liar, Liar* and *Shattered Trust: The Shari Karney Story* combine the juridical with the detective mode to shore up their respective proofs. In *Liar, Liar* a daughter's allegations that her father molested her provide the film's enigma as well as its courtroom setting: Who is telling the truth? The loving father or the daughter known for the wild stories she invents? Indeed, the CBS Tuesday Movie presentation of this Canadian film is preceded by a teaser in which a male voice announces that the film (for which "viewer discretion is advised") tells "that atrocious story that would destroy the strongest of families." "But who's really telling the truth?" the voice queries. The teaser cuts to the prosecuting attorney asking our young heroine's older sister, "Is it your sister who is lying, or is it your father?" The answer is arrived at by way of medical evidence (the presence of an enlarged and irritated rectum; the abuse was sodomy) and corroborative testimony. The older sister, Christina, ultimately testifies that, while she did not actually witness her sister's abuse (eyewitnesses are hard to come by in such intimate crimes), she believes her sister's testimony because she herself was also molested by their father while still living at home. The father is sentenced to prison followed by probation. The mother refuses to believe her daughters' testimonies and the court findings, siding with her husband and another daughter. The sisters and the eldest sister's supportive husband leave the courtroom together, along with the little brother, whom we are led to believe was also molested by the father.

Shattered Trust is the story of the real-life attorney Shari Karney, whose own memories of incestuous assault return to her while she is acting as counsel for a divorced woman involved in a custody battle for her small daughter. Although only three years old, this daughter too has a medical history including "vaginal and anal scarring almost a year old" and "rashes and pain while urinating." She also has a psychological history of "temper tantrums and preoccupation with sex" and is able to demonstrate sexual acts on anatomically correct dolls. As is wont to happen,[26] the judge finds a likelihood that the charges were trumped up for ammunition in the custody battle, and he fails to block joint custody except for a six-month period. That case, depicted in the film as having stimulated Karney's memory of her own personal history, inspires her to accept and even to seek out other cases of incest. She realizes that children's testimony is not deemed very reliable and that what she needs is an older person. This plan hits a snag when one teenager drops her case in order to reunite with her family, and Karney turns to an older, and hence more mature, client. But there is a stumbling block here too in the form of the statute of limitations. This client is willing to testify, but her abuse took place in childhood and the statutory period has run out. The client can no longer press charges. At that point Karney determines that she must resort to the "delayed discovery rule," which stops the clock on the statutory period in cases where the injured party does not realize that he or she had been injured until it is too late to go to court.

The actual history of the discovery rule has been described in the *Pepperdine Law Review*: "The evolution of the discovery rule can be traced back to the United States Supreme Court's decision in *Urie v. Thompson*. In Urie, the plaintiff contracted silicosis as a result of inhaling silica dust throughout his thirty-year career as a railroad fireman. Although strict application of the statute of limitations would have precluded the plaintiff's bringing suit, the Court held that the plaintiff's action was not barred by the limitations period. The Court concluded that because of the plaintiff's 'blameless ignorance' of his injury, his claim did not accrue until his condition became manifest and was diagnosed."[27]

The rule has since been invoked by adult survivors of childhood sexual abuse with some success, especially in what are known as "Type Two" cases. In such cases claimants could be held "blamelessly ignorant" of the harm they had endured until after the lapse of the statutory period because they had suppressed or repressed the memories of the traumas they had suffered.

Ironically, in light of popular debates that generally place more stock in the accounts of survivors who never forgot their injuries, the courts tend to disfavor claimants who have remembered all along but have waited to file suit, even in situations where the delay can be attributed to their having failed to make the connection between the injuries endured and the lasting ill effects. Very likely the battle depicted in the movie through the character Rachel is based on the landmark California case *Mary D. v. John D.*, in which Shari Karney successfully represented the twenty-four-year-old plaintiff in bringing suit against her father for sexual abuse that occurred before she reached the age of five years but that she remembered only shortly before bringing the action. The court found that "[t]he doctrine of delayed discovery may be applied in a case where the plaintiff can establish lack of memory of tortious acts due to psychological repression which took place before plaintiff attained the age of majority, and which caused plaintiff to forget the facts of the acts of abuse until a date subsequent to which the complaint is timely filed."[28] In *Shattered Trust*, therefore, repressed memory is presented as not only plausible but absolutely crucial to findings in favor of survivors of incestuous assault. The alleged phenomenon of false memory, which shortly thereafter became so prominent in the cultural discourse, is not broached here.

Shari Karney's own memories are validated by the association of her case with those of the other women and girls. Although her parents keep up their denial and Shari's sister lobbies her to return to the family fold, the sister also acknowledges the legitimacy of Shari's claims, saying, "I know something happened. I can't pretend anymore, it's not possible." Finally, as with Sybil, the presence of symptoms dating from a time before memories of abuse were consciously recovered attests to the memories' validity: Karney is portrayed as experiencing panic attacks during sexual intercourse and, to the consternation of her sister, as having always eschewed makeup, jewelry, and form-fitting clothing.

If evidence (in the form of family relics, medical histories, corroborative testimony, and ongoing symptomatology) and proof (via a therapeutic cure or a legal case) are the main concerns of these stories of incestuous assault, another of their characteristics is that they are poised between fiction and nonfiction. Docudrama is a common mode of expression; *Something about Amelia* (reportedly seen by sixty million people),[29] like *Sybil* and *Shattered Trust*, is based on a true story. *Fatal Memories: The Eileen Franklin Story*, a dramatic representation of the case mentioned in chapter 1 in which a woman recalls twenty years after the event that she has witnessed her father raping and murdering her best friend, may be added to the list. Even where the dramas are wholly fictional in terms of their specific characters and situations, they evince a streak of didacticism that avows their stake in real-world issues. *Liar, Liar,* for example, provides a veritable guide for childhood sexual assault victims: you may be disbelieved; you may be accused of undermining the family; nevertheless you should tell someone, whether your mother, a trusted teacher, or a school counselor; assault "isn't about sex . . . it's about power;" it is not the fault of the victim; coming forward and telling is a courageous act. The film also disabuses the viewer of any incorrect notions about perpetrators. They are not slimy, homeless, or perverted, but loving husbands, fathers, and pillars of the community whose wives do not necessarily withhold sex. They pass lie detector tests, and there is no "profile" of perpetrators. The film makes its chilling point with the following dialogue spoken by the father who would be found guilty of incestuous assault: "I swear I didn't do anything to Kelly that a million other fathers aren't doing right now."

In light of the battles over history and memory that would ensue, perhaps the most significant aspect of these television dramas is that they use specialized images and sounds to illustrate and verify their heroines' memories. Memories that in real life would be internal psychic phenomena are given tangible expression such that their appearance is indistinguishable from a hypothetical portrayal of actual past events. The order of the plot also supports the legitimacy of memory. Instead of beginning with childhood abuse, the films withhold the representation of crucial events (what happened in the past) for a certain time so that, when they are finally supplied, these events fulfill a hermeneutic function as the solution to the original enigma. In *Sybil* the protagonist begins a process of retrospective reflection as part of an attempt to heal her dissociation. Because this character's memories have been cordoned off from consciousness by the production of personality alters, she and her therapist must become memory detectives to solve the enigma of her mental illness. Likewise, Shari Karney has repressed her memories so that the operation of the plot is as much to peel off the repressive scarring as it is to dramatize Karney's legal victories.

Even *Liar, Liar,* which is about a child with continuous memories of assault that is still ongoing at the time of her claims, features a memory sequence at its crux. The images we see during Christina's testimony are the only visual evocations of memory in the film. Kelly's punishment by her father, presented early in the film, takes place off screen. Like the mother and her younger children downstairs, we are allowed to speculate as to the specifics of the father's actions. A good talking to? A hard spanking? Fondling? Rape? Sodomy? As in the film noir–melodrama *Mildred Pierce* (Michael Curtiz, 1945), where a reverse shot that would have revealed the killer had it been included at the start of the film is instead withheld until the film's conclusion, in *Liar, Liar* the significant encounter between father and daughter takes place initially behind the closed bathroom door. It is particularly satisfying, although horrifying as well, when at the conclusion of the film we are let into the bathroom and shown what really happened.

Upholding abuse memories is an important part of revealing the pervasiveness of the crime of childhood sexual abuse. But complications ensue to realist storytelling when the subject concerns memory. Real memories can fail to correspond to reality. Memory is not a camera; mechanically reproduced images of the past cannot be paged from an archive and publicly examined for evidence of wrongdoing. Portraying them as intrinsically true and capable of exteriorization on the television screen confers an evidentiary status that actual memory can never achieve. In presenting a situation in which images of incestuous acts *can* be referred to from the perspective of the present, these films engage in a fantasy of knowing. Television dramas are in this way more realistic than real life. But crucially, their representation of memory *as if it were a realist mode* leaves these television movies within the binaristic paradigm. Since neither inaccurate nor false memories are pictured, we are left with the impression that all abuse memories are wholly true and that parental denial is wholly wrong.

Nevertheless, although these films show a realist tendency in their tangible portrayals of recalled abuse, memory and filmic representation are both malleable enough phenomena to encourage other thoughts about the relationship between truth and memory. Even if these television movies do not break the traditional framework for presenting abuse memories, they do shake it up. The heroines' visualized memories are the least realist—and to my mind the most interesting—aspect of these films. The prohibition against speaking or showing incest seems to push these television movies into an unconventional representational realm, perhaps the only acceptable realm for the expression of such unsavory material. But whatever the practicalities involved, the heroines' memories are portrayed using editorial fragmentation; weird choices of camera angle, subject, height, and distance; alterations in light and film stock; and general ambiguity that characterizes traumatic memory images and their representation in cinema. Thus these television movies, perhaps in spite of themselves, prefigure the

explosion of radical subject and style that is more fully developed in feminist autobiographical documentary filmmaking. A close examination of
their treatment of memory is therefore warranted.

Sybil; Liar, Liar; and *Shattered Trust* all contain passages in which a character's behavior and ability to focus on the present are interrupted by
flashbacks to prior sexual abuse. In *Sybil* and *Shattered Trust*, the heroines
also experience nightmares and awful memories that cause an emotional
pain so great that their bodies can barely handle it: they collapse to the floor
in agony. In both films, while some memories occur spontaneously, others
are elicited deliberately in therapy. And in both plots the memories build
from short indecipherable fragments marked by asynchronous or distorted
sound to longer coherent sequences that allow us to piece together what
happened. Judith Herman explains that traumatic memory may present
itself "as a series of still snapshots or a silent movie; the role of therapy is to
provide the music and words."[30] Likewise, narrative resolution involves
the public disentanglement of characters' internal flashbulb memories.

In *Sybil* several scenes of physical, including sexual, torture at the hands
of her mother—for, against statistical norms it is in this case the mother
who abused her daughter[31]—are broken into parts and distributed throughout the film. Overall we see nearly a dozen sequences or sequence fragments
in which the past or personality alters appear. The first flashback of the film
occurs while Sybil is leading a line of children in a game of follow-the-
leader. She enters a state of fugue and wakes up knee deep in a fountain.
The children had sense enough to stop at the edge. What we see through
her mind's eye are flashes from the past, intercut with close-ups of Sybil's
face, which, thanks to Sally Field's brilliant performance in the role, appears
totally transformed by memory. A swing set at the park lends its sound to
an audially distorted effect of a chain being cranked. We see the upper body
of a small child being hoisted up and an instant later, after a close-up of the
adult Sybil at the park, the lower body of the child disappearing into the
loft. Later in the film we will see the whole sequence, recalled by one of
Sybil's alters, in which the child Sybil's mother binds her hands together,
slips a large hook into the bindings, hoists her up to the barn loft, and shuts
her in the grain bin where she makes her purple scribbles. Between the first
inkling of these events and their fullest depiction in the film, several associations will be made: Sybil's wrists going numb (the sense memory of their
having been bound), a woman standing on the sidewalk holding a walking
cane (which sight provokes one of Sybil's personality shifts), and a memory of Sybil's mother sucking a candy cane from the Christmas tree.

The half-circle hook shape is also linked to the buttonhook that Sybil's mother used repeatedly to perform the bizarre procedures that scarred her insides. We are not shown the image of the mother inserting the buttonhook, but we are shown the disposition of Sybil's body splayed on the kitchen table and the mother's set of "instruments" at the ready. The film strongly upholds the legitimacy of Sybil's memory. Sybil herself, and not merely one of her alters, retrieves memories in the struggle for personality integration. "I'm Sybil and I remember. And I hate her," she proclaims.

In the kitchen sequence, as in the one taking place in the barn, we are given fragmentary clues as to what happened, clues that are meant to denote the return of memory as unbidden and partial at first but insistent. The kitchen light, a bulb in its metal reflector shade, is first presented as an image that fills the frame, completely out of context, flashing four times in conjunction with a loud ticking sound. It is seen again later in a drawing made by a distraught Sybil and seen yet again, seeming to push itself into the foreground of the frame as the camera reverses past it, panning around a room to reveal a gathering of Sybil's alters. When Doctor Wilbur visits Sybil's family home (being offered for sale and therefore conveniently empty), the light hangs from the center of the kitchen and is prominently depicted in close-up. This light must have been an object of Sybil's hypnotic gaze as she lay captive on the kitchen table, for the light was right above her and served as the mooring to which her mother attached an enema bag and anchored Sybil's spread feet for the perverse gynecological torture.

Shattered Trust: The Shari Karney Story also contains memory images that are introduced as isolated shots of indeterminate origin and then consolidated into a coherent—but still complicated—sequence in about the middle of the film. Actually, our first flashback to the scene Shari will eventually remember is auditory and manifests itself in a nightmare. Over images of Shari asleep in bed, dreaming, tossing and turning, we hear on the soundtrack the wails of a crying baby. The first visual flashbacks occur to Karney during her defense of the abused three-year-old and are provoked by the court stenographer's typing. A typewriter is presented on the screen in close-up along with the sound of typing, followed by the face of a distraught toddler. These sounds and images are integrated into the recovered memory sequence in which Karney's therapist (played by Ellen Burstyn) hypnotizes her and takes her back to her childhood home. Much as we were introduced to Willow Corners in *Sybil*, we see the neighborhood street on which Shari grew up and then shots of the interior of Shari's childhood home. A subjective tracking shot down the hallway provides us with Shari's child's-eye view, a perspective supported by the high pitch in which her voice-over narration from the therapist's office in the present time is presented.

While the sequence contains some shots that recreate what Shari experienced from the physical perspective in which she saw it initially, there are also omniscient shots of the father's and daughter's actions. For example, after a shot in which a roving camera takes us into Shari's childhood bedroom and pans around the room, we see a shot taken from down the hall as Shari's father crosses from right to left, walking from his study to her room. A few shots later, the sequence switches back to first person when we see a close-up of the toddler Shari gazing upward, followed by a shot of her father looming above. The subjective aspect of the sequence makes it very like the father's approach in *Freud* as described in chapter 2. But the plot of *Shattered Trust* does not oblige the daughter to retract the report of what she has seen and experienced.

But it is the contradictory cinematographic strategy of alternating between first- and third-person narration that typifies traumatic representation, linking these television movies about abuse to a wider filmography that includes Errol Morris's documentary *The Thin Blue Line* (1988) (in which the shots that make up the numerous reenactments of the murder of a Dallas police officer oscillate between point-of-view shots and an imaginary third-person perspective) and Steven Spielberg's *Saving Private Ryan* (1998) (in which some shots represent the individual perspective of the Tom Hanks character while others are taken from behind German lines). In dramas (including documentaries) about public historical subjects such as a real-life shooting or the Normandy landing, the individual character perspectives (of real or fictional people) are used to humanize large-scale catastrophic events, bringing them to a level supposedly more accessible to audiences.

In dramas about incestuous assault, the use of both objective and subjective camerawork can confer legitimacy on what would otherwise be one individual's (questionable) perspective. The treatment of the memory sequences throughout *Shattered Trust* as a whole recapitulates this local mixing of subjective and objective material. Once Shari recovers her memory halfway through the film, the concentration shifts from her personal to her public work—pursuing court cases and lobbying successfully for the passage of California Senate Bill 108, a bill that in real life was signed into law by Governor George Dukemejian on September 30, 1990—as noted in the film's final graphic title.

Liar, Liar contains what is perhaps the most experimental memory sequence, for the film conflates the memories of two characters, the younger sister, Kelly, who has brought the charges, and the older married sister, Christina, who confirms her sister's testimony. Christina's memories seem to be the ones visually rendered. The flashbacks begin when, just after Christina has corroborated Kelly's veracity, her husband enters the courtroom holding the hand of her little brother. As the courtroom door is pulled shut, there is a cut to another door being purposefully closed. Several shots follow, all exceedingly short, all black and white in contrast with the rest of the film, shot so as to withhold the spatial context, and edited together across jump cuts. Christina, practically overcome in the courtroom, is given a drink of water. She has one more flash of memory: a longer shot of the room, which we now make out to be a bathroom, and a child's cry. Then:

ATTORNEY: You've previously testified that Kelly has never told you that she was being abused, is that right?

CHRISTINA: *(Nods, yes)*

ATTORNEY: So, what makes you now say that she was telling the truth?

CHRISTINA: She wasn't the first one.

This statement is followed by another series of black-and-white shot fragments. We see a man's lower body and legs; then a girl's bare calves and feet; a girl's hands push against the toilet tank; a man's hands cover them; the face of a small person comes into view, obscured by swishing hair as the head turns, as if writhing or resisting.

ATTORNEY: You had no idea he was doing the same thing to Kelly?

Now similar shots are repeated, followed by the big surprise: when a recognizable person finally comes into view, the face is that of Kelly and not Christina.

CHRISTINA: I was hoping he wasn't.

Thus, the older sister testifies to her own sexual abuse, and perhaps some of the shots of the bathroom might be attributed to her memory. But we also see parts of an event—Kelly's abuse—at which Christina was not present and of which no visual record could exist. The legal decision must rest ultimately on the fact that the sisters' stories—and avowed memories—support each other and not on the basis of evidence.

If we look back at the film now, from the perspective of the false memory/recovered memory debates, *Liar, Liar* seems the most vulnerable of the films for use by false memory proponents: false memories are contagious; the allegations by girls against their fathers are analogous to the witch hunt in which demons were found where none really existed. One girl's memories could actually create and not just trigger another's. The images that decide the case are extremely ambivalent in terms of perspective.

But this potential weakness in the films' feminist platform could actually be construed as its strength. In taking the risk it does, *Liar, Liar* becomes most suggestive of the vicissitudes of memory that I have delineated in chapter 1 of this book. Lacerating conventionality, these incest images present snippets of memory as impossible but nonetheless true.

Although these television movies largely cleave to realist style, the charge to represent childhood sexual abuse seems to have encouraged certain deviations from that style that I find suggestive for the contemporary retheorization of memory from a new feminist perspective. But at the time of their broadcast it was not their incipient experimentalism that was noticed but rather their unabashed acceptance of abuse memories, especially repressed and recovered memories.

DENYING INCEST

Established in 1992, as *Liar, Liar; Shattered Trust;* and *Fatal Memories* were being prepared, the False Memory Syndrome Foundation immediately began to cultivate and receive a huge amount of publicity for its strenuous refutation of the idea that women's memories of abuse, especially recovered memories (such as those of Sybil and Shari Karney), are credible.[32] These they attributed to a "syndrome" (not validated as such in the *Diagnostic and Statistical Manual of Mental Disorders*) in which "a person's identity and interpersonal relationships are centered on a memory of a traumatic experience that is objectively false but in which the person strongly believes."[33] The origin of such memories, they argued, was "a disastrous 'therapeutic' program" initiated by antifamily feminist therapists. As opposed to the clinicians and theorists (many of whom do identify as feminists) who argue that sexual abuse is underreported and that the majority of victims never see a therapist,[34] the parents and professionals of the FMSF hold that false accusations are rife, that 92.2 percent of them are made by "thirty-something daughters against middle- and upper middle-class families," and that falsely accused parents are the "secondary victims" while feminist therapists are the new "perpetrators" of the so-called false memory syndrome.[35]

Writing about feminist "survivor discourses" and their discontents, Rosaria Champagne provides an insightful critique of the rhetoric of the FMSF.[36] Whereas the organization purports to "establish reliable methods to discriminate between true and false claims of incest and abuse charges" (FMSF pamphlet quoted by Champagne), it has presented no such methods. And whereas the organization acknowledges the existence of incest, it locates this crime on an ever-receding horizon outside the white, middle-class domain of the FMSF. Through a detailed and theoretically informed analysis of FMSF literature, Champagne adds her articulate voice to those of Judith Herman, Diana Russell, and Lynn Sacco,[37] scholars who have claimed that the FMSF has done a great deal to reverse hard-won gains in the battle to bring incestuous abuse to public light. Daughters' allegations are once again being automatically disbelieved,[38] and they and their therapists are being accused of breaking up family life—as if incestuous abuse did not already do this. One can see what is at stake for the patriarchal nuclear family configuration, for, as Champagne points out, "Feminist therapy offers survivors the option to reject the tautological thinking that declares families of origin always already the final arbiters of truth."[39]

Whereas feminist researchers have striven to establish correct statistics pertaining to child sexual abuse, the FMSF has supplied a rhetoric of hyperbole. FMSF literature exaggerates the number of women who remember falsely by incorrectly maintaining that all women with recovered memories of incestuous childhood sexual abuse are suffering from "false memory syndrome." A sober perspective on this so-called syndrome must recognize that although the challenges of measuring sexual abuse multiply when memories are repressed and recovered and in cases where supposed memories do turn out to have been mistaken, many women have indeed recovered memories that are genuine and essentially correct in their particulars. As indicated in chapter 1 of this book, studies have shown that amnesia for childhood sexual abuse is not only possible but a characteristic feature of such abuse. Relying on hospital records and other means of external validation of child sexual abuse (since without such evidence an amnesiac subject would appear identical to a subject to whom nothing had happened), studies have shown that the number of women who were at some point amnesiac about their abuse ranges between 20 percent[40] and 67 percent.[41] Granted, this is quite a range, and it is clear that existing studies need to be collated and more extensive studies done. But it is also clear that abuse amnesia is a genuine phenomenon.

Moving down the inverted pyramid, one finds that, of amnesiac women (already a subset of adult survivors of childhood sexual abuse), a certain proportion end up recovering abuse memories. Linda Meyer Williams found that 16 percent of 129 adults with documented histories of childhood sexual abuse had forgotten and then recovered memories of the abuse.[42] Because the human subjects of such studies of amnesia and recovered memory are drawn, in large part, from the pool of individuals with documented histories of abuse, these are not subjects to whom false memory may be attributed.

However, some women who were not sexually abused in childhood may mistakenly think that they have recovered actual abuse memories. Judith Herman reports that estimates of the frequency of "false complaints" of sexual abuse fall between 2 and 7 percent.[43] Women who remember falsely do not constitute the mainstream of the population of sexual abuse survivors for whom feminist researchers, clinicians, writers, and activists seek to advocate. But they, along with their therapists, do constitute the target population of the FMSF, as if the problem of false remembering were as large as, or the same as, or more important than the problem of actual sexual abuse, which is known to have been experienced by millions of women.

This was the time and atmosphere of exaggeration and illogic in which the four-hour documentary film *Divided Memories* was written, produced, and directed by Ofra Bikel and aired in two installments on PBS's *Frontline* series (April 4 and 11, 1995). Long, complex, thoroughly researched, fair-minded in a time of ferocious partisanship, and with an aesthetic value that surpasses the often mundane shooting and editing strategies of many television documentaries, this is a program of exceptional quality. It is the most significant individual television intervention into the false memory/recovered memory debates that I know of.

The documentary borrows its structure from the principle of journalistic balance or objectivity—a kind of nonfiction counterpart to Hollywood classical realism. Experts appear from "both sides" of the false memory/ recovered memory debates, including Dr. Judith Herman *(Trauma and Recovery)*, Dr. Lenore Terr *(Unchained Memories)*, and Ellen Bass (author with Laura Davis of *The Courage to Heal*) on the side of recovered memory, and Dr. Elizabeth Loftus, author with Katherine Ketcham of *The Myth of Repressed Memory*, and Dr. Michael Yapko, author of *Suggestions of Abuse*, there to refute its validity. Direct cinema footage shot expressly for the program portrays various therapeutic practices, and clients and parents with pointedly different perspectives are interviewed on camera.

Differing viewer responses to the program confirm its balance,[44] although that two-sidedness is not always appreciated by viewers wishing for a more partisan orientation closer to their own ideals. For example, the following correspondents, who wrote to PBS in response to *Divided Memories* and had their letters quoted on screen, believed the program to have portrayed recovery memory theory in too positive a light: "We watched *Frontline* this week hoping that finally this memory retrieving type of therapy would be exposed for the terrible wrong it's doing to families. However, we felt there *was too much encouragement for this type of therapy.* . . . We are two falsely accused parents, Jan and Donna, Cincinnati, Ohio" (emphasis mine). In contrast, another writer, author of a newspaper review, praised *Divided Memories* for presenting an antitherapy perspective: "[Ofra Bikel] tak[es] on the feminist establishment on the issue of therapists implanting memories of sexual abuse in patients."[45]

For each of the two sides there is much at stake, including legal decisions, livelihoods, reputations, and even lives. As discussed in chapter 1 of this book, and as the program recounts, George Franklin was imprisoned on the basis of his daughter Eileen Lipsker's testimony that she had recovered the memory of his rape and murder of her childhood friend. Unlike the biographical film *Fatal Memories*, which ends with the conviction of George Franklin, the documentary *Divided Memories* reports the upshot. Franklin's conviction was overturned and he was released from prison when a judge ruled that the jury should have been informed that many of the details of the case had been reported in the media and could, therefore, have been gleaned by Lipsker from that source and not from actual eyewitness memory. "We know now that an enormous amount of repressed memory testimony is therapy driven," said the judge as explanation, even though Lipsker's memories had not been retrieved during therapy.[46] Also depicted is Gary Ramona, who earned a $500,000 settlement when he successfully argued that his daughter's therapist had implanted false memories in her mind.[47]

I appreciate the program's attempt to use journalistic balance to negotiate its way through an embattled terrain. But this balance or two-sidedness is deficient in two ways. First, the balancing act does not result in genuine objectivity. While the program does bank on an appearance of fairness, it *compels* by presenting new and powerful material. What was new to the public at the time was the antitherapy movement. Whereas childhood sexual abuse was the revelation of the 1980s, the notion of therapeutically induced or "false" memory was the notion of the 1990s. Thus, in keeping with the historical shifts in the discourse on childhood sexual abuse, and in the service of a certain marketable timeliness, the program's hook (PBS may be the public—and not the commercial—broadcasting system, but it still strives to draw an audience) was not sexual abuse after all this time, but "false memory," the new "epidemic."[48] Second, I submit that the show's very balance, while providing rich case histories, actually functions to ward off many of the complications through which adult memories of childhood sexual abuse might best be understood.

How does the show's unintended bias toward revelations of false memory get articulated? Consider the program's use of the Franklin-Lipsker case as a book-ending device. Whereas Part I begins, after the opening credits, with the successful prosecution of Franklin on the basis of Lipsker's recovery of her repressed memories of his crime, the program as a whole ends with an "update" informing us that the case has been overturned. We have moved in the four hours of the program from the judicial legitimation of repressed memory to its repudiation. Thus the program can offer itself up as a discourse that is eminently timely, going *beyond* a period when, in the words of the unseen male narrator, the "theory of repressed memories was accepted as fact on prime time TV." Here, then, is the public television version: more sophisticated, more analytical, and more up-to-date.

This rhetorical pattern lends its structure to the program as a whole. The style of the piece is to mix up the types of footage employed (interviews with experts and with affected individuals, voice-over narration, home movie footage) and to fragment each component so that, for example, an interview, instead of being presented in its entirety, is broken up and we return to it repeatedly in light of intervening and equally fragmented material. This contributes to the impression of thoroughness and impartiality. And in fact the documentary is masterfully crafted to deal with numerous perspectives along a continuum of belief in the phenomenon of repressed memory, from the subtly different to the antithetical. But though the program is in this way structured like a multifaceted crystal garden, it also traces a linear trajectory from clients (as victims/survivors) to therapists (as the professional beneficiaries of sexual abuse) to parents (as they organize around the platform of denial).

Significantly, the program's only case of *corroborated* incest and repressed memory is presented near the start of Part I. It is that of Jane Sanders, a woman who sensed something troubling in her past or emotional makeup but initially had no conscious idea what that could be. Her mother's memory, however, did extend back to the occasion when Jane as a little girl reported to her mother having been molested by her father—an act that the father admitted at the time. Reminded of the incident in adulthood, Jane experienced a "shock of recognition." This case, however, stands in the program as an exception. All of the other cases presented involve alleged rather than corroborated abuse and even, in the third of four program hours, a case of a retracted abuse testimony: that of Mara Cane. By the third hour of the program, we have seen Mara Cane several times, seated at a table contemplatively sipping from a coffee mug. But in later segments the repeated narrow shot is replaced by a shot wide enough to reveal Cane's father seated in the background of the shot. In the context of Cane's retraction of her accusation, and of her expressed fears that he will not forgive her, the ultimate revelation of his physical presence suggests visually the reemergence of his point of view—the idea that the abuse charges are unfounded in reality and induced by Mara's therapist—and of his authority over his daughter's ways of thinking. Thus the patterned change in subject matter, from allegations of abuse to allegations of false memory, (1) legitimizes the notion of false memory as the latest research findings of a controversial field, (2) reinstates the assertions of fathers over daughters, and (3) recalls the plowing under of incest stories that marked the preparation of the *Freud* scripts and film.

Of course, not only the order of presentation but also the subject's treatment makes the case for recovered memories as false and therefore invalid. Some of the most disturbing images and sounds of the program are the sobs and screams of clients in the throes of individual or group therapy sessions. For example, a passage concerning the Seattle practice of the therapist Sara Lee Blum gives us the opportunity to observe a regression therapy group in session. While middle-aged group members of both sexes huddle together on pillows against the walls, a stocky woman takes center stage. With Blum's encouragement, this woman, presumably in a regressed state, cries out, rocks back and forth, and then stands, yells, and pushes away the abuser she sees in her mind's eye. She demonstrates behaviors one rarely sees acted out by an adult, behaviors that dishevel her clothes and discompose her face and body. It is a difficult scene to watch, and its uncomfortableness gives a certain credence to various spokespeople elsewhere in the program who question why a person would desire to claim status as an abuse survivor if he or she were not one. Yet the like-mindedness and intimacy of this ragtag group suggest at the same time why group membership might be desirable even at the cost of proclaiming oneself an abuse survivor. This scene of regression therapy is soon followed by an equally emotional scene of a woman screaming in pain over the memory of having been stuck in her mother's fallopian tube and by an emotionally demonstrative session of hypnotherapy in which a woman supposedly discovers the reason for a babysitter's molestation of her as a child: she herself mistreated this same woman in a past life in which the woman was her servant.

One cannot help feeling relief in pausing between these emotionally fraught scenes for one of the intervening snippets of expert testimony with which the therapy sessions are intercut. One expert is Paul Simpson, Ed.D., a *former* regression therapy practitioner. In calm tones he describes how his skepticism of regression therapy grew as he saw "intelligent and articulate women who would come in the door, and by the next day I'd come back on the unit and they're balled up in the corner crying and speaking with a little five-year-old's voice [which Simpson mimics] about how horrible everything is." "It was shocking," he continues, "it was shocking to me to see this kind of deterioration in these in-patient people." This, he says, led him to launch his own research that led ultimately to his abandonment and repudiation of regression techniques. If one favored regression therapy, this well-spoken and self-contained individual could seem the deadliest weapon of the opposition. For undecided viewers, this island of calm in a sea of emotional turbulence would surely attract and persuade.

In addition to undermining the featured therapeutic practices by presenting them as distasteful and geared to a pathetic constituency, the program undermines *all* therapeutic intervention in cases of childhood abuse by showing mainly the most far-out. It is one thing to believe a person capable of retrieving buried childhood memories of abuse and quite another to extend the belief in memory retrieval back in time beyond conception to ovulation or to the first century A.D. Yet *Divided Memories* lumps fringe therapies together with widely accepted practices, apparently on the basis of the strong emotions they all elicit from clients, with little regard for their significantly different bases in research and testing.

But if the program bypasses the subject of childhood sexual abuse and indicts the therapeutic practices developed to treat the victim/survivors, what is left in their place? "Part II: A House Divided," suggests that a house divided is a sad house and celebrates the unified family by negative example. Here we find the dissolution of families and the cries of parents in mourning for their living children. "It would have been easier if she died," says the sister of one therapy client. The FMSF, discussed and depicted in this section as a bustling umbrella organization where heartsick parents can shelter with their own kind, conveniently steps up to fill the void. So too does a questionable therapeutic practice specializing in "detachment"—the practice of having clients break away from all loved ones emotionally and often also physically. The portrayal of detachment therapy ends the documentary on an ominous note with its suggestion that the inevitable result of recovered memories is family disintegration—and this on top of the program's overall suggestion that recovered memories and not sexual abuse are the root of the problem.

The segment on detachment therapy functions aptly as the program's conclusion, for, as the male voice-over asserts at the beginning of this segment, "It's at Genesis in Pennsylvania that all the issues of family, the recovery movement, and repressed memories of sexual abuse come together most dramatically." This final segment of the documentary depicts the practice of Patricia Neuhausel, L.S.W., and Patricia Mansmann, M.Ed., two apparently self-confident therapists whom we see in action and hear discussed by their clients, most of whom appear to be as much attached to "Pat and Pat" as they are *de*tached from actual family members. Theirs is an "in-house detachment," explain several couples. They sleep in separate bedrooms and don't speak. Another woman, Carol, explains that she is detached from her children, whom she has not seen in eight months.

In the face of these drastic arrangements, the comparatively long interview with a thoughtful and well-spoken young woman named Stacey Good rings with common sense. Surprised herself that her feelings of love for Pat Mansmann still exist, she nevertheless exposes a therapeutic practice based on the expert manipulation of emotionally vulnerable clients. "When you take everybody out of our lives that mean something to us, we're children. So Pat and Pat come in as our parents, and they knew that. They knew that if they got rid of our mothers and our fathers and brothers and sisters and our husbands and our wives and our children, that we would become children. And that to me is brilliant—because they're keeping them."

Not only is what Stacey says logical, but the deployment of this interview in the segment adds credence to her perspective. At times the authority of Stacey's words is enhanced when they are laid in as voice-over narration, as when she says that the clients become children and the image track cuts from a close-up of Stacey to a medium close-up of a middle-aged man crying "like a child." Her account is also used to fill in for images the documentary could not provide, as when her description of "rage therapy" is presented immediately after the program's male narrator has indicated that "some of the techniques we were allowed to see, others we weren't." This revelation that Bikel and her crew were barred from certain kinds of therapy sessions gives the impression that there is something to hide and attaches all the more importance to Stacey's power to present evidence. Finally, Stacey's claims that Pat and Pat are using brainwashing techniques, doing something wrong, and "hurting people" are corroborated by another former client whose wife was told by Pat to divorce him after he failed to assimilate to "the network" and by the report that eight other former patients are suing Genesis. While Stacey's words do not actually end the segment—it ends with the image of a crying mother whose daughter detached from her and from her own children—they lend it structure, and as I have argued, perspective: therapy threatens families.

The program has convinced me that Patricia Mansmann and Patricia Neuhausel are harming many of their clients. It and the knowledge and experience I bring to the viewing situation have also convinced me that therapies such as those depicted are fully capable of inducing memories and manipulating behaviors with the result, in many instances, of individual and family dissolution. But by its selection and filmic treatment of certain questionable practices and sessions over other legitimate ones, the program contributes to an overwhelming case against recovered memory. What the program does not allow is a nuanced position that winnows out illegitimate therapies from those developed to treat clients with a history of childhood sexual abuse and repressive or dissociative patterns of forgetting.

Thus, the most troubling aspect of the program has to do with the limitations inherent in its balanced (but not neutral) structure. Either abuse is present or it is not, either the memory is true or it is false, and the difficulty concerns the problems of telling the two apart. Or so goes the program's logic. Partway through "Part I: The Hunt for Memory," Dr. Salvador Menuchin, identified by the male voice-over as an "eminent psychiatrist who now works in the field of family therapy," makes a telling caveat. "Sexual violence is common," he states. But he goes on immediately to the major issue at hand: the claim that "therapists are creating, together with patients, memories that may be false." Menuchin's rapid dismissal of the former proposition in favor of the latter serves the program's focus on therapeutic practice rather than past events and their ramifications. The implication is that the real scandal is not childhood sexual abuse but the ability of "iatrogenic" or therapy-created abuse memories to masquerade as real. But what if things are actually more complicated? What if truth does not reside in a "one or the other" proposition but in a "both/and" formulation?

This is the scenario that the trauma theorists discussed in chapter 1 of this book strive to elaborate. Consider as well the work of the philosopher and historian of science Ian Hacking. In *Rewriting the Soul: Multiple Personality and the Science of Memory*, Hacking explains that "[o]ld actions under new descriptions may be reexperienced in memory."[49] An actual event may be reexperienced, remembered, and described differently at different times depending on the kinds of descriptive possibilities available to the person at the time of the description. To illustrate, Hacking offers the 1921 case of Bernice R., who told her doctor, H. H. Goddard, that her father had had sex with her.[50] H. H. Goddard "was convinced this was a fantasy." Hacking reminds us that there *is* a fact of the matter, although we may never be able to determine what that fact is. Either the father did have intercourse with his daughter or he did not. However, he also suggests that "the vast amount of memory work does not end with such plainly cut-and-dried facts-or-falsehoods." Perhaps Bernice's father "did sexually abuse her, but in less flagrant ways than Bernice seemed to remember," and she may have "acquired a set of new descriptions in the form of horror stories at the home for wayward girls." Invoking Freud's insight that for an individual the meaning of the primal scene is not immediate but deferred, Hacking explains that in Bernice's case her life experience as it unfolded allowed her a new interpretation of old actions.

Hacking makes the point that the phenomenon of "false memory syndrome," understood and formulated by the False Memory Syndrome Foundation as "a pattern of memories of events in one's own past that never took place," is merely one possibility in a far more varied set of memory responses. Hacking affirms, at least in theory, the possibility of "false memory," which he renames "contrary memory," and acknowledges that "[i]n the prototypical example, a 'recanter' says that she seemed to remember being regularly raped by her uncle, but now she realizes that nothing of the sort ever occurred. Nobody ever raped her. Her uncle was gentle and caring."[51] But he argues that there are other, much more common possibilities for the shifts and vicissitudes of memory. He groups these, with "contrary memory," under the general heading "deceptive memory." For example, in what he terms "merely-false-memory," the uncle in the above example could be "a screen for the father, the real perpetrator. Thus, the memory *is not contrary to all reality, but the past has been radically remolded"* (emphasis mine).[52]

As Elizabeth Waites reminds us, this sort of "radically remolded" but not absolutely untrue memory may be one of the most characteristic responses to traumatic experience. This is especially true for childhood sexual trauma, where traumatic experiences tend to be repeated and often occur prior to the child's development of integrated identity patterns. "Memory itself," writes Waites, "and the integration of memories into coherent patterns, is often markedly affected by trauma."[53] An exogenous trauma, a trauma from an external source, is very likely to trigger a memory pattern marked by gaps and misperceptions that might be explained by the phenomena of repression, fantasy, and/or dissociation rather than a memory pattern marked by simple factual accuracy.

Given this research that expands the possibilities for the relationship between memory and real events, it becomes conceivable that women who, in the absence of virtually all corroborating evidence, tell bizarre tales of satanic/ritual abuse may nevertheless be victims of a less imaginative form of childhood sexual abuse: plain old father-daughter incest. Again, we can turn for clarity to Louise Armstrong's suggestion that despite all its vile and gory qualities, or perhaps precisely *because* of them, satanic/ritual abuse "is far less socially threatening" than "everyday child-molesting dads."[54]

But the possibility that a woman's embellished memory might itself be a *symptom* of her real abuse is a messy notion that the neat two-sided structure of *Divided Memories* abrogates. Actually, it is a possibility that the program runs up against repeatedly but from which it ultimately veers away. The whole last section of "Part I: The Hunt for Memory," from the program's intermission to its conclusion, is devoted to the case study of a woman with the given name of Anne Norris who wishes now to be called Kate Rose. Through home movie footage of Kate's childhood and her senior recital as a voice major, through interview footage and audio track, through the words of an unseen male narrator, and, more enigmatically, through the repeated image of Kate seated in a rocking chair rocking back and forth, the program tells Kate's story. It recounts her traditional upbringing with three siblings in an upper-middle-class home in Santa Monica, California, her painful relationship with her mother, her breakdown and attempted suicide, her entry into therapy, and finally, her rape at a party. The latter incident precipitated the recovery of memories first of paternal rape and then of satanic/ritual abuse by her parents and grandparents. The story is a tragedy. We mourn for this beautiful and talented girl's seemingly senseless descent into a life of horrifying mental images—images, for example, of having been ritually and sexually tormented by family and cult members who stuck broomsticks, spiders, and wires into her vagina, or of having been tortured with tools from a hardware store. Hers is a descent from singing to rocking, from active family life to a state of isolation and despair that is visually expressed through shots of Kate alone on a beach at sunset. As one viewer responded, "I am devastated by her transition from an accomplished singer to a lonely lost person. . . . I think of who she might be now had her therapist helped her to become whole."[55]

But how does the program explain or make sense of this mental descent? Here too the viewer letter is revealing in its suggestion that therapy, or rather the lack of proper therapy, is the key. "What was going on?" questions the male narrator. This query is followed by interview footage of several therapists, each with a different perspective on "what was going on." The first to speak in this section is Dr. Laura Brown, who asserts that there are documented cases where one child in a family gets singled out for sexual abuse. In context, her words suggest that Kate Rose might have been just such a singled-out sibling.

But this implication is buried as the sequence unfolds. "The answer is not to be found in reality but in therapy," intones the narrator. There follow interviews with two other psychotherapists who deal with the problem of "reality and therapy" and have differing responses to it. The most radical is that of Kate's own psychotherapist, Dr. Douglas Bruce Sawin, M.D., who opines that "we all live in a delusion." For Sawin, since the client's pain is real, it is of little importance whether her account of its origin is veridical. He is not interested in entertaining the possibility, suggested by Dr. Brown, that Kate may well be a singled-out incest daughter. But neither is he interested in the idea that it matters one way or the other. This therapeutic philosophy disturbs the majority of people who have grown up in a world where historical facts and notions of accuracy carry great weight and serves in the documentary to discredit Kate's "side" of the argument.

Thus it is Dr. Yapko, the final psychotherapist to speak in this section, who sums up what is very likely a popular position on the question. Authoritatively, dressed in a dark suit and a red power tie, Dr. Yapko explains that the "narrative truth perspective," (the idea that "if a patient believes it, it may as well be true") becomes problematic in "a unique context where truth matters." And what is that context? The program has just provided it by including, between the interview with Dr. Sawin and that with Dr. Yapko, the information that Kate, with the support of Sawin, has filed suit against her parents and grandparents for twenty million dollars in damages. Thus, Dr. Yapko's words ring with the logic that truth indeed matters here. In the series of interviews with psychotherapists, we have moved from the possibility that Kate's troubles are the result of actual past abuses to the suggested conclusion that they are the product of interference by a therapist without regard for the truth and that they are, by extrapolation, *untrue*. Furthermore, we have moved from the suggestion that Kate is the victim/survivor to the implication that the real wronged parties are the unjustly accused parents.

This is powerful *narrative* logic, but is it really logical? What about the possibility, couched in the works of Hacking, Waites, and Armstrong, that *part but not all* of what Kate believes she remembers is true? It appears that filmmaker Ofra Bikel herself has entertained this notion, for, moments from the end of the sequence on Rose, we hear her make a crucial inquiry. "What hurts you more," Bikel inquires of Rose, "the fact that your mother was cold to you or the fact that she ritually abused you?" "Would it have made a difference," she asks trailing off, "if sexual abuse didn't happen, if ritual abuse didn't happen, but everything else, mother the way she was . . . ?" With these questions, Bikel seeks an explanation that goes beyond the "bad therapist" formula to address the unmistakably real emotional pain felt by Rose from a time preceding therapy.

In fact, Bikel seems as much to advance an explanation as to seek one: the explanation that Judy Norris was indeed cold to her daughter Anne (a.k.a. Kate Rose) and that that is "something [she'll] have to live with." As Bikel states through the mouthpiece of the male voice-over and illustrates through the use of interview footage of the parents intercut with home movies, this is Al's and Judy's "own version of reality." Over the footage of a two-year-old Anne patting the head of her baby sister as she lies in the cradle, we hear Judy Norris's voice. "When my husband walked out on me when Anne was two," she explains, "I just shut down. Holding my little baby [Anne's younger sister] in my arms and rocking her I felt a real sense of bonding even though my feelings had shut down toward the two older children at that time." "Anne seemed devastated," the narrator reports Judy Norris as having said about that period. The moment is quite affecting, rendering what could easily have appeared a heartwarming scene of sisterly love a heartbreaking image of motherly love usurped. Thus, the program brings in the parents to corroborate Kate Rose's prior testimony that her mother was cold and abandoning and to advance a third alternative explanation (other than sexual abuse or therapy-induced memory) to explain Kate's emotional pain.

But there is a second question that remains *unasked* of Kate. "Would it have made a difference," Bikel might have asked, "if ritual abuse didn't happen, but sexual abuse did?" This is the obvious question that the program avoids: another potential partial truth, but one that is met with parental denial rather than parental corroboration. And, indeed, given the lack of corroborating evidence, there were probably good moral and legal reasons for the documentary to avoid the question.

I am most interested, however, in the ideological reverberations of throwing the baby of incest out with the bathwater of ritual abuse. As I have been maintaining, the program's perspective is one that discounts the reality of childhood sexual abuse and argues for family integration even in the absence of family integrity. What Armstrong has proposed about society is also applicable to the program: namely that, paradoxical as it might seem, satanic/ritual abuse is more socially palatable than incestuous abuse, not only because the perpetrators are faceless and outside the family (Rose currently asserts that the Norrises are not her biological parents), but because the claims of satanic/ritual abuse are more easily dismissed as fabricated, especially in the real absence of documented cases in any significant number.[56]

The shift from allegations of paternal sexual abuse to satanic/ritual abuse supports the disgusted dismissal by Kate's younger sister Caroline of Kate's accusations. "It [Kate's story] just started winding and winding and all of the sudden it, you know, wasn't just my father, it was my sister, and then all of the sudden, you know, satanic cult [Caroline rolls her eyes] and all these just absolutely crazy notions . . ." For Caroline, the story becomes "crazy" at the precise point where it involves satanism. It is there that the father is let off the hook. Before the allegations of satanism emerged in real life, and early on in the chronology as presented in the program, an uncertainty creeps in. Regarding the lone allegation of paternal molestation, Bikel asks Caroline, "Did you believe it?" "No," she replies. But then she goes on: "But again there's that doubt, you know. Am I crazy, you know, was I in a fugue state throughout my entire childhood? . . . I mean, you know, you second-guess yourself. You think, you know, what could I have missed?" This is the doubt that the thought of satanism demolishes. "If I had had a doubt in the beginning when I first spoke to her when she first told me, by the time, you know, this craziness had come out it was, like, what is going *on* here, you know?" Kate can retain the status of dutiful daughter in the eyes of her parents as long as her explanation includes the element of satanic/ritual abuse; for this is the element that strains credulity and supports, therefore, the dismissal of Kate's incest claims. This is the shift, from incest to satanism, that supports the Norrises' position that their love for Kate is intact.

But what about that doubt? Perhaps, for Caroline, it is dispatched. But what about the viewer of *Divided Memories?* Is it possible that the doubt abides in our memories? I would suggest that, in spite of the program's general and ostensibly sensible dismissal of Kate's charges of both incest and satanic/ritual abuse, the documentary material opens to an alternative interpretation. Why did Kate's parents separate for eighteen months when Kate was two years old? And why did Judy Norris take it out on her daughter? These questions are never pursued in the program, yet they remain on this viewer's mind as loose ends, gaps in the overarching narrative of the abandoning mother and deluded daughter. Could the separation have been the result of paternal sexual abuse? Could the price of the parents' reconciliation have been the cessation and complete denial of said abuse? I do not claim to have the answer to these questions, though I would assert, following Hacking, that one exists. There is a historical fact of the matter in terms of actions performed and received, no matter how they are remembered, reexperienced, or interpreted.

I would suggest too that while the words and gestures of Kate Rose's parents and sister in the program's interviews are used to present an explanation for Kate's illness other than past abuse, these same words and gestures could have been put to different use. The mother's anger, the father's tears, and the sister's eye-rolling dismissal of the satanic explanation, considered outside the program's dominant interpretive framework, are no more expressive of their innocence than they would be of their (albeit unproven) guilt. In other words, the possibility of childhood sexual abuse, though overtly denied by the program, is also inadvertently suggested by the tenor of the denial itself.

Linda Williams describes a process through which a certain group of contemporary documentary films dealing with past traumatic events reveal "the power of the past not simply by dramatizing it, or reenacting it, or talking about it obsessively . . . , but finally by finding its traces, in repetitions and resistances, in the present."[57] Drawing on the work of Shoshana Felman, Williams discusses how Claude Lanzmann's film *Shoah* (1985) uses present-day testimony to deepen the understanding of the past. When Polish peasants are asked by Lanzmann to explain what they knew and understood about the deportation and extermination of the Jews of Chelmo, their replies seem inordinately matter-of-fact, even to the point of callousness. The villagers emphatically quote a rabbi's desperate explanation that the Nazi persecution of the Jews was just retribution of the Jews' condemnation of Christ: "The rabbi said it. It was God's will, that's all!" Perhaps what we are seeing is a persistence of the very attitudes that held sway during the German wartime occupation of their town. The Polish peasants deny their own culpability while simultaneously demonstrating a chilling sanguinity about the execution of their Jewish neighbors. This "repetition in the present of a crime of the past" is characteristic of the postmodern documentary, suggests Linda Williams, extending Felman's ideas from *Shoah* to other films. "[T]he vérité of catching events as they happen is here embedded in a history, placed in relation to the past, given a new power, not of absolute truth *but of repetition*" (emphasis mine).[58]

The case of the Norrises in *Divided Memories* is somewhat different. We are dealing here not with a mammoth historical event independently corroborated from uncountable quarters but rather with an uncorroborated event that *might* have taken place within the confines of a family. But the mechanism of the interview that relates past and present is similar in that the Norrises' denial in the present, while it might be legitimate, might be, on the contrary, the present indication of the very discourse of denial through which the past abuses were perpetrated.

This is the alternative light in which one might read Judy Norris's strenuously dispassionate demeanor, both toward her daughter in the past and on camera in the present. Kate Rose characterizes her mother as having been not only abandoning but angry. She testifies to childhood feelings of fear. And she tells how her mother's anger emerged again after her senior recital, when "it felt that she was just peeling off layers of my skin." "Like with a potato peeler," Bikel offers encouragingly. This account of Judy Norris's past capacity for contained anger rings true in light of her manner in the present during the interview process and Bikel's probing. Discussing her daughter's previous hospitalization and in answer to Bikel's question as to what was wrong with Kate, Judy Norris snaps, "Well, in *my* opinion what was wrong?" Thus, she implies her contempt for the views of the medical establishment, which do not jibe with hers, but she notably expresses no emotion regarding what brought Kate to the hospital—a suicide attempt. Then, after Al Norris tells of his emotional response to Kate's accusation, Judy Norris offers, "[I]t was just an unbearable sound coming out of a man." Unbearable, perhaps, for Judy Norris but heartfelt, we see, for Al Norris. Unlike his wife (or ex-wife by the time of the program's release), he does express emotion during his interviews. His eyes tear up on camera, ostensibly for the loss of his daughter, and he puts into words his love for Kate.

Now, I feel compelled to state again that there is no way for me, or for anyone but those involved, to know for sure whether Al Norris sexually abused his daughter Anne (Kate Rose). But I want to suggest that Judy Norris's demeanor in the present is expressive *either* of frustrated innocence *or* of a capacity for deeply felt anger and the strenuous rejection of unpleasant thoughts. This *could be* the demeanor of a woman whose resuscitated marriage was built on her denial (at the cost of abandoning her daughter) of another "unbearable sound": the voiced suspicion that her husband may have molested their two-year-old daughter.

In a sense, then, Judy Norris's denial stands as the mark of what *Divided Memories* itself denies: the continuing social significance of childhood sexual abuse. To be sure, the program is not about childhood sexual abuse. It is about the rise of a therapy movement specializing in recovered memory, and it is unconcerned with the factual status of the memories in which the movement traffics. To the extent that the program is able to expose the practice and problems of false memory implantation or inducement, I must admit that it has a point.

However, the deck in *Divided Memories* is stacked. To make its point that the more timely social issue is not childhood sexual abuse but rather false accusations of it (and the program is based in a morality where false memories become a problem at the moment they translate to false *accusations*), the program elides corroborated cases of abuse and takes special heed of marginal (one might even say "crank") therapeutic practices. Thus, although the program, through its experts, ostensibly acknowledges the existence of childhood sexual abuse, none of these experts simultaneously exposes illegitimate therapeutic practices *and* indicates what he would do therapeutically with a client presenting a legitimately remembered history of childhood sexual abuse. Moreover, therapists who both acknowledge a difference between true and unfounded claims and maintain a clinical practice including survivors are present within a panoply of experts but missing from the program's glimpse of therapeutic practice in action.

What the program denies is disremembering—the possibility that embellished and mistaken memories (for example, memories of satanic/ritual abuse) can be the result of sexual trauma (paternal incest) and that therapeutic intervention can be genuine and helpful. Judith Herman might have broached such a view, but in *Divided Memories* her words are fragmented and perhaps also elided (left on the cutting room floor?) in the service of a far simpler and also misleading equation between misremembering and lying, between the mistaken detail and the utter untruth. Thus the balanced structure of *Divided Memories,* the idea that two sides may be presented and evaluated, militates against the operative principle of the subject matter of trauma and memory: the principle that the relation between the two may be especially uncertain where the trauma is the most real. This, and not a lack of effort, is the undoing of *Divided Memories.*

The television dramas and the documentary film discussed in this chapter all concentrate on the truth status of incest memories. This is true even of *Sybil,* which was made long before the recovered memory movement began. And this very similarity highlights their salient difference: whereas the television movies "believe women," *Divided Memories,* made after the inception of the antifeminist antimemory backlash, diverts attention from the problem of child sexual abuse by centralizing the phenomenon of repressed and recovered memory and discrediting it and its female rememberers in the name of the false memory syndrome.

It would have been more difficult for *Divided Memories* to retake the ground won and then lost by relevant feminist sociocultural interventions of the 1970s and 1980s if these latter discourses had not represented memory as an either/or (true/false) proposition. That sort of binaristic thinking is introduced through the realist tendencies of the television docudramas and sustained in *Divided Memories,* where it keeps at bay the potentially productive complications inherent in the subject of traumatic memory. Thus, while it was an achievement for television dramas to break through the prohibitions against representing incest on the screen, formal experimentation in autobiographical documentary practice—as in the films discussed in the following chapters—holds a greater potential for representing both the vagaries and the validity of incest memory.

FOUR

Strange Bedfellows—
Incest in Trauma Documentaries

Daughter Rite; Some Nudity Required;
the *Electronic Diary* Series; *Just, Melvin;*
and *Capturing the Friedmans*

Fully two decades after the release of her film *Daughter Rite* (1979), Michelle Citron returned to consideration of that work in an essay she contributed to the volume *Feminism and Documentary* and in her prize-winning book *Home Movies and Other Necessary Fictions,* where the script for *Daughter Rite* also appears.[1] In the intervening years the film had achieved a measure of fame, becoming well known and respected in feminist film circles and well represented in feminist film studies literature.[2] Autobiographical, experimental, and recursive, the film intermixes home movie footage from Citron's childhood, faux documentary passages, and poetic first-person narration in support of its meditation on the relationship between mothers and daughters. But why return to this film, which is already, in and of itself, a critique of documentary's realist pretensions and of society's normative sex roles as well as a revelation of the anger daughters harbor toward mothers?

It turns out that Citron had a lot to add to her previous insights. In both books she writes eloquently from a filmmaker's perspective about the creative process and the recourse to fiction that may become necessary in the pursuit of truth: "Autobiographical fiction presents a paradox. It allows for more authenticity by giving voice to that which we both consciously *and* unconsciously know. Yet at the same time, it works by deception, which ironically, by opening up a space of safety, may ultimately lead to honesty and truth."[3] Moreover, in her monograph she reveals that the daughter's anger was not the only "dark secret" of the film. In truth Citron's mother and she herself were incestuously molested during their respective childhoods. *Daughter Rite* as a finished film forged a new relationship between mother and daughter and in so doing brought the secret to light—making it possible, retrospectively, for Citron herself and for audiences of book and film to read the latter's deepest meanings.

As Citron recounts, she hesitated to show the film to her mother. Finally, two years after its initial release, she showed her mother an abridged version of *Daughter Rite* from which she had excised two scenes, including one in which a woman addressing the camera relates the story of her rape by her stepfather when she was a teenager. But still the full extent of incest's important position in the film remained obscured for another two years until Citron's mother viewed the film at an art museum screening in her home city. Then Citron's mother finally told her daughter that she (the mother) had been sexually abused by her brother, the filmmaker's uncle, between the ages of eight and twelve: "I am the first person my mother ever told this secret to; she was sixty-four years old when she told me, the day after seeing *Daughter Rite*. I think she believed that if I could make *Daughter Rite*, I could hear her secret. And she was right."[4] But this is not all. In her book Citron reveals that she too is an incest survivor, having been sexually abused in childhood by her grandfather, and that her mother's revelation had helped her "to come to terms with" her own experience of incest. Also it "changed forever the meaning of the home movies," Citron reports:

> I had read my family's narrative in the home movies. I had appropriated the medium that was complicit in preserving the idyllic vision of my family, though I was unconscious of what I was doing at the time. And my mother had read my film back to me. As a family, we finally remembered and started to understand and speak our secrets. . . .
>
> I go back to the home movies. I sift through the images, looking for evidence of my abuse. A clue. A visual symptom. Freud said the repressed always returns. Trauma always leaves a trail, if only you know how to read the markings. I want to find evidence of the incest secreted in the behaviors I see on the screen.[5]

Citron's film had been partially a work of her unconscious. The meaning of the home movies is legible only after a fashion and after a delayed return with the benefit of external stimulus.

In this chapter I too want to enact a return: to *Daughter Rite*, a studied film that has become unstudied with the dawning of new consciousness about incest and the vicissitudes of memory; and to the continuum of memory, the continuum of traumatic documentary, and the psychic symptoms of post-traumatic stress disorder (PTSD) listed in chapter 1 of this book. These I want to sift through again in light of the new perspectives provided by *Daughter Rite,* several other autobiographical traumatic documentary features, and one video diary about incest memory.

I have argued that the television dramas and documentary discussed in chapter 3 are concerned with the archeology of memory and the achievement of proof. They present childhood sexual abuse memory as an artifact buried by the sediments of time, and they trace how it is excavated, publicized, dated, tested, and authenticated by legal and therapeutic social institutions. But I have also argued that such proceedings rely overmuch on a concept of memory whose solidity is actually belied by contemporary memory research. Because these television programs do not couch the meaningful vicissitudes of traumatic memory, they cannot effectively restrain the popular tendency to dismiss out of hand incest memories that include elemetns known to be mistaken.

Traumatic documentaries, on the other hand, particularly those that are autobiographical, are very much concerned with the ephemeral nature of memory, and they suggest, self-reflexively, that the representational forms of screen-based media (film, video, the computer screen) can parse memory's complicated grammar. Here, using as the core example a group of traumatic autobiographical documentaries on the theme of incest, I will describe the characteristic features of the traumatic documentary and argue that the nature and arrangement of these features constitute a trauma aesthetic that relies on the psychic disposition of traumatic memory.

Traumatic documentaries are not representative, in their approach, of documentary or nonfiction films as a whole. For one thing, they are historical, as many documentaries are not. Reality television, an exceedingly popular nonfiction form that has been proliferating since the mid-1980s, represents one vector in the development of the documentary form, a vector pointed away from documentary's historiographic potential. At its furthest extreme, reality television can become fully presentist, as when events are broadcast or cablecast as they unfold, with the editing function reduced to the selection of signal from one camera or another. One of the first examples of this, airing in 1985, was *American Vice: The Doping of a Nation,* a two-hour program conceived and hosted by Geraldo Rivera, in which drug busts were carried out live on camera. An on-screen time-code readout joined with Rivera's frequent assertions that what we audiences were seeing was happening at that very moment. Now shows based on the premise of liveness proliferate, including the veteran show *Cops* (very likely inspired by *American Vice*); the recent crop of medically based shows, such as *Trauma: Life in the E.R., Paramedics,* and *Code Blue* on the Learning Channel and *Hospital* on the Discovery Channel; and the situation shows such as *The Real World, Road Rules, American High, Big Brother, The Osbournes,* and the famous *Survivor.* These shows involved or involve real people in real situations, but they are usually edited for future and repeated airing—the Survivors were already home by the time the show aired. Perhaps, then, it is on the Internet where the promise of liveness is best kept though webcam sites such as Jennycam or HollywoodVoyeur. At the latter site, launched in 1999, a visitor could click on a button to activate one of several cameras mounted in the rooms of a house in Tarzana, California, to view what was going on in that particular room. It would be worth questioning the extent to which such programs may be said to be documentaries or even nonfiction, but I shall leave that to others, for these are not the historical films with which this book is concerned.

But historical documentaries are not necessarily traumatic by my definition, not even when they treat disturbing cataclysmic events such as war, famine, or ecological disaster. To be construed as a traumatic documentary, a film must place in abeyance the traditionally assumed correspondences between image and reality and between imagination and reality. For example, Ken Burns's groundbreaking nine-part documentary *The Civil War* (1990) evokes the horrors of battle and the divisions of people and the nation, but it does so in a way that reaffirms constantly the legitimacy of its own historical project and the clarity of the cinematic lens as a scope through which the past is sighted.

Traumatic documentaries are distinguished by their aesthetic and formal properties as much as by their subject matter, taking what Linda Williams describes as a "postmodern approach" to "the trauma of an inaccessible past." The taxonomy I began in chapter 1 and will elaborate here builds on Williams's identification of "a special few . . . documentaries" that recognize the ultimate inaccessibility of perfect historical truth but aim nevertheless at the truth that lies on the cusp of a "receding horizon."[6] My own interest, as should be clear by now, is to contextualize the group of traumatic documentaries made over the last twenty-odd years in relation to popular debates on, and more traditional representations of, history and memory and to describe in some detail their characteristic features.

One more qualification. Whereas all trauma documentaries meditate on the historical representation of catastrophe, not all trauma documentaries are biographical or autobiographical. Here I will concentrate on traumatic documentaries that do place a documentary protagonist or protagonists and his, her, or their testimony about tragic past events at the center of the work in order to interrogate the uses and limitations of a historiography of traumatic reminiscence. Particular attention will be paid to works in which the film- or videomaker is the work's protagonist or is in a highly charged relationship with that person. As P. Adams Sitney observed in his seminal "Autobiography in Avant-Garde Film," "[T]he very making of an autobiography constitutes a reflection on the nature of cinema, and often on its ambiguous association with language."[7] My concern is the construction—and deconstruction—of traumatic memory as it pertains to a self and its history.

In chapter 1 I identified and arrayed the various tendencies in traumatic documentaries on a continuum ranging from fiction to nonfiction. The past may be shown through archival photos or footage, represented in the form of relics, talked about by people in a given documentary, and/or reenacted. So far I have suggested that each way of representing the past corresponds to a certain point on the continuum, with the middle portion, as in cases where actors reenact events that really took place, harboring the most complications.

The already complex matter of fictional/nonfictional modalities of representing the past is further complicated by filmmakers' subtle modifications of these modalities to change their position on the continuum. For example, one might expect to find the home movie near the right end of the continuum, since it is a kind of filmic primary document—what you see is what was, selection and perspective notwithstanding. But when Michelle Citron manipulated her own home movies for *Daughter Rite,* slowing and repeating short sequences, she was in effect sliding those images along the continuum to the left. The child Michelle did not have her barrette refastened ten times, only once. The home movie images are no longer documents simply lifted from the real events that they depict. Rather, they bear the marks of subsequent aesthetic choices about their appearance and disposition.

In the (auto)biographical traumatic documentary the most suggestive affinities lie not between a given way of representing the past and its location along the continuum but rather between a given way of representing the past and the features of memory linked to PTSD. (Auto)biographical traumatic documentaries may be recognized by their use of three strategies or three categories of footage: (1) home movies, (2) direct address to the camera or to an unseen interviewer, and (3) enacted and reenacted sequences. These, I will argue, are woven together in the films such that their formal design echoes that of the traumatized mindscape, with its characteristic recurrent memories, dissociative tendencies, and involuntary reenactments.

HOME MOVIES AS RECURRENT MEMORY

Home movies and old photographs are a recurring feature of traumatic autobiographical documentaries, both from film to film and within a given film. Whereas in traditional historical documentaries these imagistic artifacts are often used to define and anchor the historical narrative (providing us, say, with the knowledge of what a president or general looked like at age eight as his "character" is being introduced), in traumatic documentaries old pictures appear at odd points, their placement unobservant of temporal logic. Neither do they serve a strictly referential purpose in traumatic documentaries, for often the same images are repeated time and time again. Moreover, their integrity as indexical signs may well be tampered with by filmmakers eager to tease out unexpected or deeper meanings, and home movies used in traumatic documentaries are often slowed, reversed, and/or duplicated.

Given their characteristic use, home movies and photographs take on the same role vis-à-vis the signifying context of the traumatic documentary as that played by recurrent memories in the mind of a person suffering from PTSD. Home movies, like recurrent memories, intrude repeatedly upon textual consciousness, fragmenting its potential cohesion and disturbing its narrative linearity. Unlike actual recurrent memories, which come unbidden, home movies in autobiographical works are deliberately incorporated, but, as we saw with the example of *Daughter Rite,* their shifting meaning is not always fully anticipated by the filmmaker. In fact, the relationship between home movies and recurring memories is more than metaphoric, for the autobiographical works in which these home movies figure as memory may themselves exist as the tangible memory work of their makers. But I am qualified to speak only of the psychology of the text and not of the psychology of the filmmaker per se.

In *Daughter Rite,* home movies, mainly of two sisters and their mother, are dispersed throughout, alternating with mockumentary sequences of two adult sisters, and accompanied by first-person voice-over reflections about the present or recent past of a filmmaker who is partly a fictional creation and partly Citron herself. Twelve of the nineteen sequences numbered in the published script are home movie sequences. At any given point in the film, therefore, viewers are aware of an intrusive past, the significance of which they are invited to read in relation to the present-tense material. But the relationship is not the usual one. For one thing, while we assume that the eldest sister in the home movie footage is the filmmaker herself, the eldest sister in the mockumentary footage is named Maggie and not Michelle (Citron). As students as well as critics have noted, this offers us a hint that what appears to be cinema verité footage is not genuinely such. The 8mm sequences themselves are undated, but we can see that they are used out of chronological sequence.

Citron's manipulations of the home movie footage also work against any sense of its being self-evident or directly reflective of past occurrence. As mentioned above in passing, the 8mm images have been magnified, slowed, repeated, and reversed (for example, several times we see the mother and her daughters walking forwards, backwards, and then forwards again along the sidewalk). As Annette Kuhn noted during the film's initial critical reception, "The magnification and graininess of the image and its slow movement and repetitiousness suggest also a close scrutiny of the past for clues about the present." And, as she continued, "The irony is that however hard the image is examined for clues, it cannot in the end deliver the goods."[8]

Or perhaps one might say that in the end it does and does not "deliver the goods." Citron's own scrutiny of these images continued for many years subsequent to the release of her film, and she discovered what she now believes to be a very telling sequence—if one has the language to read it. Citron contends that several of the home movie sequences, including one in particular, show the results of the sexual aggression that was being perpetrated against her at the time the footage was shot. In that sequence she forcibly hugs and kisses her younger sister and grabs her ass while the sister struggles to break free and the child Michelle laughs. These are Citron's words to describe that sequence: "I want to attribute this filmic moment to the incest: an acting out on my sister of the sins of my grandfather, a displaced sexual aggression forced onto a child younger, smaller, and more helpless than myself. I am mean and corrupted and I laugh. I seem thrilled by the coupling of sexuality and power. In the harsh, flat glare of the camera's floodlights, the film is profoundly disturbing. This image breaks my heart."[9]

What we now know further convinces me that the sequence, like its counterparts in other films, bears a relation to truth similar to that of a recurrent memory. Recurrent memories, as we have seen, may not be wholly veracious in terms of the fullness or correctness of the details they reflect. Certain details may be absent, others added. Or the memory may focus on a shard, a seemingly innocent object—or a horrifying one. Or another scene entirely may be substituted, as when a person suffering from PTSD has amnesia for the event itself but obsessively remembers its sequelae. Yet such memories, however large the loss of correspondence to the scene of trauma itself, may still reflect the "gist" of the catastrophic occurrence. So too with the 8mm footage in *Daughter Rite*. The most crucial actions— what occurred between Michelle's grandfather and herself behind closed doors or when nobody else was around—are not shown. The time of the filming is shifted in one direction or another. Grandfather and grand-daughter were not caught in the act. Rather, the granddaughter was caught, before and after, in interludes that alternated with the incestuous abuse to which she was being subjected during those years. But we do see the child's past abuse transposed to her own dominating actions in relation to her sister. What Citron "remembers" by refilming 8mm as 16mm and by sifting the images over time is correct in the gist but skewed in the details.

The trauma remains elusive. Understanding increases in retrospect but will perhaps remain incomplete. In the chapter she contributed to *Feminism and Documentary*, published just prior to *Home Movies*, Citron revealed that her mother's reaction to *Daughter Rite* was significant. But Citron stops short of revealing exactly what that reaction was. "[T]hat's a story for later," she wrote.[10] Finally, in *Home Movies*, she revealed the role of incest in the etiology of the film. Who is to say that more does not remain to be seen? Or that what was revealed will now be embraced to the fullest by future viewers of the film? In this regard it strikes me as significant that the script of *Daughter Rite*, included near the back of the book *Home Movies*, presents the telling sequence whose meaning was interpreted in the book's previous pages with the innocuous words "Images of the two young Sisters, dressed in pajamas and curlers, mugging to the camera."[11]

Like *Daughter Rite*, Odette Springer's superb autobiographical feature documentary *Some Nudity Required* (1998)[12] presents home movie footage of the filmmaker at various stages from toddler to teen interspersed with images from more recent times. (These latter images are not "faux," as in *Daughter Rite*, but they are somewhat manipulated, as we will see below.) Structured into the film like memories reasserting themselves in a trauma-tized mindscape, Springer's home movie frames take on more explicit meaning as the film progresses. Finally, with the help and guidance of Springer's thoughtful first-person narration and the cinema verité sequences, we realize that the images shown near the beginning of the film and repeated in part near its end reflect the family situation of a child who was being sexually abused. In fact, we learn that the home movies themselves were very likely deliberately staged, shot, and later viewed for personal pornographic purposes. Continuing the comparison with *Daughter Rite*, it would be as if Citron's abusive grandfather and not her naïve father had operated the home movie camera.

Whereas *Daughter Rite* is a pioneering film made in the late 1970s by a filmmaker working during the earliest stages of second-wave feminist research and writing about the prevalence and proclivities of childhood sexual abuse, *Some Nudity Required* reflects its own contemporary context. Made after the explosion of feminist literature on childhood sexual abuse and in the fallout of the recovered memory debates, the latter film is savvy and informative about the web that interconnects male dominance and female submission, violence and sexuality, institutionalized film industry practices, representational conventions, parent-child relationships, childhood sexual abuse, and personal memory. It combines many of the insights of Citron's film, essay, and book in one impressive package.

And where Citron's film locates her personal reflections—and the home movies that represent them—within the broader social context of mother-daughter relationships, Springer's memories are posed in relation to, and indeed are spurred by, her work as a composer, singer, and music supervisor in the B movie industry, whose best-known creative executive is Roger Corman. At the same time, therefore, that *Some Nudity Required* is a meditation on the filmmaker's familial history, it is an exposé of what Springer sees as the exploitative practices of the B movie industry, which include an extremely formulaic and unbalanced allocation of gender roles: women in these films are young, beautiful, and big breasted, and they often end up dead;[13] men are unattractive, sexually desirous, and often violent. The film includes interviews with B movie producers, directors, and writers (including the late Samuel Arkoff, Roger Corman, Dan Golden, Bob Wynorski, Chuck Moore, and Catherine Cyran), many of whom defend the genre but some of whom are well aware and even critical of its gender inequities. Also included are interviews with several female B movie stars, including Julie Strain, Maria Ford, and Lisa Boyle, who speak eloquently about their respective views of the industry (Strain is proud of her work; Ford feels exploited and wants to break into A pictures) and whose girlhoods are photographically illustrated.

The key home movie sequence in the film appears near the beginning and provides us with our first image of Springer as a child. "That's me," reports

Springer's voice on the soundtrack, as a little girl who looks to be about three years old marches into the room dressed in a bonnet and a white quilted coat (or could this be a bathrobe?). We have only a moment to take in this image before the film cuts to a second entrance. The same little girl appears in the doorway, dressed now in a salmon-pink party dress (or is it a short frilly night-gown?). She trips along into the room, past a man seen from the waist down seated at a table in the background, and twirls for the camera and for her live audience. In the third shot a woman's hands enter the frame. The hands spin the girl around and then draw her back again toward the entrance of the room. Now, assisting with the preschooler's reentry, another rehearsal to get the performance right, the hands lift the child's dress, revealing that she is not wearing any panties. In another shot a seated woman watches. The child twirls as the camera moves in on her naked bottom. The next shot is the same graphically, but now the child wears only a short undershirt—still no panties. And then, there she is, completely naked. She tries to run off but is pushed back into the scene. "I can still hear their voices, 'She's so cute'; they could-n't get enough of me performing," explains Springer in voice-over.

Viewers might not know what to make of this sequence. On one hand, it could be received as an innocent romp, a celebration of the chubby tod-dler body. On the other hand, it might be regarded as sexually inappropri-ate both as a series of actions and as a series of filmed images. I assume the film-processing lab personnel read it as the former. And in fact, at this point in the film, we are encouraged to shrug off intimations of creepiness. For this short sequence is inserted into a montage that includes typical home movie images of the growing child and her family members to whom we are being introduced in voice-over. We see Springer at various ever-increasing ages playing the piano and starring in a school opera production at the age of thir-teen years. The sequence ends with a still image of Springer at perhaps eleven or twelve years of age seated at the piano as the adult Springer remarks in voice-over, "I bet her mother never dreamed her classically trained daugh-ter would end up scoring erotic thrillers in Hollywood." At that point there is a dissolve to the present, and we see Springer wearing headphones and recording a song. The emphasis here is on the contrast between the career she was being groomed for and the career that actually resulted.

Yet the hint of sexual exploitation in these home movie images is sec-onded in another passage. Speaking of Julie Strain, Springer exclaims, "I've never known anyone so confident in her self-image. Certainly not a wo-man." But then she continues, "Actually, I take that back." On the image track we see a teenager in a bikini smiling into the camera and then a

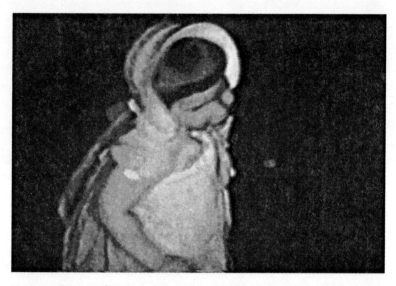

Figure 2. "Dance for us, Sweetie"; *Some Nudity Required.*

younger Springer in a blue sundress. "I was an uninhibited little girl until about five or six. And then, although nobody seemed to notice, I became afraid of everything." We see the child Springer checking her downward motion on a slide, moving slowly, carefully, until the image freezes on her look into the camera lens.

Not until the last fifteen minutes of the film does Springer finally provide the information with which to read the full import of these images. For Springer's film is structured as an enigma. Unlike Citron, whose conscious insights about the relationship between her molestation and her thematic preoccupations postdated the making of *Daughter Rite,* Odette Springer obviously incorporated her own insights along those same lines into the structure of *Some Nudity Required.* She made an autobiographical documentary that explained her choice to work in B movies in terms of her personal history of molestation and explained as well her ultimate need to get out of that branch of the industry for the sake of her own well-being.

The home movie images from the beginning become legible at the end of the film in conjunction with dreams and memories that Springer reports as having come to mind *and* in conjunction with some particular B movie images that Springer says she was becoming obsessed with. Moreover, embedded within the sequence in which Springer reveals her own ingrained motivations is a minisequence featuring another B movie worker, actress

Lisa Boyle, who is the one to speak out loud the term *molestation,* a main subject, we now realize, of the film as a whole.

Over multiple dissolves of the present-day Springer at her piano, we hear the following:

> VOICE-OVER: I'd been having a recurring nightmare. I'm three years old dancing on my mother's grand piano. I'm wearing her gold spiked heels. The grownups are clapping, stomping in rhythm. My ankles twist in the big shoes. I want to stop dancing but they cheer even louder.
>
> IMAGE—THE PRESCHOOLER SPRINGER IN UNDERSHIRT AND UNDERPANTS, DANCING FOR THE CAMERA
>
> VOICE-OVER: I don't know what they want from me.

The camera then pulls back from a mirror image of Springer, which is followed by another moving shot that begins on a burning hearth and pulls back over a rumpled bed. Fade to black.

There follows the sequence featuring Lisa Boyle. This sequence both delays the coming revelation about Springer's own childhood sexual abuse and at the same time broaches and contextualizes it. The sequence contains in miniature the components of the film as a whole, for we see Boyle interviewed, Boyle in a film role, some footage that has the look of home movies, and a photo of Boyle as a baby. What Lisa Boyle says is that "almost every stripper I know has come from a difficult childhood" that included "molestation or very dysfunctional family." "I have a lot of issues of that in my own childhood." These words are intercut with a sequence from a B movie featuring Boyle's character dressed in little-girl clothing, flaunting her buttocks for audiences within and of the film. Also interspersed is a cut-up film sequence in which a man calls to a little girl (we see his mouth in close-up as he lures her to him); the door shuts slowly behind her as she enters the room. The additional element, which has the look of a selection from Springer's own home movies and in any case harks back to the earlier image of the child Springer on the slide, is a shot of a child reaching the bottom of a slide and being swung high into the air by a larger person.

We do not return immediately to the memories Springer has begun to broach. Another sequence, this time featuring Maria Ford, contributes to the buildup. Finally, though, we do see Springer sitting in front of her monitor watching over and over a scene from a film in which Maria Ford plays a woman who ended up being inadvertently choked to death in the course of a sexual experiment. "That's when I finally remembered," announces Springer over a close-up of her at the console. There follows the film's revelation: that Springer was sexually molested in childhood by her aunt and uncle. The home movies from the beginning return in shortened form—the hands spinning the salmon-pink garbed girl and the little naked body—this time interspersed with close-ups of Springer remembering and overdubbed with Springer's account of their past actions.

> VOICE-OVER: Aunt Lina and Uncle Johnny liked to play this game—
> "Dance for us, Sweetie"—I lie down on the floor and
> Johnny watches as she hovers over me. When I hear the
> clanking of her gold charm bracelets I know her hand is
> reaching for me. She always laughs when she touches me,
> slowly sliding her finger inside until she makes me laugh
> back at her. The little electric rushes feel good, but I'm
> really nauseous at the same time. Where is my mother?
> I am so scared. I hate those pictures they take of me.
> Whenever I'm with them I feel like a bad girl.

One additional moving image is shown: the girl Springer dressed in a garment opened at the front like a tent flap to reveal her genitalia. The child bends down to look into the camera's lens, as if preferring even then to be shown full face rather than naked and from the waist down.

Springer tells us in voice-over that her older cousins corroborated her memories with their own, although her mother denied that anything like that could have happened in their family. We see sepia-toned shots of Springer packing to leave and a shot of her car proceeding down the road and around the bend.

> VOICE-OVER: It became clear why these images so attracted me. Degra-
> dation, pleasure, fear. That's the basic formula for an erotic
> thriller. When I was violated, it felt good . . . and bad . . .
> kind of like getting your wires crossed.
> It was time to get out. I quit my job.

I like the elusiveness of Citron's film *Daughter Rite,* where the meaning of images is never fully exhausted, for it reconfirms what we know to be the uncertainty of memory. But there is something to be said as well for the explicitness and supreme control exercised by Springer's film: the dark secret, finally and masterfully revealed, is that she was sexually abused in childhood, as were a number of actresses in the B movie industry. Yet this satisfying—if disturbing—certainty is accompanied by an equally satisfying complexity. Even though the film presents Springer's incestuous molestation by her aunt and uncle as a corroborated fact of history, the film does broach memory's inherent ambiguities. For one thing, one gathers from Springer's narration that she had been amnesiac for a time about the abuse by her relatives ("That's when I finally remembered"), which would qualify her memory as having been repressed and recovered rather than continuous—and therefore subject to an extra measure of reconstructive work. And unlike in the TV movies, where questions about the idiosyncrasies of recovered memory are ignored, here they are enhanced by the film's formal structure. The 8mm images on which portions of the aunt's and uncle's vile acts are recorded, metonymically, are included in the film prior to Springer's avowed recall. They announce themselves periodically, like a traumatic memory that returns unbidden. Shall we assume from this that the repression was incomplete and the remembrance more complicated than a sudden bolt of lightning? Handled as recurrent memories, these 8mm flashes introduce a fascinating ambiguity as to the completeness of forgetting and the relationship between home movies and memory. Moreover, according to the film's narrative, it was not Springer's constant sifting of her home movies that triggered her abuse memories, but rather her constant sifting of sexually explicit and violent scenes from B movies that did so: "I watched Maria's scene over and over. I thought my fascination was just about kinky sex. But now the violence was turning me on too. I was horrified. *That's when I finally remembered*" (emphasis mine). The substitution suggests that representations of sexuality and violence for profit, for personal consumption, and for the sake of memory, are thoroughly connected and thoroughly meaningful as indicators of social and cultural authority and the powerlessness of women and girls. But at the same time it suggests that the connections are mysterious and shifting.

Used in the traumatic documentary, home movie and photographic images insinuate themselves into present consciousness, promising knowledge about, and at the same time marking our distance from, the past.

DISSOCIATION AND DIRECT ADDRESS

In a monologue delivered in direct address to the camera, Stephanie in *Daughter Rite* recounts the story of her rape by her stepfather when she was a teenager. But as I have discussed above, by the end of the film—in the credits if not before—we have come to realize that "Stephanie" is not a real person but rather a character played by an actress. If we had felt this revelation as a betrayal (the rape was a fiction; our sympathies were improperly solicited) or become smug in our superior understanding of the use of the artifice, Citron throws us for another loop in *Home Movies.* There she reveals that the story was that of a real person after all, a sixteen-year-old girl whom Citron had interviewed while doing preparatory research for the film. The direct-address style as used here touches on both truth and artifice and departs dramatically, so to speak, from the conventional use of direct-address interviews in informational documentaries.

We learn about the past when individuals speaking into the camera lens, and/or to an unseen interviewer positioned to the side of the camera, report what they know. This is a major way—along with the use of archival footage—that historical knowledge is conveyed in the documentary mode in its broadest definition. In traditional news-style documentaries, experts pass along information and eyewitnesses offer corroboration. Think of the government and military spokesmen who proliferate in World War II newsreels or Edward R. Murrow's sincere plea for our compassion in *Harvest of Shame* (1960). Or, for a less dictatorial but still authoritative use, consider the centrality of direct address in *Vietnam: A Television History,* the renowned thirteen-part series that aired on PBS in 1983. There, striking use is made of direct-address reminiscences by people with very different perspectives, including both American soldiers and North Vietnamese villagers.

The potential of the direct-address technique to expand historical discourse is even more fully realized in the traumatic documentary. Along with home movies and (re)enactment, to be discussed below, direct address epitomizes the traumatic documentary's historiographical practice. For traumatic documentaries tend to use direct address and the closely related technique of the full-face address to an unseen interviewer, not just to disseminate information, but also self-reflexively to interrogate the testimonial form itself. Following the trail of direct-address and other interviews in the traumatic documentary, we find that there can be myriad different points of view on any given matter and that testimonials, like the memories from which they are derived, can be true to the gist of an event while being ambiguous or mistaken in the details.

Lynn Hershman Leeson is a San Francisco–based performance and multimedia artist who, over the course of a career spanning more than thirty years, has explored questions of self and identity and their construction. In her video works, particularly her autobiographical *Electronic Diary* series (1984–96), her explorations of selfhood have proceeded via the technique of documentary direct address, but direct address pushed to its most radical ends and complemented with other forms of expression that irrupt strategically into the text. Hershman's *Electronic Diary* videos are structured around her intimate address to the camera. In *Binge* (1987) she confides to the camera, ironically, "I would never ever talk this way if someone were in the room."[14] And what she confides in particular are almost unbearable (her word) truths (her word) about her personal history of physical and sexual abuse and about how that history forms a link in the chain of human rights abuses worldwide.

For Julia Lesage, what makes Hershman's work radical is more than David James's observation of "video's [medium-specific] ability to represent—to construct and deconstruct—a self."[15] Lesage argues further that Hershman's is a specifically feminist endeavor to bring to light the relationships among psychic fragmentation, the physical and sexual abuse of children, and patterns of men's domination and women's masochism under patriarchy.[16] That women may identify with their oppressors and/or derive sexual pleasure along with feelings of violation is an aspect of sexual abuse that Hershman has brought out but that other feminists have had a difficult time facing. Springer suggests something similar at the end of her film, saying, "[W]hen I was violated it felt good . . . and bad." But Lesage indicates that this troubling aspect of Hershman's work has been partially responsible for her neglect by feminists. I concur with Lesage's reading of Hershman's video oeuvre as a place where virtually unspeakable connections are made. The *Electronic Diary* series teaches us, explains Lesage, that "[w]omen's consciousness itself is shaped by our living in a violent world, and . . . there is an ever present connection between the abuse of women and our perceptions, behavior, and art."[17]

For me, the additional element of great interest in Hershman's tapes is their concentration on revealing the naked truth of her abuse while at the same time calling into question the memory processes through which that abuse is remembered *and* forgotten, communicated *and* denied. In other words, while one self-avowed purpose of the diary is to speak aloud dirty family and social secrets, its actual work is to make connections that are elusive and abstract rather than bald and technical.

At the end of *First Person Plural* (1989), Hershman makes it perfectly clear that her history involves childhood abuse. "I showed this tape to friends," she states, "but they didn't get it. I'll just have to come right out and say that when I was very young I was physically abused and sexually abused." And in fact *First Person Plural* begins with a monologue repeated from an earlier tape,[18] *Confessions of a Chameleon* (1986): "When I was . . . uh . . . small. I mean, when I was little, there would be these . . . uh . . . kinds of episodes of battering. And I would go up into my attic and almost retreat into myself." Or in *Binge* she says bluntly, "I will acknowledge the incest." Equally important to disclosing a history of abuse is the exploration of how events that took place were at one time cloaked in secrecy. Hershman includes passages about the prohibition against admission. Several times throughout *First Person Plural* we see a shot of her in the dark, whispering, "[Y]ou're not supposed to talk about it," and we see several times a giant close-up of her lips mouthing, "[D]on't tell." The close association of revelation and the prohibition against it is further illustrated by a shot of the talking head of Hershman in front of a wall covered with the words "Do not say it" and "Don't talk." Hershman does talk, speaking of how she was harmed and how as a later result she would tend to be attracted to abusive men, and ultimately the prohibitive graffiti is wiped out by her image grown large.

Yet as I have indicated, Hershman interjects doubt about the statements she makes to the camera/to us and about how perfectly or imperfectly the past may be preserved in her memory. She "toys with her own credibility. She drops us in an abyss between belief and denial," astutely observes David James.[19] For one thing, some of the autobiographical facts Hershman reports sound improbable. In *Confessions of a Chameleon* she states that she started attending college when she was going into the third grade. This was indeed the case. Hershman had been part of a pilot educational program in which a handful of elementary school–age children were selected to attend college courses. But the tape provides only the bold, incredible statement, which we are left to grapple with and possibly disbelieve in the context of the rest of the material. Another way in which she casts doubt on her own statements is by revealing that she has lied to others in the past. For example, she states that when her husband left her she didn't tell anybody for years. "I kept saying that he was on vacation," she explains.

But the major way through which Hershman calls into question the same facts that she asserts is through reference to personality dissociation. This theme was present in Hershman's work prior to the *Electronic Diary* series, particularly in the performances and exhibited works concerning Roberta Breitmore, a persona embodied by Hershman for nine years ending in

Roberta's enacted exorcism and death in Italy in 1978. Roberta Breitmore had her own slate of biographical data (born August 19, 1945, educated at Kent State University, etc.) and her own identity artifacts (a checking account, a driver's license, a wardrobe, a diary, and responses to an ad she placed for a roommate), which were exhibited in various museum shows.[20] Roberta was and was not Hershman: "Many people assumed I was ROBERTA. Although I denied it at the time and insisted that she was 'her own woman' with defined needs, ambitions and instincts, I feel in retrospect that we were linked. ROBERTA represented part of me as surely as we all have within us an underside; a dark, shadowy anaemous cadaever that is the gnawing decay of our bodies, the sustaining growth of death within us that we try with pathetic illusion to camouflage through life . . . . She was my own flipped effigy."[21] Autobiographical personae, especially Roberta Breitmore, are works of artistic expression drawn from Hershman's own life.

In the *Electronic Diary* series Hershman refers to a personal history of dissociation. When she was small, she says, she would react to episodes of battering by creating other "characters"—by "dissociating," we would say with the benefit of psychological terminology. In other words, the child Hershman, like Sybil, invented personality alters to experience and remember events too horrible to comprehend as an integrated personality. "I would create these characters, each of which had their own life. Very completely. And sometimes it was hard to tell who was who or what the real truth of the . . . uh . . . incidents were. And . . . uh . . . what was fantasy" *(Confessions of a Chameleon)*. She describes this method, used consciously and/or unconsciously, as carrying on into her adult life. "For years I would pretend I was other people" *(First Person Plural)*. Was Roberta Breitmore one of these? Furthermore, Hershman's use of the multiple selves in *First Person Plural* suggests that memory can be a matter of perspective: "I always told the truth . . . for the person I was. But the personas kept fluctuating. They would see things from all sides . . . [a]nd be afraid from all sides."

For our purposes, the most significant aspect of this dissociation is its incorporation as a video technique. Because the *Electronic Diary* videos are each shot over the course of a year before being edited, each contains various images of Hershman photographed at different times. The practical result is that, over a tape's duration of ten or thirty minutes (depending on the specific work in question), we see her dressed up or casually garbed, wearing makeup or not, and with different hairdos, and even, in *Binge* (which is about Hershman's compulsive eating and dieting after becoming separated from her husband), at different body weights. Moreover, the

Lynns that we see are often further multiplied by digital effects so that at points in *Confessions of a Chameleon* and *Binge* (tapes entirely made up of Hershman speaking to the camera)[22] we see up to thirty-one duplicated head shots, arranged in successive columns of one, two, four, eight, and sixteen. In other words, her splitting image is like that of a cell dividing; the initial Lynn divides into two Lynns, which then divide into four, and so on. The opening passages of *Confessions of a Chameleon,* in which she talks about her childhood coping strategy of creating characters, are delivered by a relay team of Lynn Hershmans. First we see her as a full-screen image speaking to us. Then that image reduces in size and a small double appears in a box to the left. The duplicated images of Lynn look left while the large one freezes and the smaller head is replaced by a new image of Lynn, dressed in the same clothing but looking screen right instead of screen left. This image is followed by four new head shots, rapidly cut together, including one that contains its mirror image reflected upside down in a shiny table surface. All this takes place in the first two minutes of the tape and continues in the same manner throughout.

This multiplication of her image in conjunction with the suggestion that "it was hard to tell who was who or what the real truth of the [past] incidents were" might seem like the ravings of a woman completely out of touch with reality. But this admission allows Hershman to illustrate what is also a central argument of the psychological literature discussed in chapter I of this book: namely, that one of the effects of real trauma can be a split self constructed partially of fantasy components. In fact, although she indicates that what she tells people cannot be taken at face value, specifying that "we deal with things through layers and copying and *fiction* and faction" (*Binge;* emphasis mine), this is not to say that the abuse did not happen. We might say, rather, that the abuse itself *caused* the alternations in personality here manifested through the video medium. Her assertions are difficult to believe—even for her in retrospect:

> It was always that . . . uh . . . in my situation the truth was much more difficult to believe than anything I'd made up. (*Confessions of a Chameleon*)

> I thought when I remembered things that were, might have happened to me as a child . . . very young child . . . that I was making it up, confusing things in my mind. But I believe that the fantasy was real, that the unspeakable horrors that were the framework for my childhood and for my understanding of who I am really did happen. (*First Person Plural*)

But the response she attempts to elicit is not one of disbelief; rather, it is an understanding that the episodes of battering were exceedingly difficult to experience and are equally difficult to remember and communicate.

Textual dissociation in Hershman's work is the key enabler of her complex and contradictory representation of memory and history. Unlike classical Hollywood productions, where the theme of sexual abuse is left behind in the source novels and early script versions that remain as the unrealized artifacts of a whole productive entity, Hershman's *Electronic Diary* series itself encompasses the traumatic material and the multiplicity to which it gives rise. And if another version of a certain tape should be created (Hershman is known to reedit her own material),[23] a further multiplication of the text whose logic is the multiple, it is for purposes not of censorship but of further investigating the properties of traumatic representations of selfhood.

I want to extend the use of the concept of dissociation for the analysis of trauma films. For while we cannot say that other film- and videomakers are as directly involved as Hershman with personality dissociation and with the technologically facilitated multiplication of their own images, we can say that others are equally interested in shards of testimony that cohere as a crystalline history of incest. For *Daughter Rite,* Michelle Citron developed a new mode of autobiographical discourse that involved the creation of a surrogate self (a fictional personality alter?) who could speak the secret of incest. For *Just, Melvin* (James Ronald Whitney, 2000), a Web site was built in which the names of family members are arranged in a circle. Clicking on a given name activates an audio recording of a few snippets of that person's dialogue from the film. Together they tell what could not be told alone.

'JUST, MELVIN'

Just, Melvin is a genealogy of incest. A stunning feature-length autobiographical work by James Ronald Whitney, the documentary includes interludes of direct address in which Whitney tells his own history of childhood incest. These are interspersed with family photos, archival television sequences featuring Whitney's youthful appearances on game shows and in televised dance contests, and individual and group interviews with more than a dozen family members. There is even a home movie sequence of Whitney's wedding. In fact the whole film has a home movie quality, being about a filmmaker and his family as they are today, crying and laughing before the camera lens. Only this film documents as well the filmmaker's and his family's quest to bring to light the truth about their past and to bring to justice the perpetrator: patriarch Melvin Just.

I do not want to make the concept of dissociation a procrustean bed. With one or two possible exceptions—Aunt June has evidently forgotten parts of what happened, Aunt Denise has had flashbacks—there is no evidence here that any family member suffers from a dissociative disorder or even creates personality alters deliberately, as does Hershman. Nor are there any James Ronald Whitney surrogates as there are Michelle Citron surrogates in *Daughter Rite*. But in *Just, Melvin* the recourse to other personae (different people, same family) and the multiplication of their testimonies are clearly necessary for the autobiographical project. If in the case of Hollywood cinema one might speak, as I have, of other textual versions— the finished film's intertexts—as dissociated remnants of what could not be represented in the mainstream, here one might speak of the proliferation of voices in the film as a kind of intratextual dissocation.

James Whitney's personal history is narrated in direct address to the camera, and he appears to be alone in the room, à la Hershman, when he shares these confidences. That the film invites us to join Whitney in this self-exploration, and in the havoc that Melvin Just has wrought, is suggested by one shot that is an homage to *Citizen Kane* (Orson Welles, 1941)—a film about the impossible desire to really know a man. At one point in *Just, Melvin* the camera pans across a city skyline and down and forward toward a skylight through which we see Whitney seated below. In *Citizen Kane* the camera seems to pass right through the corresponding skylight to focus on what Susan Alexander has to say about her ex-husband, now dead; here the film cuts to a medium shot of Whitney revealing, "I was five years old when one of my uncles molested me." Recurring throughout the film, Whitney's own addresses to the camera speak of two childhood sexual experiences and then proceed with a chronology of troubling events and how he responded at the time. We learn what it felt like to have a suicidal mother who once hooked a hose up to the tailpipe of her car: he would pretend she was dead so that if she died he would not "freak out and just lose it." He encouraged himself with the thought that "if your mom kills herself, shame on her. But you can't let it destroy you." Whitney also acknowledges a debt to his mother, from whom he must have inherited his exceptionally high IQ. As in *Daughter Rite*, anger at the mother, at both her power and her powerlessness, are here expressed.

But crucial to the film as they are, these passages of direct address do not stand alone. Rather, as I have indicated, they are purposefully intercut with Whitney's investigation of his family's past, which is carried out mainly through a series of interviews with others. To learn about Whitney we have his unflinching statements *and* we must go back two generations:

> I didn't even know what fucking was in the second grade. And nobody said not to do it or not to fuck your cousin. Our parents were in the front of the mobile home playing cards and we were in the back. She lost her virginity when she was four years old.
>
> But it didn't start with us and it didn't start with our parents. It started with our grandparents a long long time ago. I decided to go back home and put the pieces of a long forgotten puzzle together for the first time.

Thus, in its reliance on survivor testimony and corroboration, in its dogged accumulation of gruesome details, in the presence of an interviewer (Whitney) who is an interested party, in the extent of the injuries inflicted, and in the truth gleaned from discrepant claims, this film is the *Shoah* of incest documentaries. I use the comparison advisedly. I am not *equating* the incest perpetrated by one man on his families with the massive scope of the Holocaust and the Final Solution. Rather, I am saying that the two films representing these different events may be compared in style and structure, for while they are not identical in this regard they do contain some telling similarities. As in *Shoah* (Claude Lanzmann, 1985), whole biographies of trauma are elicited from each of the film's subjects, stories that are then cut apart and shuffled together with one another so that the individual interviews thus joined create a choruslike effect. And as in *Shoah,* here in *Just, Melvin* the filmmaker witnesses testimony about what Felman, talking about *Shoah,* refers to as "the *event-without-witness.*"

Melvin Just sexually abused three stepdaughters, including Whitney's mother, Ann, and the twins Jean and Jan. He also abused two biological daughters from one marriage, three stepdaughters and a biological daughter from a different marriage, and a granddaughter, many from the time they were toddlers. The parties in the film agree that Melvin Just deliberately left the first family for the second precisely because of the young daughters in the second home. As for Melvin's stepson, we do not know that there was childhood sexual abuse, but Jim, as an adult, makes no secret of the fact that he invited his homeless stepsister to cohabit in a sexual relationship. "I can't sleep with you; you're my brother, don't you get it?" she responded. Melvin Just also attacked a county nurse who was the second family's caseworker, killing and burying her in full view of several of his children. A police detective interviewed in the film states that physical evidence of his guilt exists—including a semen specimen, for he also violated the nurse's corpse. But for his crimes of incest, which began in the early 1960s, Melvin Just spent only eight years in jail, from 1980 through 1988. By then his eldest stepdaughter was thirty-seven years old and his youngest eleven. He was never arrested for the murder.

We might say that in this family history there was an erasure of witnessing. Each child apparently realized and despised what was happening to her: "Oh man, I hated that. That was in the summertime, 'cause I knew I was going to get *fucked* every day." And as a group they observed what was happening to one another: "He looked at me and goes 'Shut that fucking door!' and he was humping on her." But what emerges from their testimonies throughout the film is that they figured what they were suffering went on in other families, or they told their mothers and the authorities but received the answer that they "couldn't prove nothing," or they blocked it out. They did not have a choice. Incest in this family was, to borrow Felman's words about *Shoah*, "an event, thus, not empirically, but cognitively and perceptually without a witness both because it precludes seeing and because it precludes the possibility of a *community of seeing*: an event which radically annihilates the recourse (the appeal) to visual corroboration . . . and thus dissolves the possibility of any *community of witnessing*."[24]

"When I'm finished with him [Melvin], he'll either be in jail or he'll be dead," vows Whitney in voice-over. But the more significant accomplishment, in my view, is the elicitation of all the testimonies. By questioning his mother, his cousin, his uncle, his aunts, and his grandfather, by listening concentratedly to their responses, and by documenting these responses on film, *Just, Melvin* brings the "*event-without-a-witness* into witnessing, and into history."[25]

Whitney's pattern is not to quantify. He does not ask how many counts of incest took place, nor is he terribly interested in dates or locales. He is interested in the texture and color of specific incidents. As Patricia Erens has written about *Shoah*, "We learn specifics"; "Always there is a point."[26] For example, we learn the gruesome details of how this adult man prepared tiny girls for intercourse. He would give them crayons to stick up their vaginas, instructing them to increase the number in the bundle until they had four or five, at which point they were to let him know. There was a hard rubber hot dog, meant as a doggie toy, that was to be used for the same purpose as the crayons. Eventually it ended up out in the yard in a tree, where it became green with mould. Then it had to be sheathed with increasing layers

Figure 3. Melvin Just with one of his daughters; *Just, Melvin.*

of condoms so that it wouldn't be gooey. Melvin Just would pay the girls twenty-five cents if he could get his penis one quarter of the way into their vaginas, fifty cents for halfway, a dollar for all the way. When they were older he'd pay them with tampons for having sex with him. These things we hear from more than one woman and from testimony scattered throughout the film. One of the most affecting moments is near the end of the film, when we learn that Melvin had intercourse with his mentally and physically disabled stepdaughter Pambi when she was a woman in her thirties as recently as two years before the film was shot. "He told me to keep it a secret, but he did pay me," she reports. "He did pay you," echoes Whitney. "He paid me a dollar because it went in all the way. But it did hurt," she replies.

But like other trauma films, this film simultaneously presents the naked truth of familial incest *and* draws attention to the frailty of testimony. Some events are not known or not remembered by all. "I didn't hear about that," one sister remarks about a story another tells. There are some events about which people disagree. "He was a real sweetheart, very caring person," Faye says about her husband, Melvin. And if her grown son Jim corroborates this view, saying, "As far as I can tell they were happy; I never saw him beating on her," she herself reverses it an instant later: "I was a punching bag to him." Little by little as the film progresses, we begin to realize that denial in the family was a feature of experience, especially because Faye evidently overlooked or perhaps even colluded in what was happening to her children. She put her toddlers and older children into bed with Melvin and went along with his innocent act. "No one wanted to believe it, especially not our mother," says one of the twins about Melvin's fatal attack on the nurse. June's little sisters would not corroborate her childhood claims to the police. And Melvin himself apparently persisted in his denial until death delivered him from the pressure to speak. Confronted on camera by his grandson filmmaker and on the audio track with a repetition of the testimonies we have by then heard, and confronted as well by Whitney's statement that he has read the court transcripts from the trial that resulted in Melvin Just's conviction for incestuous child molestation, Just continued to deny the charges. "But I'll never let him forget," swears Whitney.

At the same time that the film witnesses the collective testimony about what took place *and* about what had been missed as a dispersion of bits and pieces of evidence and memory, it dramatizes in the present the relationships that sustained over time a familial culture of incest. Here lies the innovative brilliance of the film. If silences, discrepancies, and denials during the time Melvin Just was molesting his children obviously prevented these atrocious events from being interpreted for what they were, we come to understand this failure of the community to see and intervene by observing the persistence of denial in the present. As Linda Williams writes about the postmodern documentaries of Errol Morris and Claude Lanzmann, so too with *Just, Melvin*: these films "do not so much represent th[e] past as they reactivate it in images of the present."[27] Home movies, interviews, and reenacted sequences are three categories of footage in the traumatic documentary, three means by which the past is accessed. The past may also be "reactivated"—returning to haunt the scene—when actions in the present correspond unmistakably to those that are behind us.

The final scene of the film is crucial in this regard. Watching it, I am outraged. By the end of the film Melvin Just has passed away and Whitney is able to keep his vow (that Just would be in jail or dead) and to shoot footage at the gravesite service. There the daughters eulogize their father. Some choose to avoid what one would have thought would be the determining factor in their relationships with their father. "I love him and he was my father," attests Jenise. "My dad was an awesome man; he has his faults as does everybody. . . . [H]e was a damn good man," pronounces June. Alternatively, Jerri is painfully honest. She stands up next to the pastor and attests that her father was "mean and ugly to her," that he was a "child molester and a murderer." She pours beer on his grave. But it is as if the pastor hears only the socially acceptable words of the daughters who have forborne to speak of Just's crimes. Previously the pastor had elected to preach from the Bible as follows: "Children, obey your parents in everything, for this pleases the Lord. It also pleases your parents, and they turn around and please you again because they'll treat you nice." After and in spite of Jerri's testimony, he continues in the same vein: "We've heard some good thoughts; we've had some good memories, Lord," he intones. He admonishes the daughters to behave, opting for decorum over honesty, for "good memories" over memories bad and true. Here we have before us tangible evidence of how, when it comes to the relationship between fathers and daughters, religious tenets combine with social organization to discount crimes and disarm testimony. The film further consolidates its anatomy of denial by letting us know that even Jerri was circumspect in her eulogy. Alluding to a barter system mentioned earlier in the film, Jerri is filmed shoveling dirt at the gravesite and giving a post mortem of the service: "At least I didn't say, hey, I had to go ask to get permission to come up and see about having sex or something so I can have some tampons."

Jerri might not have added her comment about what she kept back during the service if Whitney and his crew had not been there filming. Thus, face-to-face and off-the-cuff interviews fall into the category of documentary "enactment" in that, while they involve actual people in real situations, they would not have taken place if not for the presence of the camera. *Just, Melvin* is a work of history not only because the subjects reveal their collective past but because the film writes into history the acts of revelation— the telling—that would not have occurred in so extensive a manner if a film were not being made.

Such performative historiography is even more pronounced in an earlier scene in which Just's grown daughters pay him a visit in a health facility where he is being cared for. Comments by the daughters suggest that many of them have not seen their father in some years, and the way some of the women linger in the hallway suggests a great reluctance on their parts to see him now. One gathers from Whitney's narration that the reunion has been encouraged by Whitney and enacted by the group for the sake of family catharsis and perhaps also so that it might be filmed for the family record— and to provide closure to the film.

Consider, in relation to this, a central feature of *Shoah*: Claude Lanzmann's act of returning Holocaust survivors to their childhood towns to trigger memories for the interview process and, importantly, to confront the remaining non-Jewish townspeople. Simon Srebnik's return visit to Chelmo is a significant case in point. *Shoah* begins with a title card explaining that Srebnik was one of only two survivors of the four hundred thousand-person massacre at Chelmo, Poland, and that Lanzmann brought him back from Israel, where he was then residing. In the sequence discussed previously, the boisterous villagers are interviewed beside a subdued Srebnik. They had witnessed his captivity and observed the comings and goings of the gas vans through which the execution of the other Jewish inhabitants of the town was carried out. They recall how the Germans made him sing for their amusement and how one woman tried to convince his captors to let him go. But in the same passage, some of the villagers exclaim about the gold and valuables they found in the forcibly abandoned suitcases of the Jews. Lanzmann has effected what Shoshana Felman terms a "*seeing again*" of "what remained *originally unseen* due to the inherent blinding nature of the occurrence."[28] And yet, the result is the "*re-forgetting of the Holocaust*."[29] "The film does not so much give us a memory as an action," suggests Linda Williams.[30] By creating an encounter that would not have happened if not for the filming, Lanzmann causes the Polish peasants not only to express but actually to *enact* the anti-Semitism that led them to both deny and profit from the killings in their midst.

Likewise, in the care facility scene in *Just, Melvin,* we see that the family dynamic from decades past, the one that allowed the perpetration of incest, still operates at full force near the end of Melvin's life. For if the image and synchronous sound passages in which the daughters interact with their father were taken out of the context of the rest of the film, we would have no idea that molestation ever occurred. The daughters greet their father, hugging and kissing him. They ask him what he is up to. Pambi says she is glad to see him up and about. June asks, "How do you like me now?" Melvin answers, "I love you now." The lack of confrontation, or any discussion at all of what happened in the past, and the very evident mutual love enact a "repetition," "a renewed reduction of the witnessing to silence." Silence then and silence now.

But certain filmic choices break that silence. For one thing, one sister remains in the hallway and speaks to the camera of her inability to forget and of her pain:

Life is not like that to put back on the shelf to forget, my ass, you can only forget so long until someone brings it up or a bottle breaks. Then you have to go clean the shit up. Fuck.

I don't want to hurt myself because of him. 'Cause I don't know how to release it and I just keep stuffing it in and it feels like this ball inside of me that just wants to explode.

It seems that she leaves without going into the room to greet her father. Another way Whitney maintains a hold on ugly memories is by weaving audio interviews into the synchronous dialogue of the reunion with Melvin. While seeing June and some of her sisters in the corridor of the care facility on her way to find Melvin, we hear one sister (perhaps it is June) say, "I'm not going in running in there hugging and kissing on him. No way." But that is just what we do see. "That's my daddy," June says fondly on the synchronous soundtrack. Then, just prior to another embrace between father and daughter, we hear the following exchange between Whitney and his aunt:

> JUNE: I don't believe I was ever penetrated by him for the simple reason that when I was fifteen and when I was engaged I finally gave my virginity away and I bled . . .
>
> WHITNEY: Is that what it would have taken for you to consider you were molested is for him to have penetrated you?
>
> JUNE: Oh no, no no no no. Fondleism, it's all molestation.

June is apparently living with contradictory feelings that are illuminated by the editorial choice to lay in interviews as commentary over the direct cinema presentation of the reunion. Taken as a whole, the scene effectively displays the double consciousness of ongoing and past survivors of incest. And, taken in relation to the film's use of survivor testimonies, the scene may be seen and recognized as contributing to *Just, Melvin*'s presentation of the past as perfectly preserved in images, sounds, feelings, thought patterns, and actions in the present and, at the same time, subject to the analytical and reconstitutive operations performed by the scalpels and sutures of filmic representation.

REENACTMENT, PSYCHOLOGICAL AND FILMIC

Just, Melvin employs the strategy I'm calling "enactment," and it also employs what I will identify as a special form of cinematic "reenactment." As discussed in chapter 1, to reenact cinematically is to replay for the camera an event that took place previously. Nanook and company in the eponymous documentary classic *Nanook of the North* (Robert Flaherty, 1922) reenacted a walrus hunt, putting down their rifles and picking up spears to satisfy Flaherty's desire to show how Inuit hunted walrus a generation before. Nowadays reenactments are liberally sprinkled into reality shows such as *America's Most Wanted* and *FBI: The Untold Stories* when producers desire visuals to spice up retrospective crime stories. The majority of the scenes in *Just, Melvin* are genuine direct cinema or cinema verité. But there are traces of reenactment, as when Ann recounts how once, when Melvin was beating her mother, she (Ann) got a shotgun and fired it at him (it was not loaded). We see a photo of an old car (presumably theirs) and hear a man's voice on the soundtrack yelling, "Get away from that car." Perhaps the audio snippet is borrowed from a contemporary interview with Melvin, or perhaps it is a recorded performance by an actor. In either case, introduced here it reads like a furious command from the event itself, an echo from the past.

Far be it from me to imply that reenactment is an improper documentary strategy. On the contrary, the device has great potential to evoke the past. Unlike filmicly rendered dreams, which tend to bear oblique or fantastical relationships to concrete past events, and unlike home movies, which tend to represent events temporally or spatially adjacent to a given traumatic occurrence, documentary reenactments are flexible enough to represent the traumatic event itself *as if a camera had been there when it was originally taking place.* Reenacted sequences function in documentary film texts much as psychic reenactments function in a traumatic psychic landscape. That is, in their textual figuration, reenactments offer the film viewer an experience that parallels (without being equivalent to) that of a traumatized person who acts or feels "as if the traumatic event were recurring" and who has a sense of "reliving the experience."[31] The point is to appreciate the historiographic properties of the reenactment without losing sight of its fictive aspects. Reenactments are powerful not just because they resurrect what was but because they constitute something that is not there. Like the psychic impression that an event is recurring, documentary reenactments reexplore and help work through events that are in the past but still refuse to release their grasp on the present. I believe that their potential to evoke the vicissitudes of traumatic memory is best realized when the fictive aspects of reenactment are enhanced and not inhibited or disavowed.

Some Nudity Required and the *Electronic Diary* series, for example, contain reenactments that evoke genuine autobiographical events in a self-reflexive manner, thus making us aware in the very reexperiencing of events the ultimate impossibility of that proposition. Lynn Hershman's fifth electronic diary is *Re Covered Diary* (as Hershman Leeson, 1994). Unlike the earlier diaries, which are dominated by direct address, this piece contains a variety of elements, including direct address, cinema verité interviews with several other women, footage of an all-girl chorus, archival photos, scripted scenes of children shot at an abandoned building and of the mythological Furies, and recurring reenacted sequences featuring two types of subject matter: (1) an actress portrays Hershman, ten years earlier, fighting with her two daughters (although in reality she has only one), who are played by young actresses; (2) a child's head is pushed into the lighted burner of a stove and her hair is burned; she lies on a bed; she sits up, pulls off the wallpaper above her bed, and digs a hole in the plaster.

The burning sequence begins the film, makes up its penultimate sequence, and appears several times in between. It is the film's meaningful core sequence, for it represents Hershman's own childhood abuse from which she is struggling to recover through her diaries. Near the end of the film we see the following shots (with which we are already familiar): a hand removing a pot from a lighted stove; a big close-up of a little girl's eyes staring into the camera; the face and head of a doll being held to the burner, where the flame ignites the hair; the back of what looks more like a real girl's head but is probably a doll or wig being forced into the flame by a woman's hands; a close-up of the girl with a special effect making it look as though her hair is on fire; this then superimposed with a photograph of the face of Hershman as a girl. On the soundtrack and then in direct address we hear Hershman speak the following words:

> It was hard to do this scene and figure out how to get the props that would make it look like that girl's hair was burning and not hurt anybody. 'Cause that girl was me and I remember my hair being set on fire and my head being pushed in an oven like my dead aunts and uncles [who died in the crematoria]. And from that time, maybe before that time when I was about two, I became a survivor without knowing it. I remember the smell of burnt hair, burnt skin, wax paper and butter about my head and it healed and nobody talking about what happened. It didn't hurt; the healing hurt.

The sequence is not handled realistically, and is all the more strange and revealing for its departure from verisimilitude. Part of the reason for the antirealism must have been Hershman's stated goal to achieve the scene without harming anybody. But the obvious use of the doll and the special effects suggests the importance of establishing a distance between the present and what happened in the past. Nobody should be hurt. Nobody should have been hurt. But the healing hurts, for it involves facing up to and intervening in painful memories through their video re-presentation as abnormal occurrences that cannot be overlooked as was the childhood abuse.

In *Some Nudity Required* it is not Odette Springer's childhood sexual abuse that is reenacted. The technique of reenactment is not needed to make the past visible since we have the home movies, which, as I have discussed, show us images from a time perhaps only hours out of synch with abusive incidents from Springer's past. Thus, in this film, reenactment—used sporadically throughout—fulfills the function of representing not the abuse itself but the process through which Springer came to consciousness about her past abuse. Reenacted sequences are used to illustrate Springer's initial glimmer of disillusionment with the B movie business and her literal departure from it. Our first view of Springer in the film comes in such a sequence. We hear her voice on the soundtrack describing her entrance into the business: "In the early nineties I arrived in Hollywood and actually got a job. Me, Odette Springer, music supervisor for the largest producer of B movies in the world. This was exciting. Until my first screening." From the landmark Hollywood sign the film cuts to the beam of a projector in a darkened room. Then a scene from a B movie fills the screen. Springer is introduced from behind, seated in the audience, watching the movie, which we see over her shoulder. The sequence then alternates between the erotic thriller filling the screen and Springer watching in mounting horror. "Of course these films are perverse, even stupid, but I never thought they would affect me. By the end of the screening I had to stop myself from throwing up all over the floor. Not that anyone would have noticed, the floor was so dirty they spray-painted it black on a regular basis. I should have quit right then and there. Instead I stayed on and made the music drive the violence even harder. Something beyond my control was pushing me all the way to the bottom."

We then see Springer, from the back and in slow motion, walking down an outside corridor at the studio toward the light of day. This prefigures her departure from the industry, which, as I have mentioned, is represented in sepia tones, included near the end of the film. What I did not emphasize previously is that this sequence is clearly reenacted. In slow motion we see her putting books and clothes in a bag and walking out of the room. The film cuts to a shot taken from a moving car as she drives away. Over images of the road, the car, and her in it—images that must have been created after the fact—we hear her reasons for getting out of the industry: "Degradation, pleasure, fear; that's the basic formula for an erotic thriller. When I was violated it felt good . . . and bad. Kind of like getting your wires crossed. It was time to get out. I quit my job."

The crucial use of reenactment, though, is the one that precedes this driving sequence. As I have indicated, Springer tells us that her abuse memories were recovered while she was satisfying her obsession with watching a particularly violent and erotic sequence. The watching is also pictured through stylized reenactment. Just prior to the repetition of the home movie images, this time with accompanying commentary that reveals their true meaning, we see a number of shots of Springer seated at her computer. Intercut with images from the film she is watching, we see shots of her, face sweating, stopping and starting the images that compel her. I believe we can make the assumption that she was in fact alone, without a camera on her, when she initially remembered the abuse. What we see here is a reenactment of that moment.

The main insight of the film is that watching B movies produced in Springer a psycho-physiological effect that duplicated what she felt while being abused in childhood: "The little electric rushes felt good, but I'm really nauseous at the same time," she says of her childhood feelings. "Degradation, pleasure, fear; that's the basic formula for an erotic thriller," she also concludes. The use of documentary reenactment in this particular sequence may be said, therefore, to redouble *and convey to the viewer* the reliving of experience that Springer underwent and intends to express.

Of course, the viewer is in fact seeing Springer at the screening, Springer on the road, and Springer at the computer for the first time and not for the second. For viewers, reenacted events are not exactly relived, but they are given a sensory dimension. Their use and characteristic repetition and fragmentation in traumatic autobiographical documentary texts constitute a *textual* recurrence that evokes, without being the exact equivalent of, the psychological reenactment that is a symptom of PTSD.

EXPERIMENTAL DOCUMENTARY, SOCIAL HISTORICAL RECONSTRUCTION, AND 'CAPTURING THE FRIEDMANS'

To those who have been traumatized, the past returns unbidden, unannounced, in snippets, and perceptually altered. Likewise, in the documentaries discussed in this chapter, everyday images from the past are made strange by repetition, context, or graphic design, and extraordinary images impinge upon our consciousness: a little girl clasping her smaller sister in a tight bear hug, a doll's hair burning, an aunt's hands lifting the hem of a child's dress. Shots like these come at us suddenly and take us by surprise, emanating from a source beyond our control. But because they were deliberately selected and combined by film and videomakers from the raw materials of footage and memory, these sequences also stand as evidence that some measure of control may be exerted over how, when, and where traumatic memories may appear. James Ronald Whitney's vow to see Melvin dead or in jail is carried out in part through the consecration to film of his relatives' and his own memories. "It helps me to talk about it," reports Lynn Hershman. Or, as she says about the reenacted sequences of herself as a little girl digging into the plaster of her bedroom wall, "[M]y memory is a powdered past pouring out into this camera." In creating and disseminating their works, experimental autobiographical documentarists necessarily concretize personal memory and launch it into a wider orbit.

Although the films discussed in this chapter seem much more personal or individualized than the topical television movies discussed in chapter 3, they recognize the widespread social dimension of incestuous abuse that they convey to us. *Some Nudity Required* suggests (1) that Springer's *own* "crossed wires" led her to take pleasure in viewing violent, erotic thrillers; (2) that quite a few people working in the B movie industry are there for deep-seated reasons of individual psychosexuality; and (3) that B movies resonate with large numbers of people because their institutional and representational forms are derived from human psychosexual features—including unsavory ones. In the *Electronic Diary* series, successive entries offer broader and broader social perspectives. *First Person Plural* and *Re Covered Diary* link Hershman's childhood history of sexual abuse to personal traumas experienced by others and to other collectively experienced traumas. In *First Person Plural,* for example, one of the devices for reading the personal through the social—and in this case the mythic as well—is that of approaching footsteps. "The story of Dracula has always had a special meaning for me," Hershman says in direct address to the camera. As she continues to speak ("It's always been kinda close to my heart . . . the story of a diabolical craving in which you give up your vital fluids through seduction"), the image shifts to that of Nina Harker writhing in her bed in F. W. Murnau's *Nosferatu* (1922). We then hear the sound effect of footsteps and Hershman's account: "[W]hen I was small I would feel that he was coming down the hall into my room. . . . I mean, often I would hear the footsteps." At the same time we are given the unforgettable image of Nosferatu's silent approach up the stairs to Nina's room. Hershman finishes with

Murnau's Nina superimposed over live-action highly diffused footage of an actor Hershman has directed to play Dracula. "I would be both excited and repelled. He's always been there and I've always felt his presence," she reports. But whose footsteps do we hear? Those of the shadowed father of the dark nights of Hershman's childhood, or those of the vampire, Dracula? The point of the sequence, I believe, is that the two are intimately connected; that the popularity and longevity of the Dracula legend may be explained by its covert representation of the simultaneous excitations and repulsions inherent in sexual violation of whatever sort. Springer's and Hershman's works make apparent the way in which personal memories already exist in the social dimension but are unrecognized on some levels while acknowledged on others.

The echoes of footsteps remembered from childhood are given still further resonance in a passage in which Hershman discusses her Jewish grandparents who fled Austria and Germany during Hitler's rise. "They heard the footsteps that were not quite on the ground," says Hershman. This commentary is illustrated by the boxed and slowed image of Hitler's march from *Triumph of the Will* (Leni Riefenstahl, 1935), followed in turn by a boxed and superimposed image of the sea rising in an upward wipe to blot out the background as Hershman discusses the number of European family members exterminated during World War II. Through the recalled and recorded sound of footsteps, *First Person Plural* as a whole joins remembrance, fantasy, and the material cosmos to explain incest in relation to and as an act of social domination. "The blood won't clot," says Hershman to evoke the generational march of a "dominant force" that overtakes "the weaker parts" in a connective history of sociopolitical and domestic violation and abuse.

Capturing the Friedmans (Andrew Jarecki, 2003) is even more adamant that memory is absolutely instrumental to the maintenance of the social contract yet at the same time dramatically unreliable. The documentary, about a family in which the father, Arnold, and his youngest son, Jesse, were incarcerated for child molestation, is advertised on the "Free Jesse" Web site.[32] There, in conjunction with printed documents pertaining to the case and correspondence from Jesse supporters, the documentary serves the continuing effort to cleanse the latter's reputation following his release from prison and to appeal the requirements of his parole, including his existence as a registered sex offender. But along with this practical application comes the film's challenge to any unproblematized linkage between evidence and conclusion. As Nick Poppy puts it, the film seems to ask "how we know anything and why we think we do."[33]

To one way of reasoning, the film's simultaneous presentation of evidence and refutation of its ability to be meaningful creates no contradiction. As in *Divided Memories* (Ofra Bikel, 1995), and as is the wont of False Memory Syndrome Foundation claimants, *Capturing the Friedmans* winnows out falsity parading as unvarnished truth. The film rebuts claims by the police and would-be witnesses and victims that boys were sodomized and otherwise sexually abused in basement computer classes conducted by Arnold with the help of his teenage son. It does so by presenting several individuals who indicate that the interview procedures used by detectives on the case led to misrepresentations of the truth by alleged victims. The film also provides analysis by the investigative journalist Debbie Nathan, who discusses the fact that the case broke at a time of hysteria about child molestation and denies the validity of supposed abuse memories recovered under hypnosis, a technique that was used in the collection of evidence against the Friedmans. In addition, photographic evidence in the film gives the lie to the assertion by a retired detective that piles of child pornography were found lying around the Friedman house. Through quantitative analysis of the dozens of counts of sodomy against Arnold and Jesse, the film suggests that, given the numbers of hours that the classes met, the charges must be inflated at best. Under this logic, the only troublesome evidence is false evidence.

To another way of thinking, however, the film is a remarkable expression of sleight of mind. Here, the truth itself is susceptible to disremembering, and raw footage thickens to nontransparency. When I saw *Capturing the Friedmans* after it won the Grand Jury Prize at Sundance in 2003 and went into theatrical release, I recognized it as a textbook example of how trauma cinema socializes the vicissitudes of memory. This is a film about the tricks a person's mind can play, not to fabricate trauma where there is none, but rather to survive traumatic events that are all too real.

When the police showed Mrs. Elaine Friedman one of the pornographic magazines found at her home, she simply could not take it in. "My eyes were in the right direction, but my brain saw nothing," she observes in the film. She had eradicated the memory of having seen this material until she was shown it again at a later date because she "had no concept that this existed in the world." Might this operation be related to how she managed to live and raise three sons as the wife of a pedophile with less and less self-control? If so, then her statement in the film is one example of how *Capturing the Friedmans* reveals "the power of the past" not by returning to what was, but by "finding its traces, in repetitions and resistances, in the present."[34] The film also reanimates the past through a kind of abridged reenactment in which the camera visits places where significant events once took place. At one point in the film Jesse's attorney describes how he and Arnold had to move tables in the visitors' room of the federal prison where Arnold was already serving his sentence because the latter was becoming sexually excited and distracted by a four- or five-year-child at a nearby table bouncing on his father's or stepfather's lap. While the attorney is speaking, we see the exterior of the facility and then a graphically satisfying shot of a row of crossed chair legs seen from a foot or so off the ground. Whether or not these are the actual chairs in the actual room in Wisconsin, the weirdly subjective shot, from a low height that cannot possibly match the attorney's eyeline, guides us into a time warp in which past and present are coeval. This is and is not what he saw. This is both then and now. Likewise, two time-lapse photographic shots taken of the spinning hands of a clock in a tower in Great Neck against backgrounds of rushing cars and clouds suggest not only that the everyday is not what it seems but also that the past could somehow catch up with the present. This is the clock as it was when Arnold lived his superficially normal existence as one of the town's eminent citizens; this is the clock as it looked when it was filmed after Arnold's suicide in prison. Our job as assigned by the film is to try to reconcile the two.

The film's home movies, though, best exemplify the transferential aspect of trauma cinema in which old conflicts are replayed in a new arena. The home movies in *Capturing the Friedmans* are culled from fifty hours of footage made available to filmmaker Andrew Jarecki by the eldest Friedman son, David. About twenty-five hours of the original material were shot on 8mm film during David's childhood, mostly by Arnold Friedman. The other twenty-five were shot on videotape by David at home and at the courthouse after Arnold's and Jesse's arrests but before Arnold's and later Jesse's incarceration. The scenes from the early years are of happy times: trips to the beach, a Thanksgiving dinner, playing the piano, a boy riding on his father's shoulders. The scenes from the later years feature arguments around the table about how best to fight the legal charges. In one sequence Arnold tells his family outright that nothing happened in computer class. These two epochs in the life of a family are brought together in the film, where they are interspersed with interviews and other footage shot by Jarecki more than a decade later. In this context, we are led to ask ourselves how the ostensibly happy family of the early years could have deteriorated into the dysfunctional family in crisis.

Obviously, the home movie camera of the early years failed to bring to light the secret of Arnold's sexual history. As he wrote in his prison memoir, his first sexual partner when he was thirteen years old was his eight-year-old brother (although his brother, Howard, who is interviewed in the film and shown with his partner, Jack, remembers nothing).[35] Arnold later had sex with boys his own age and, as he grew older, became absorbed by pedophilic fantasies. Apparently, he acted on these fantasies on at least two occasions without getting caught, according to his memoir and according to Elaine and Jesse's attorney, who report on conversations in which Arnold admitted as much.

Nor does the home movie camera definitively portray Jesse as a victim of incestuous abuse by his father. That he was molested is a possibility raised by the film through interviews but never definitely proved or disproved. Jesse's attorney states that Jesse at one time represented himself as an incest victim, but on camera Jesse denies both that incest occurred and that he ever reported anything of the kind to his attorney. As this doubt builds, we attune ourselves to every nuance of the home movies and family photos, and we reflect back on those that flashed by when we as viewers were innocent of the possibility of incest.

In Citron's book about *Daughter Rite* and in Springer's film, secret trauma is revealed behind the home movie veneer. Key passages are subject to analysis, and, as discussed above, a new interpretation encompassing incest is attributed by the respective autobiographers. The Friedmans resist the notion that incest lurks in the family history and archive. But the innocence of the home movies notwithstanding, this was a family destroyed from within and, as presented by the film, a family in denial about abuse that did take place. True, the testimony of the child witnesses upon which the police and prosecutors would have built their case seems induced. The film also explains that Arnold and Jesse were forced by prosecutors to cop guilty pleas even though they apparently believed themselves to be innocent of the charges. To that extent, the family's denial seems valid. Arnold and Jesse may not have—probably did not—perform the numerous acts of abuse for which they were sent to prison. That a game of leapfrog could have included sodomizing every bent-over boy—without anyone reporting it at the time—seems highly unlikely. However, we are given Arnold's admission of having perpetrated two acts of molestation at the family's beach house, and we are shown computer games with sexual content inappropriate for boys that we are told were provided by Arnold for play during computer class. These latter facts are never explained away by family members during the course of the film. They stand as evidence of a biographical perspective that exceeds and is distinct from the autobiographical impetus of the home movies and direct-address interviews with family members. It may be that the allegedly abused children's statements to the police were not "merely-false-memory," in Ian Hacking's term, but rather an exaggeration of less flagrant abuses that felt wrong. As in the cases Hacking discusses, these abuse memories may be, not "contrary to all reality," but "radically remolded" to fit the scenario developed by law enforcement.[36]

How, then, do the home movies speak the family's tragedy? Two sequences in the film use editorial juxtaposition to mark, without vocal narration, the possibility of an incestuous relationship between Arnold and Jesse. A title against a black background informs us that it is the night before Arnold is to begin serving his sentence. David's home movie footage has captured his father at the piano playing the Irving Berlin standard "Cheek to Cheek." Intercut with this action, and borrowing its soundtrack, is a *pas de deux* by Arnold and Jesse in the form of a stop-motion animated home movie. The sequence was dreamed up and created by Arnold and Jesse, who appear before the camera, with David operating. The two enter from opposite sides of the living room, their eyes locked together. Without taking a step, they appear to move toward each other until they are eye to eye and nose to nose. In a kind of couples dance without touching—Arnold's arms are at his side, Jesse's hands are in his pockets—they circle one another. Then they move apart, backwards to the edges of the room, and we return to shots of Arnold at the piano. The romantic overtones of this sequence are recharged retrospectively when the topic of incestuous molestation is overtly raised. This occurs in a later sequence, the one in which the attorney states his belief in Jesse's molestation and Jesse states his denial. The attorney distinctly explains Jesse's admission that his father molested him; while he did not enjoy the sexual aspects, he did enjoy the attention. Under the soundtrack of the attorney's words, we see two photographs of the boy with his father: seated on a rock at a scenic overlook, and at a table before several lighted Chanukah menorahs. In the later shot, Jesse clasps his father to him. The film uses David's home movie footage and family photographs to advance a theory of the past with which David and Jesse disagree.

This is not to say that David and Jesse do not acknowledge the contradictions of their history. David's and Jesse's participation in *Capturing the Friedmans* is carried out in loving memory of a father they must know, on some level, to have been a child molester. After its title, the film opens with a young Jesse hamming it up on camera with his father. "Hi, hi, it's me, it. Oh we're not ready yet? Hi, hi, it, it's me, Jesse . . . . Well, this afternoon after that very lousy sketch about yo-yo-ing, I figure we'll, for lack of anything better to do, take it to a more serious side right about now and we're going to conduct an interview with Arnold Friedman." The latter pops into the frame from the bottom corner, and the two cut up in a distinctly unserious manner. At a certain point, their voices are potted down, and Jesse's words from a later, sadder day are superimposed. What I find remarkable is Jesse's capacity to hold in his mind and heart the knowledge of his father's pedophilia and his abiding love for this parent: "I still feel like I knew my father very well. I don't think that just because there were things in his life that were private and secret and shameful that that means that the father who I knew and the things I knew about him were in any way not real." Elaine's explanation, that her sons' idealized love for their father is that of the child for an abusive parent, has merit but appears overly limited in the context of the film as a whole. Neither David nor Jesse has publicly protested the film's presentation of their father's admissions of acts of molestation. David and Jesse both state in the film that they would have welcomed a confession from their father that the latter had done *something* that started "this crazy mess." The brothers reject simple either/or explanations: their father "did it" or he did not; their father is not a molester and they love him, or he is a molester and they do not love him. The brothers manifest a tremendous, and I believe truly admirable, ability to live with contradiction. He did something *and* they love him. After all, David is (or was before the film's release) New York's number one birthday clown as well as being a child of this tragedy.[37]

Transferring this lesson to film viewing, we are taught that what we know from images is not "in any way *not* real." There is no secret film behind the happy home movies. The several home movie shots and family photographs of Arnold and Jesse with their arms around each other are all we have. They are it. They are precisely it. This is the image of a father whose sexual fantasies spilled over into criminal actions that may have involved his son Jesse as well as other boys. This is the image of a son who adored his father. This is the image of a loving pair. What *Capturing the Friedmans* teaches us, among other hard lessons, is that meaning can be hidden in plain sight. Even if you have tape, even if you have an unmanipulated record of catastrophic past events, those moving shadows must still be read in context. Meaning is neither self-evident nor unitary.

David's video diary is achingly sad and beautiful, and self-contradictory.

Dated November 18, 1988, the entry is of David directly addressing the camera in Lynn Hershman's confessorial mode: "This is private, so if you're not me you really shouldn't be watching this because it's a private situation between me and me. It's between me now and me in the future. So turn it off, don't watch this, this is private. If you're the fucking cops, go fuck yourself." The paradox of addressing an other precisely to deny the other's right to look and listen epitomizes the paradox of the film as a whole. We, the viewers, are introduced to terribly private things that must be made public because Arnold Friedman sexually exploited minors including, very possibly, his own sons. But the knowledge we gain, like that of those directly involved, is forever distanced by time and memory in its very conveyance via trauma cinema.

These filmic acts of intercourse between the personal and the public, the individual and the collective, the familial and the social, and knowing and not knowing are to be applauded for their refusal to bracket off incest as a purely familial and/or purely individual matter. Following this lead, I am adamant that films about incest should not be bracketed off from films on alternate themes. The next two chapters are approached with the thought that, although the traumatic documentaries that they study deal with the Holocaust, these films, like films on the theme of incest, also translate into representational terms the psychological features of the traumatic mindscape.

PART III

The Personal Is Public Historical: (Auto)Biographies of the Holocaust

———

FIVE

The Last Days *Is Not* Shoah— *Experiments in Holocaust Representation*

The March and *Tak for Alt*

Dwarfing the Fortunoff Video Archive at Yale University, the Survivors of the Shoah Visual History Foundation revels in its achievement of having collected nearly fifty thousand videotaped interviews for its visual history archive to be preserved "for all time."[1] Jewish survivors of camps and ghettos; Jews who hid successfully or escaped, some to serve as members of the resistance; homosexual and Gypsy survivors; and gentile rescuers and witnesses are included among those interviewed. The interviews, conducted by trained professionals in the interviewees' homes, and in their most comfortable languages, are designed to elicit testimony reflecting the amplitude of people's catastrophic experiences before, during, and after World War II.

To the date of this writing, the collection amounts to more than 120,000 hours of videotaped testimony, which, if watched twenty-four hours a day, seven days a week, would take fourteen years to consume. According to the foundation's director, the historian Douglas Greenberg, this is the largest public database in the world by virtue of its existence in the form of a Digital Library System with a four hundred–terabyte storage capacity.[2] Catalogued and digitally indexed, these testimonies are being made available at educational institutions both in the United States and abroad. Founder Steven Spielberg has said that he considers the Shoah Visual History Archive to be the most important work of his life.[3]

This evident zeal to archive is understandable in light of a particular convergence: from one direction, the advanced age and passing away of Holocaust survivors, witnesses, collaborators, and perpetrators; and, from the other direction, the growing legions of Holocaust deniers.[4] The culture of the mid-1990s further strengthened the archival project by giving weight and dimension to minoritarian experiences, including the wave of hatred that pounded European Jewry. The U.S. Holocaust Memorial Museum in Washington, D.C., was dedicated in April 1993 and has been crowded by visitors ever since. Citing that museum opening and the release of *Schindler's List* (Steven Spielberg, 1993) several months later, Michael Rothberg, writing advisedly, has dubbed 1993 "The Year of the Holocaust."[5]

Because of this evidently powerful impetus to speak and listen to Holocaust stories and to secure the memories of them, one is loath to question the Visual History project. But all the same, a certain critical perspective is necessary to secure the legitimacy of the archive by taking cognizance of its strengths *and limitations* as a repository of historical evidence. Historian Harold Marcuse has observed that the majority of survivors whose testimonies have been recorded since the project's inception in the 1990s were children during their wartime experiences and are not, therefore, first-hand witnesses to the larger workings of the Final Solution. Moreover, as Marcuse has also noted, people's memories of events that took place a half century ago *may not be wholly veracious.*[6] Indeed, in view of the preceding pages, it will come as no surprise to the reader that I too must broach the subject of the frailty of memory, now with regard to Holocaust recollection. Why has the foundation made elaborately high-tech plans to cross-reference statements made by interviewees but no similar plans to check facts? But how can one suggest that there may be a need for empirical proof without sounding like a denier?

My ambition, of course, is to *take back from the deniers* the ever-present amnesias and slips of memory that mark the return path to historical occurrence. Whereas deniers pounce on discrepancies between and among histories and testimonies as evidence of deception, the studies of memory discussed previously and Deborah Lipstadt's analysis in *Denying the Holocaust* teach us that misremembering is a prominent feature of catastrophic memory, and interpretation an intrinsic feature of history; in contrast, it is utter consistency that may signal the possibility of confabulation.[7]

Thus, while the many valuable focused books on the Holocaust demonstrate the worth of close studies of this single but extremely complex topic, an emphasis on the resonances between incest and Holocaust discourses has the ability to highlight historiographic issues that would otherwise be passed over. The fact that the Holocaust happened is no reason to neglect the vagaries of memory as regards historiography or the vagaries of historiography as regards the processes of memory. Both of these are glossed over in some studies that are brilliant in other respects. For example, Lawrence Langer's *Holocaust Testimonies: The Ruins of Memory* groups Holocaust testimonies from the Yale archive by textual trope—"deep memory," "anguished memory," "humiliated memory," and so on—purposely sidelining issues of referentiality. [8] This strategy seems to limit the study's historiographic application because it does not differentiate between fantasies with no discernible referent and fantasy structures that relate, however obliquely, to definite external events. As I have argued previously, following the insights of the literary critic Shoshana Felman, the psychiatrist Dori Laub, and others, we know more about memory formations when we have access to outside material. So, yes, one *could* say that Langer's work is important precisely because it concentrates on self-avowed memory instead of some misguided notion of empirical truth. But saying as much would underestimate the importance of referentiality in making memory legible. Likewise, James Young's analysis of film and video testimony is extremely valuable for its attention to the ramifications of filming testimony as opposed to listening to it without such recording devices and ambitions: "[A] survivor's memories are necessarily unified and organized twice-over in video testimony: once in the speaker's narrative and again in the narrative movement created in the medium itself."[9] But he too is interested in the textual aspects of ostensible memory without regard for its fantasy elements.

In keeping with the book's foregoing chapters, here I will take a position that is both the extreme and the opposite of the empiricist's stance on survivor testimony. On the one hand I advocate enhanced corroborative efforts to secure the historical legitimacy of documented survivor testimony. As one of my favorite historians, Errol Morris, would say, the truth is difficult but not impossible to know. On the other hand, I believe that the role of mistaken memory and even forgetting has been too little considered in the historiography of Holocaust testimony.

This chapter, therefore, will celebrate Holocaust documentaries that use experimental strategies to represent, paradoxically, the impossibility of representation, and it will critique documentaries that assume a transparency between event and image. The sheer magnitude of the Holocaust in combination with the existence of denier rhetoric suggests the courage it takes for Holocaust filmmakers to go beyond realist representational strategies.

It would be so much more convenient for experimental documentarists to present a succession of facts in the form of unimpeached personal memories, archival footage of various ghettos or the liberation of camps, filmed official documents, and expert testimony. In fact, these are the very materials marshaled by *The Last Days* (James Moll, 1998) in its salvage ethnography of the Holocaust, its program to capture survivor culture before those who lived through the Holocaust pass away. The courage of filmmakers to do otherwise—to use the remarkable plasticity of film form and style to question what we know or how we know this epic catastrophe, or who "we" are as remembering and forgetting souls—is thoroughly impressive. For example, Deborah Lefkowitz in *Intervals of Silence: Being Jewish in Germany* (1990) has created a sound collage of contemporary interviews with Jewish and non-Jewish Germans of different ages and has juxtaposed this with an image track from which the speaking subjects are absent. Lefkowitz uses cinematic techniques such as "bipacking" (related to superimposition) and photographic negatives to encourage awareness of the epistemological dimension of both film and history.[10] Daniel Eisenberg, the son of Dachau survivors, also "invite[s] the viewer to be as active as the maker" in his experimental documentary *Displaced Person* (1981). By rhythmically piecing together fragments of found footage, including shots of Hitler and boys on a bicycle, Eisenberg seizes on "a structure that was open enough for multiple readings" and even "for readings that were contrary to each other."[11] This chapter understands experimentalism in Holocaust documentaries as a particularly productive mode and as a basis of comparison among various Holocaust films. Holocaust films and videos also—productively—disremember.

'THE LAST DAYS' IS NOT 'SHOAH'

A corollary of the marked difficulty of bearing witness to and just plain *bearing* incest and the Holocaust is the taboo against representation that has been applied to both. Lynn Hershman's experimental video rendition of the imposed childhood refrain "[D]on't talk" is one artist's attempt both to speak out about incest and to represent the prohibition itself—a prohibition that was strongly enforced in Hollywood cinema and strongly challenged by Hershman and her fellow autobiographical documentarists. In the case of the Holocaust, challenges to evocative representation have often referred to Theodor Adorno's famous dictum of 1949 that it would be barbarous to write poetry after Auschwitz,[12] linking this injunction to the biblical second commandment against the creation of graven images.[13] As to the former prohibition, Gertrud Koch has explained that Adorno himself took issue with those who would construct a "normative moral taboo" on the foundation of his earlier insight:[14] "Perennial suffering has as much right to expression as a tortured man has to scream; hence it may have been wrong to say that after Auschwitz you could no longer write poems."[15] For Koch, it is Claude Lanzmann's film *Shoah* (1985), and not so much the literary testaments of first-generation survivors (their "legitimate clai[m] to expression" notwithstanding), that effects a "radical aesthetic transformation" of the problem of representing the Shoah. Or, as LaCapra has argued, sounding like Morris, Adorno's statement is best taken as a "statement concerning the difficulty [but not the impossibility] of legitimate creation and renewal in a posttraumatic condition."[16]

Steven Spielberg's *Schindler's List* was widely recognized as the most significant treatment of the subject of the Holocaust since Claude Lanzmann's *Shoah,* and its release became a significant media event in the United States, Europe, and Israel. Whether positively heralded or excoriated, the major studio film drew in large audiences, and the film's reception included an Academy Award for Best Picture, a presidential endorsement, an impulsive but well-publicized rejection by black students at Castlemont High in Oakland, California, a book of critical essays, and two ice-skating routines at the World Professional Figure Skating Championships choreographed to the film's score.[17] But the comparison with *Shoah* variously served and undermined the Spielberg work.

A number of journalists have latched onto the convenience of distinguishing and celebrating the two films on the basis of their modal difference: *Schindler's List,* the greatest historical *fiction film* on the Holocaust; *Shoah,* the greatest *documentary.*[18] But others, those more intent on traditional historical values as well as those less comfortable with unproblematized representational strategies "after Auschwitz," criticized Spielberg's film for its debt to entertainment, melodrama, spectacle, stereotype, and the Hollywoodian happy ending. The film, they argued, is less than great.[19] Elaborating such responses and to some extent sympathetic to them, Miriam Hansen is at the same time critical of thinking that would reject out of hand a film that "relies on familiar tropes and common techniques to narrate the extraordinary rescue of a group of individuals."[20] "*Schindler's List* Is Not *Shoah,*" asserts Hansen in the title of her well-known essay, nor need it be. Yosefa Loshitzky warns against a too pat distinction between documentary *(Shoah)* and fiction *(Schindler's List).* Lanzmann, she points out, has described *Shoah* as a "fiction of reality,"[21] while "the assimilation of documentary style into *Schindler's List* is part of the broader postmodernist aesthetics of the film."[22]

I agree that the documentary/fiction distinction is specious in this case, as it was in the case of the documentaries discussed in chapter 4, where fictive strategies at work in the general context of nonfiction were seen to contribute to the films' historiographic designs. And, here, the proof is in the sequelae. For the Spielberg-produced *The Last Days,* although a documentary in name and one that relies, like *Shoah,* on personal testimonies, bears a closer relation to *Schindler's List* than to the Lanzmann film when it comes to the question of a film's relative ease or reticence to represent the Holocaust. Hansen's characterization of *Schindler's List* as a film that "does not seek to negate the representational, iconic power of filmic images, but rather banks on this power," also applies perfectly to *The Last Days.*[23] Spielberg himself, though perhaps unaware of (or uninterested in) the intricacies of the discussion about the impossibility of representing the Holocaust, does explicitly identify the Visual History Archive as the most significant legacy of *Schindler's List.* In an infomercial for the Survivors of the Shoah Visual History Foundation, Ben Kingsley (who played Itzhak Stern in *Schindler's List*) narrates the story of how, during the shooting of the film on location in Poland, survivors would approach him and Spielberg to tell their stories. She survived by a miracle, exclaims one woman to Spielberg in "making-of" footage that illustrates Kingsley's narration.[24] And if the Survivors of the Shoah Visual History Archive is the most significant legacy of *Schindler's List,* then *The Last Days*—created in tandem with the oral histories collected by the Shoah Visual History Foundation— is the further legacy of that endeavor. Therefore, if we are to affirm Hansen's insistence that *Schindler's List* is not *Shoah,* it behooves us to contemplate a companion premise: *The Last Days* is not *Shoah* either.

'SHOAH'

The deluge of writing on *Shoah* is testimony to the film's particular attributes and perceived uniqueness. Film reviewers and academics, historians of the Holocaust, literary critics, philosophers, and psychiatrists have grappled with the nine-and-a-half-hour film in essays and book chapters that present an assembled page count in direct proportion to the length of the film itself.[25] Here, in deference to the quality of preexisting ideas and writing on the film, I will keep my remarks on *Shoah* short. But I do want to differentiate the reactions of the film's various reviewers and confirm a sense of its extraordinary features. I aim to explore the contrasts between *Shoah* and *The Last Days* and, alternatively, the similarities among *Shoah*, *The March* (Abraham Ravett, 1999), and *Tak for Alt* (Laura Bialis, Broderick Fox, and Sarah Levy, 1999) as films that engage a "problematics of memory."[26]

In her exclamation that "*Shoah* differs from all that has come before, even though almost everything related by the film's multiple speakers is knowledge already known," Patricia Erens goes to the heart of the matter: the film's paradoxical existence as a historical but simultaneously antiempirical text.[27] The film "remains on the level of document," asserts Erens. But "the experience becomes hypnotic, obsessional. . . . [T]he more you know, the more you want to know."[28] The film is distinct and radical, but how is it distinctly radical when it comes to historiographic practice? This latter question is the one that divides the film's committed scholarly audience.

Dominick LaCapra's criticism of *Shoah* rests on his contention that the film is overly invested in the work of "retraumatizing" survivors so as to traumatize secondary witnesses—the film's spectators. And this, LaCapra argues, undermines the film's historiographic potential. Obviously, this objection coming from LaCapra must be understood very differently from an ostensibly similar objection (say, that the film is overly melodramatic) coming from empiricist quarters. LaCapra has been for years a preeminent philosopher of history and one of the most sophisticated thinkers about the relationship between psychoanalysis and historiography and in particular about the transferential dynamic between historians and their objects. It is not, therefore, any dearth of historical detail or correctness that inspires LaCapra's critique. Rather, what troubles LaCapra is precisely the film's lack of analytical distance from its human subjects (including Lanzmann himself as a character in the film) and its inability to "work through" rather than simply "work out" or, worse, "act out" problems of historical epistemology. LaCapra is skeptical of the film's use of certain techniques: Lanzmann gets people talking by returning them to the camps where they were incarcerated or to surrounding areas where they suffered, and his use of staging goes even further, as when he elicits Abraham Bomba's testimony in a hired barber shop, with Bomba cutting hair while he speaks. In its concentration on grieving and lamentation, the film, to LaCapra's mind, falls into the very same antitransferential patterns as positivism; the past is "reincarnated" or "relived" by the witnesses, by Lanzmann, their interviewer, and by the very structure of the film, rather than merely being "repeated *in the discourse* of the observer."[29] The spectator's position as offered by the film, LaCapra argues, is overly empathetic, collapsed, and melancholic, rather than being analytically mournful.[30]

LaCapra's critique of *Shoah* is homologous to his critique of Shoshana Felman's treatment of the film. Whereas the film displays an inordinate closeness to its human subjects, Felman's essay displays an inordinate closeness to its filmic subject. LaCapra complains that in Felman's "authorized" reading, "history is marginalized in the interest of History as trauma indiscriminately writ large."[31] The style of Felman's essay is "to repeat themes or motifs of the film in a fragmented, often arresting series of comments," such that "the 'infinite task' of 'encountering' a film seems bizarrely to displace the 'finite task' of 'making sense of the Holocaust.'"[32]

Michael Rothberg and Joshua Hirsch are much more cognizant than is LaCapra of *Shoah*'s use of distancing strategies and are therefore much more sympathetic and indebted to Felman's delineation of *Shoah*'s representational limits. Where LaCapra sees Lanzmann, character and director, as wallowing in his subjects' pain, Rothberg argues that the film "maintain[s] an unbridgeable gap between testimony and 'being-there.'" He continues the thought by indicating that Lanzmann "marks the desire for the real without arousing the suspicion that he might attempt to simulate it."[33] The film is obliquely historical, Rothberg believes, and he turns to Felman for affirmation: "What is being stalked . . . is history," writes Rothberg, "or perhaps more accurately, in Felman's words: 'new possibilities for understanding history, . . . new pragmatic *acts* of historicizing history's erasures.'"[34] Hirsch, for his part, engages directly with and refutes LaCapra's contention that the film doesn't "work through" the trauma of the Holocaust. "Though the witnesses in the film may themselves be acting out trauma . . . , the point is that they do it for Lanzmann, and, more importantly, for the camera, for the public, for history," writes Hirsch. "Thus through the film," he continues, "the terrible burden of witnessing genocide may be relayed (but not removed) from their shoulders to a public who can lend to traumatic memory the degree of awareness, of consciousness, possible only to the outsider."[35]

Rothberg's and Hirsch's readings of *Shoah* recognize the film's historicity because they attend more thoroughly than does LaCapra to the intricacies of form and style, especially as regards *Shoah*'s unconventional use of testimony.[36] Joshua Hirsch's discussion of *Shoah* is particularly impressive because it is developed in the context of a full-length history of documentary representations of the Holocaust. Echoing the larger categories of historical documentary, Hirsch delineates the following loosely historical approaches: (1) the raw footage Holocaust documentary, which consists of archival material presented without narration or with only a minimal use of it (Hirsch discusses a two-minute film of the execution of Jews as the premiere example of a film in this first category); (2) the newsreel form, in which archival footage pertaining to a certain historical moment is compiled, edited, and presented with verbal commentary (Hirsch discusses the 1945 film *The Death Camps* by Actualités Françaises in this context); (3) the historical compilation form, in which archival footage and commentary combine not just to provide information about a certain point in time but to create an explicit historical narrative with explanatory and emotional power (the Swedish film *Mein Kampf* from 1960, written and directed by German Jewish refugee Erwin Leiser, is discussed in this connection); (4) historical verité, in which location shooting and direct address by the film's subjects lessen the need and desire for commentary (the reference here is Jean Rouch's Parisian ethnography, *Chronicle of a Summer*, 1960); and (5) the post-traumatic form, distinguished by its break with documentary realism and its relationship to postwar modernism (Hirsch discusses both *Night and Fog* (Alain Resnais, 1955) and *Shoah* in these terms, demonstrating the variations of this form and its development over time). Thus, Hirsch, like Rothberg and also like Gertrud Koch, Linda Williams, Bill Nichols, and myself, understands *Shoah* as a film that exemplifies a "a recent transformation in the documentary representation of history—a transformation that has been variously identified as postmodern, reflexive, or posttraumatic."[37]

What, then, are *Shoah*'s extraordinary attributes that contribute to its reputation as a groundbreaking film and distinguish it from Spielberg's later but more conventional documentary effort? Or what are the attributes that make the film what Felman, Rothberg, Hirsch, and I take it to be (and what LaCapra wishes it were):[38] a radical historiography of the Holocaust? First, of all, the film contains nary a frame of archival footage. This is evident from the film itself and has been much remarked upon, both before and after Lanzmann's incendiary comment in *Le Monde* on the occasion of the opening of *Schindler's List* in France. Criticizing Spielberg's choice to recreate the gas chamber at Auschwitz, Lanzmann affirms: "[I]f I had found a film—a secret film, because it was strictly forbidden—made by an SS man showing how 3,000 Jews—men, women, and children—died together, asphyxiated in the gas chamber of Crematorium 2 at Auschwitz; if I had found that, not only would I not have shown it, I would have destroyed it."[39] That Spielberg's choice would be the opposite is suggested by the inclusion and handling of archival footage—and certain images in particular—in *The Last Days* (executive producer, Steven Spielberg), released four years after Lanzmann's *Le Monde* statement. I will return to this point below.

The second remarkable thing about *Shoah* is that the use of contemporary but retrospective interviews is just as exceptional as the nonuse of archival material. A number of the survivor interviewees had to be tracked down and many were induced to break their self-imposed silence about past events. Then, once Lanzmann gets them talking, it is the accumulation of minute detail that he concentrates on rather than the larger picture. "The interviews seem incredibly simple, sometimes even trivial," explains Patricia Erens. But "by the piling of fact on fact, detail on detail, he leads us slowly to our own conclusions."[40]

This is not to say that the details always "add up." Another extraordinary aspect of the film is that, taken as a whole, it approaches truth by contextualizing all and giving the lie to some of the individual statements. For example, the Polish peasants' claim that they risked their lives to bring water to the desperate evacuees shut up in boxcars takes on a different cast as the sequence continues and interviews shot at other places and times are cut in. By the side of the Treblinka railroad track Lanzmann is seen interviewing a group of Polish peasants. "Who gave the Jews water?" he inquires. "We did, the Poles," they respond emphatically. At that point one is skeptical. But then we hear Abraham Bomba's testimony that it was so unbearably hot and airless in the crowded boxcars that people were offering diamonds in exchange for water. What we come to realize, therefore, is that the words of the Polish peasants may not be bald-faced lies. Perhaps, and this may be worse than lying, the peasants did bring water, profiting, thereby, from the serendipitous passage of the boxcars. Or perhaps the diamonds were accepted but no water was handed over. This is Bomba's claim. But the film never makes (refuses to make?) the point absolutely clear. What we do come to understand is that nothing is simple; that words are one thing, meaning quite another; and that individual testimonies have a limited historical value.

Apart from what is said by witnesses (as in "witnesses to history," including survivors, bystanders, collaborators, and perpetrators), how and where it is said are of paramount importance. As has been discussed by others, Lanzmann opted to show the part of the interviewing process that involved the work of a translator, rather than cutting out that intermediary stage and adding subtitles to the final product. I disagree with LaCapra's statement that the "problem of translation (as well as the role of the translator) is not thematized in the film despite its major importance."[41] As Patricia Erens argued in her 1986 review of *Shoah*, this elaborate means of translation is used throughout the film, and it is self-reflexive. By showing himself on camera conducting interviews with his female translator at his side, Lanzmann foregrounds the difficulty and the internationality of the interview process. As Erens remarks, audiences are made privy to the lengths to which Lanzmann had to go to extract evidence, from buttering up Polish bystanders whose overt anti-Semitism must have surely offended him to lying to an SS Unterscharführer. In the latter case Lanzmann opts to include shots of the remote van from which the interview was clandestinely filmed and direct evidence of his own broken promise to former SS officer Franz Suchomel—named in the film—that his name would not be used. Film students tend to divide over the ethics of Lanzmann's actions. Some believe that in lying to a documentary subject Lanzmann begins his descent to the low moral level of this former Nazi. Others defend Lanzmann for doing what was necessary for posterity. My own view is that—*because it is revealed to the film audience*—Lanzmann's subterfuge makes his integrity as filmmaker and historian (though not as interviewer) all the clearer.

We can say that this sequence involving the secret filming of Suchomel is staged, meaning that it would not be occurring if not for the purpose of being filmed. But almost all interviews are staged. Unless the person *just happened* to be speaking anyway (as American direct cinema of the 1960s would have us believe of the many drivers of vehicles who *happen* to be monologuing on school integration or states rights),[42] an interview is an event that comes into being because filming is underway. What is special, then, about the Suchomel passage, or about the sequence in the film in which Lanzmann interviews Abraham Bomba cutting the hair of volunteers in a rented barbershop? It is not, I would argue, that these sequences are staged and others unstaged, but rather that here the staging is more elaborate, involving other people and elements of the mise-en-scène as well as the main interview subject. More elaborate staging constitutes what I call "enactment," as when James Whitney brings Melvin Just's daughters to see him at his care facility, or, as discussed previously in this regard, when Claude Lanzmann brings Simon Srebnik back to Chelmno, Poland.[43] Another remarkable thing about *Shoah*, therefore, is that almost every sequence involving people is staged to a greater or lesser degree. Perhaps one could construe the odd cart passing by unexpectedly as a direct cinema element—something that would have taken place with or without Lanzmann's presence but is captured incidentally by the camera. But the majority of the spoken word sequences are staged. This does not mean that the film is not a documentary.[44] As discussed previously, staging is a venerable documentary technique.

But if staging is a prominent feature in the film, what about reenactment? Lynn Hershman's *Re Covered Diary* (1994) and Odette Springer's *Some Nudity Required* (1998) use staging and reenactment both. But *Shoah* seems just as leery of reenactment as it is of archival footage. There are no passages in the film in which people act out or "reenact" events that occurred previously. There is no use of reenactment—unless one considers the special form of reenactment that is the mainspring of *Shoah*'s originality.

In *Shoah* enactment becomes reenactment in the crucibles of history and psychology. "The film makes testimony *happen* [emphasis in original]— happen inadvertently *as a second Holocaust* [emphasis mine]," writes Felman.[45] Or, in Williams's words, "Morris [in *The Thin Blue Line* (1988)] and Lanzmann do not so much represent th[e] past as they reactivate it in images of the present."[46] Returning with this in mind to the sequence in which Simon Srebnik is brought back to Chelmno and made to stand and interact with villagers in front of the Catholic church, Williams, following Felman's lead, shows that the extraordinary aspect of the sequence is that the anti-Semitism of the villagers lives again. The very anti-Semitism manifested in the 1940s as they watched their Jewish neighbors being deported and listened to the captive boy singer is here revived in their gestures and comments as they surround Srebnik. Thus, one might say that the sequence is not simply enacted but also *re*enacted.

Michael Rothberg is even more explicit than Felman or Williams in his application to *Shoah* of the concept of reenactment, although it must be said that he is at the same time more critical of the use of the technique. Rothberg points to a sequence involving Filip Müller, a survivor of the Auschwitz Sonderkommando, as evidence of the film's deployment of reenactment as a subjective device. Accompanying Müller's testimony, and instead of Lanzmann's characteristic slow tracking campscapes, are subjective shots "of a steadily moving hand-held camera and an itinerary [the camera's passage through camp-adjacent fields] that closely matches that of the narrative." Or, when Müller twice describes the floor plan of the gas chamber/crematorium complex, "it is the shifts between the 'imitative' sequences [in which the camera stands in for a mobile human figure/gaze] and the non-'fictionalizing' context of the rest of the film that prevent viewers from reading the imitative shots as part of a 'realist' mimetic universe."[47] Therefore, as I understand him, Rothberg means to suggest that while reenactment is used to "stalk" history, it may also draw the film into what Rothberg sees as a dangerous "desire to touch the real in a more direct way."[48]

The evaluations of *Shoah* by Felman, Erens, Hansen, Koch, Hirsch, LaCapra, Williams, and Rothberg do vary somewhat. Nevertheless, however high or low they rate *Shoah*'s success in this regard, these scholars all peg documentary film's potential to give us access to historical events after Auschwitz to a redefined and complicated use of the documentary mode. *Shoah* is important because it succeeds to a greater or lesser extent (depending on critical perspective) in calling to mind both the past itself and the indirection of the means through which we represent it.

A preference for adventurous depictions over conventional ones does not necessarily require the out-and-out rejection of the latter, and one discerns a generous measure of tolerance in scholars' comparative surveys of various different Holocaust representations. According to Rothberg, "Despite the risks of distortion and displacement, representations of all sorts—including documentary footage, historical documentation, fictional and nonfictional narratives, and so on—remain the only access to historical events. No preconceived evaluation of which media are appropriate or inappropriate (i.e., the image) to a particular event can come to terms with either aesthetic representation, historical documentation, or the event they both seek to capture."[49] And Hansen notes that "whether we like it or not, the predominant vehicles of public memory *are* the media of technical re/production and mass consumption. This issue is especially exacerbated for the remembrance of the Shoah in light of the specific crisis posed by the Nazis' destruction of the very basis and structures of collective remembering. . . . In a significant way, even before the passing of the last survivors, the remembrance of the Shoah, to the extent that is was public and collective, has always been more dependent on mass-mediated forms of memory—on what Alison Landsberg calls 'prosthetic memory.' "[50] My own sense, though (am I less tolerant?), is that Spielberg does not need professional academicians to defend him against negative opinion, since his fictional and nonfictional Holocaust representations circulate widely, to say the least. But I believe we academics can be of use not only in defending but also in publicizing *unconventional* representations of the Holocaust. It is in this spirit that I offer, advisedly, the following critique of *The Last Days* and, in the following section, a celebration of experimental Holocaust films.

The Last Days is definitely not *Shoah*. It contains archival footage and also family photos. In fact, it features the closest thing we have to Lanzmann's "secret film" of killing (that he claims he would destroy if found) in the form of what is known as the Weiner footage or Liebau film, shot by Reinhard Weiner, who was at the time a sergeant in the German Navy. The film consists of less than two minutes of footage depicting the firing squad execution of Jews standing in a trench. [51] The inclusion of this material in *The Last Days* is all the more noticeable given that the filmed executions took place along the Latvian-Lithuanian border, as indicated in a subtitle, whereas *The Last Days* is a film about the Jewish Hungarian experience. The footage, then, which is on deposit both at the Yad Vashem Holocaust Museum in Israel and at the U.S. Holocaust Memorial Museum in Washington, D.C., is included *in spite of* its lack of direct relevance to the topic at hand and presumably *because of* its status as the ultimate in archival material.

The Last Days is also very different from *Shoah* in its use of testimony. Whereas testimonies in the earlier film are cumulative but often contradictory, testimonies in *The Last Days* are additive and similar. That is, individual experiences are presented as representative of the experience of many. This must be true in general. While the particular details of any two survivors' stories will certainly differ, the trajectory of occurrence will be more or less the same. As four of the five interviewees in the film explain, their early childhoods were spent in Hungarian villages or towns surrounded by loving families until the sudden shock of the Nazi entry into Hungary made them refugees, deportees, and finally orphaned concentration camp inmates. A fifth interviewee, raised in Budapest, was arrested during the occupation and deported to a forced labor camp, from which he escaped to join the underground. For all five interviewees, liberation initially meant life as a displaced person and then readjustment to a new situation that involved, apparently—the film does not dwell on this aspect—emigration to the United States.

The striking similarity among subjects' stories is intensified by the film's editorial structure. Instead of opting to present complete stories in sequence one after the other, the filmmakers have opted to break apart each story and to intercut it with the others so that a pattern of alternation persists throughout the film. And, crucially, whereas this technique could have been used to raise discrepancies between and among purported facts, it is used instead to emphasize historiographic consistency. Even the details of experience are similar according to the logic of this film. For example, an early sequence in the film presents interviewees describing an idyllic prewar mix of religions in their respective towns. "We had a church, we had a synagogue. Everybody knew each other; it was beautiful," reminisces Irene Zisblatt. "The bulk of Jews in Budapest were utterly assimilated and deeply patriotic," explains Tom Lantos. "We felt Hungarian." Or, taking similarity to the level of minute detail, the film includes the following cut between two interviewees talking about being transported to the death camp. Renée Firestone: "It was total darkness; the light seeped only through the cracks of the cattle car." Irene Zisblatt: "My father found a crack in the cattle train and he looked out."

The film's use of a structuring principle of similarity is not incidental. Rather, it is intimately related to and in fact produces the film's ideological perspective on the history of the Shoah and on Holocaust representation. Here, to seek similarity is to inhibit difference. Is it really true that no Hungarian child experienced anti-Semitism before the rise of Nazism? Even I experienced it. Growing up in a small town in northern California in the early 1960s, I remember the neighbor girls who were my friends taunting me one time by saying that Jews have horns. If *The Last Days* had included such anecdotes, then the film might have introduced the possibility that simmering anti-Semitism made the Hungarians vulnerable to Nazi ideology, or the possibility that there might be two ways to read the climate of this early period, or the possibility that people might forget or misremember aspects of past experience, especially unpleasant ones. As it is, with interviewees expressing surprise that their Hungarian neighbors could turn on them in an instant, the film is able to paint a picture of anti-Semitism as confined to or emanating from a certain unique moment of history and a certain group—Nazis, not Hungarians. In the terms of the film, the Hungarians were not originally anti-Semitic; rather, they "turned" with the arrival of the Nazis. Perhaps partly because it is based on the testimony of people who were children during the time they are reflecting back on, *The Last Days* idealizes the prewar period in Hungary, figures the Nazi occupation of Europe and Hungary as an historical anomaly, and seeks to instill a sense of continuity between the prewar years and the present. *The Last Days* does not heed the warning of the Jean Cayrol commentary in *Night and Fog* that such events are not completely "of a certain time and in a certain place" but rather continuous. Anti-Semitism predated and postdates the Holocaust. But *The Last Days* is at least partially "deaf to the endless cry" that in *Night and Fog* signals the ongoing human capacity for evil.

The film's use of "objective" footage intercut with personal testimony contributes to the impression that history is perfectly accessible as well as noncontradictory. Throughout the film, the life stories being narrated are illustrated with black-and-white archival footage and also with color footage presumably shot by the makers of *The Last Days*. For example, an early passage in which the interviewees are describing their towns is handled as follows. Over a color panorama of a town we hear a woman's voice relating, "We lived in a town called Sárvár." The next shot reveals the woman seated in her dining room; she is introduced via a subtitle as Alice Lok from Sárvár, Hungary. "It's in Hungary," she continues. There follow four shots in black and white: (1) a man with a bicycle, (2) women in a marketplace with baskets of what appear to be potatoes, (3) a boy facing the camera but looking at a woman's embroidery work, and (4) a group of women, including, very prominently, a woman with a bundle slung over her upper back. These images are accompanied by Lok's lilting narration: "Every day the peasants would bring their wares from the neighboring villages in big baskets, and they would carry it on their head or their shoulders." That image then dissolves into the image of another town, which we understand as such because it is introduced by a man's voice explaining, "Szaszova was a very small little community consisting of three thousand people, no electricity and no utilities at all." We then see our narrator, Bill Basch, as he continues his story. The fact that these images correspond nicely to what is being described verbally—the woman with the bundle appears just at the moment when Lok's voice is heard mentioning peasants carrying wares on their shoulders—lends credence to the interviewees' stories as well as lulling the viewer into the sense that the archive is full. There is an image for every occasion, and that image suffices. Such reassurances are redundant, however, since the very structure of the film is based on the presumption that history may be told through autobiography and that eyewitness testimonies are the basic and unimpeachable building blocks of history.

The Last Days relies on eyewitness testimony to describe not only the social practices of prewar Hungary but the political machinations as well. For just as "ethnographic footage" of various towns is intercut with personal testimony, so too is archival footage of the Nazi occupation. For example, in a passage that follows a capsule history of Hitler's military successes, interviewees tell of the Nazi entrance into Hungary. Again interviewees' stories are intercut with one another, and again the film alternates between direct-address presentation of interviewees and archival footage accompanied by voice-over. "Hitler moved into Hungary on the 19th of March,

1944," Tom Lantos narrates over images of Hungarian boys reaching up to touch the hands of soldiers riding tanks into Budapest. The film then cuts to a shot of Lantos saying, "I was sixteen years old." There follows an immediate cut to Alice Lok recalling, "1944, March 19th. Germans, the SS, entered our town." We see in sequence a truck moving down a small-town street, a townscape, and then a motorcycle on the road. The film then cuts to Irene Zisblatt relating, "[T]wo motorcycles was the whole Nazi regime that occupied our town." In this way the film slides easily between footage that illustrates events at which these witnesses really may have been present—or perhaps not; we cannot know for sure—and events that happened at a distance. The result is to confer a larger historical expertise on people whose direct experience was actually of local events that occurred when they were children.

This slippage between personal and public history is further lubricated by the inclusion of black-and-white photos of the individuals themselves. When Renée Firestone, to take one example, speaks of being forced along with all Jews to wear the yellow star, we see archival footage of Jewish people with stars sewn into their clothing. We then hear a painful memory recounted by Firestone. Preparing hastily to be taken away, she made a futile attempt to hang onto her happy childhood by impulsively donning under her clothes a colorful bathing suit that had been a gift from her father. This story is followed by a photo of Firestone taken in 1943 when she was nineteen. She is wearing a (the?) bathing suit. The personal photo and the archival footage are woven together by Firestone's powerful memoir. No wonder that slightly later, when Bill Basch is speaking about eluding soldiers in the street by "jump[ing] into the group of Jews" being deported to Buchenwald, we cannot help imagining that the archival images accompanying the narration depict the very group of which he speaks. But, upon reflection, that is highly unlikely. It is this mixing technique, however deceptive, that nevertheless emphasizes the interviewees' personal connection to, and concomitant authority to speak of, historical events.

I do not dispute that the Nazis occupied Hungary on March 19, 1944, nor do I dispute that *The Last Days* is well researched by professional historians. I also accept that individual interviewees witnessed and experienced all too directly the Nazi occupation and its fallout. The stories they tell are deeply evocative and moving. I watched the film with my twelve-year-old daughter and we cried together. I fully support the various oral history projects involved with the preservation of such accounts on tape; we must have such reports from ground zero.

My critique is on the level of historiography. The film relies overmuch on spectators' deep-seated trust in what Michael Frisch has called the "Anti-History" approach, where oral historical evidence is seen as being "beyond interpretation."[52] Because they directly witnessed some things, the film employs the interviewees as stand-up witnesses to History writ large. And it does so without regard for the frailty of memory and without regard for the mediated nature of historiographic forms, including film. How different this is from the conflicting and recursive testimonies of *Shoah,* and from the retrospective profundity of *Capturing the Friedmans* (Andrew Jarecki, 2003) as well. In the latter film, as discussed in the previous chapter, sit-down interviews and home movies are a much more complicated duo. At certain points their import is mutually supportive—but never in the simply illustrative manner of *The Last Days.* Moreover, *Capturing the Friedmans* uses the juxtaposition of these two types of evidence to undermine any expectation that meaning resides on the face of things.

Actually, moments in *The Last Days* reveal gaps in its characteristic seamlessness. Speaking of her work as an artist, Alice Lok states, "I always felt that my language is inadequate, and if I wanted to tell the story of my experiences I have to talk through a medium. And I found art. Because art transcends; it's beyond words." Significantly, the works of Lok that we see in the film are large and abstract, created through the layering of wrinkled paper. "It should look like a crumpled wall, like it's papered over with yesterday's news, because people want to forget about the past, about the Holocaust," Lok explains. We, as spectators of *The Last Days,* may take this as an opportunity to reflect on whether the film we are watching also "transcends." Does it go beyond words—the words of the interviewees—or beyond realist style to an expressive realm more adequate to the subject matter of catastrophe? I believe that the film's goal is to inject feeling into historical narration. This it does well. But I would welcome more moments like this one with Alice Lok when representational possibilities and limits are foregrounded.

Another exceptional moment is the sequence involving Renée Firestone and Dr. Hans Münch, a former Nazi doctor at Auschwitz. Firestone has gone back to Auschwitz to look for documents pertaining to her sister's death. With the help of an archivist, Firestone locates a card listing her sister's name and the date of her death. Apparently her sister was experimented on in Dr. Münch's clinic. But when she confronts Münch himself, presumably thanks to arrangements made by the filmmakers in another example of filmic enactment, she finds him evasive. As she reflects in a passage included in the film before her research trip but obviously recorded after, "I was hoping that going back to Auschwitz is finally going to give me some closure, and I was shocked to find out that it opened up new questions and new doubts." Here is one place in the film where tangible evidence is used to link personal narrative to large-scale history. Notably, this is also the very spot where the film suggests that historical knowing is not at all a straightforward proposition. The apparent contradiction of these two historiographic impulses is a tension I believe we must embrace to write history effectively.

Overall, though, the film seems to strive for the very closure its subjects know to be impossible. Whereas Firestone comprehends at the time and expresses later that dropping the bathing suit into the pile of clothing at Auschwitz created an uncrossable chasm between before and after, the filmmakers seek to fill the hole with images, archival images recruited not to represent the loss as such but rather to paper it over. Moreover, I would argue that the plentitude represented by the bathing suit, while genuinely expressive of the Firestone family bond, must have been illusory when it came to history. Yes, Firestone's father was once free to travel on business trips and bring back presents for his children, but the collaboration of Hungarians with Nazis suggests with hindsight that the Jews were never as fully assimilated as they believed themselves to be. Irene Zisblatt indicates that her family's ostensible friends "turned overnight and went with the other side." But she also indicates that two motorcycles were enough to occupy the town because "they were already there with the people that live there the whole time and did their dirty work." Thus, interviewees make many thoughtful comments suggesting that the Holocaust is a catastrophe that must be remembered in fits and starts and may never be perfectly understood. Their historiography often seems appropriately rough and unresolved. The film, on the other hand, confers what I take to be an unwarranted and unwanted authority on witness observation. Its raison d'être is the assumption that filming these survivors will fill up the gap between prewar events and present mastery. As the film would have it, the bathing suit and all it symbolized of family, joy, and life is not forever an absent referent but rather one that is still present in the photos and archival footage that the film somewhat facilely provides.

Closure is sought not only through the plentitude of articulate remembrances and images but also through the project of returning these five survivors to Hungary, Germany, and Poland. As in Lanzmann's return of Simon Srebnik to Chelmno, the survivors' returns in The Last Days are occasioned by the filming (which is not to say that any given survivor did not also have her or his own reasons to make the trip). As such they qualify as documentary enactment. However, whereas in *Shoah* enactment turns to reenactment in the emphasis on the retrospective, historical aspect of the documentary performances, in *The Last Days* the future is what matters. Rather than using the return of survivors to trigger residual, continuous anti-Semitism in European villagers, *The Last Days* returns survivors to emphasize the differences between the Nazi occupation and the present day. In this aspect too the occupation is presented as being anomalous.

Just as *Schindler's List* ends with a documentary passage featuring the descendants of the "Schindler Jews" (along with some of the survivors themselves), so too *The Last Days* celebrates the presence of the interviewees' offspring. Tom Lantos reveals that his own children came to him and their mother with a special promise to bear many children to make up for their parents' losses, and we see footage of kids of all ages running and jumping on a spacious lawn. For the most part, though, the children and grandchildren of interviewees are seen in the sections of the film involving travel back to Europe. Renée visits her hometown in the company of her daughter Klara, the namesake of her murdered sister; Irene conducts her daughter Robin around a ghetto brickyard where she was forced to labor; Bill tours Dachau with his son Martin while Alice tours Auschwitz with her son Bill; Tom recounts his history to grandchildren on site at a railroad bridge where he was once forced to labor in Danube Bend, Hungary. The generational progress indicates that time has moved on. This may be regarded as being all to the good. Interviewees—and audiences—are empowered by the presence of the children to revel in survivorship. But, again, the film's ideological stake in a circumscribed and temporally limited concept of the Nazi occupation is evident.

In *Shoah*, incomplete and contradictory testimonies recounted haltingly enhance our perception of the challenges to historical understanding. Insight comes not through well-chosen words (and certainly not through archival images—these were dismissed from the beginning) but through the remnants of affect. The past is not. In *The Last Days*, in contradistinction to the situation in *Shoah*, the past is eminently available to be either idealized or transcended.

'THE MARCH'

On the bases of comparison advanced above, *The March* has more in common with *Shoah* than with *The Last Days*. Constructed almost entirely of contemporary interviews and devoid of archival footage, the film also shares *Shoah*'s animating paradox: that it is just as impossible to gain a purchase on the past as it is to outrun it. The ravages of time tell on the filmmaker Abraham Ravett's mother, Fela Ravett, who ages before our eyes as the film proceeds with seven interview segments shot between 1984 and 1997. And still her tale remains unfinished—in part by her own choice, one assumes. Her last words of the film, addressed to her son, are "I just had a stroke. Do I have to remember? Think about it." Thus we are left to "think about it," knowing at the same time—as the film seems to suggest—that "history can be grasped only in the very inaccessibility of its occurrence," to quote Cathy Caruth.[53]

The teller and the tale both differ markedly from those of *The Last Days*. Whereas the five subjects of the latter film are interviewed in beautifully decorated and furnished homes and are impeccably coifed and dressed, Fela Ravett and her surroundings bespeak a working-class existence as well as an un-self-consciousness about her son's filming process. In one sequence Fela Ravett is filmed wearing what appear to be striped pajamas and a bathrobe. This difference in life circumstances may have to do as much with the respective class origins of the subjects in the two films as it does with the effects of the war, but the comparison highlights the selection process at work in the "casting" of *The Last Days*. That film probably could have included fewer well-to-do subjects. As it is, the obvious material success and articulate self-possession of the interviewees softens the horror of their stories, since it appears—and the film delves no deeper—that things come out all right in the end.

Unlike the stories told by survivors in *The Last Days*, stories elicited with attention to a deliberate "before, during, and after" pattern, Fela Ravett's story is a mere shard of her wartime experience. Although it is told in more or less chronological order, the story of the forced march Ravett endured at the time of the liquidation of the Auschwitz camp is not only fragmentary but also halting, repetitive, presented in dribs and drabs over a period of years and punctuated by resistance and forgetting.

What she *says* is that the death march took place from January through May; that the prisoners were given a loaf of bread, a blanket, and a can of meat; that she walked in wooden shoes (clogs) together with a friend, sharing one blanket after giving away her own; that she found some sugar in a barn where they were sheltered for the night and she shared it with her friend; that the man who would become her husband (the filmmaker's father) made his escape from the march; that many people fell down dead or were shot along the way; and that she was near to dying when the American liberators appeared and took her to a hospital. These details are clearly important as historical data and presumably important to the filmmaker for personal reasons; otherwise why would he have pressed his mother sporadically over more than a dozen years to tell about the march?

But these details do not make the film. Very striking are Fela Ravett's reluctance to narrate, her evident sadness in reflecting on past times, and the sense that she tells to oblige her son—and *only* to oblige him. "Abe, don't ask me any more because I start feeling bad," she begs. The other striking thing about the film is, of course, its experimental nature. Working against any tendency to smooth Fela Ravett's halting and fragmentary tale, *The March* not only roughens it through the use of the dated interview segments but also employs unconventional documentary techniques that interfere with the possibility of our getting lost in the story. For one thing, Fela is hard to understand and sometimes even to hear. The first time she appears she is speaking into the camera, but the footage is silent (and her image is stacked on top of its ghostly double). This practice went out of style with the advent of the sound era, so that, used here, it immediately signals a different approach to filming Holocaust testimony, one that deliberately erodes the primacy of the word. When sound is brought in, in the following interview sequences, Fela's words are sporadically muffled by wind or traffic noise. Now, this muffling might be attributed to the difficulties of a filmmaker working outdoors and alone. In one shot we see Abraham Ravett's own hand adjusting the microphone on what appears to be a stool placed in front of Fela Ravett. However, the fact that this particular example of sonic interference is completely consistent with the film's overall handling of Fela's story would suggest a larger pattern. That the filmmaker is willing to abide and even to introduce distance between the tale and its audience is further confirmed by his invitation to his mother to speak in Yiddish, which would necessitate the use of subtitles—another layer of mediation between subject and audience. Again, as with the wind and traffic noise, the question arises as to whether the distancing is deliberate or inadvertent on the part of the filmmaker. Perhaps Abraham prompts his mother to speak Yiddish so that she will feel more comfortable speaking. But her surprise at the invitation, which she immediately declines, asserting that she is more comfortable in English, suggests that the use of the Yiddish language (which is spoken and written out elsewhere in the film) may indeed be regarded as another of the film's planned distancing devices—however conscious or unconscious on the part of the filmmaker.

As the foregoing points indicate, the film is not only experimental but reflexive and interactive, to maintain Bill Nichols's definition of and distinction between the latter two.[54] Whereas *The Last Days* strives to make invisible the joins between archival images, personal photographs, and direct-address interview footage, *The March* takes every opportunity to draw the viewer's attention to the process of filming Fela Ravett's tale—to acknowledge, reflexively, the relationship between *filmmaker and audience*. The most conventional aspect of the film is the opening title card providing the history of the forced march. We are surprised, therefore, to see film leader—film stock generally used as filler at the heads and tails of movies—rolling by in what is in fact the second shot of the film. This alerts us to the shaping presence of the filmmaker and prepares us for segments throughout the film where crude white lettering on a black background introduces or repeats words or phrases from Fela Ravett's narrative: "trepches," "blanket," "Estrusha was her name."

The film is also *interactive* in that it displays overtly the relationship between *filmmaker and subject* and their collaboration in the filmmaking process. Abraham Ravett invites his mother to clap her hands or say "testing 1, 2, 3" to establish synch, and his questions to his mother are left to form part of the soundtrack. Both of these devices make it clear that Fela's is not a spontaneous narration but rather one that Abraham instigated for the purposes of the film.

But interactivity takes a somewhat unusual turn when Fela Ravett forces Abraham to specify his goals by asking questions in return: "You want me to start with the march or first of all that they put people like cattle?" This may be a mother trying her best to please her son. As Michelle Citron has discussed, autobiographical filmmakers may have a special ethical obligation to family members because, in wanting to please, they become easily exploitable.[55] But the relationship depicted seems more complicated than that, and it is not at all certain that Abraham is the one in control.

If *Shoah* is profoundly transferential in that the dynamics of past relationships are reactivated in the present, so too is *The March*. The last on-screen interview with Fela Ravett is shot in her hospital room, where she lies fitted with a breathing tube. Her decline from one filmed interview to the next has been frighteningly obvious. Now, apparently, the bar mitzvah of Abraham's son, Chaim, is approaching, and Abraham asks his mother for a message for her grandson. She obliges with more eagerness and animation than she manifests elsewhere in the film.[56] He should "be a mensch" she advises. But in the following sequence, when Abraham returns, again, to questions about the march, his mother finally refuses outright. "Mom, do you remember anything more about the march?" he asks. Watching the sequence, I feel for Ravett. With his father already gone and his mother lying in a hospital bed, this may be one of a few last chances to learn his parents' wartime history—his own heritage of catastrophe. Over black leader marked with clarifying subtitles we hear her response:

> "No, I don't want to talk about that."

> "Enough, my son!"

> "You have enough."

> "They say in German, English . . . 'Overdo.'"

That got a laugh from the audience at the Denver Jewish Film Festival.[57] Some audience members evidently thought the film itself, with its experimentally patterned repetitions, "overdone." Yet there is so much more to know. "Why didn't you ask your mother for the story before she was so old and so much less lucid?" inquired an audience member at the screening. I hope I am not overstepping the bounds of etiquette in offering my own response to the question addressed to Ravett, who is an extraordinarily articulate and poised speaker. It seems to me that the point of the film is that he did ask, and ask, and ask. But the answer he received was never fully satisfying. We have replayed before us in the film the very reticence—indeed resistance—that must have characterized Fela's lifelong responses to her son. Indeed, she seems to me perfectly lucid in the filmed sequences; the issue is not her lucidity but her *refusal* to discuss the march. Perhaps we can read Abraham Ravett's choice to write out "Repeat Repeat" against a black background as evoking both his own drive to repeat his question and his mother's view that his questions are repetitive and even tiresome.

And then there is the issue of forgetting. On one hand, forgetting is a survival tactic. As Shalom Asch has written, "[N]ot the power to remember but its very opposite; the power to forget, is a necessary condition of our existence."[58] On the other hand, remembering is a survival tactic. If we recognize and remember the Holocaust we can keep the deniers at bay, and perhaps we can also keep at bay any potentially holocaustal situations. But forgetting and remembering are the two extremes. It is likely that the middle ground is more common. Certainly, as with incest survivors who have post-traumatic stress disorder, there are Holocaust survivors whose memories are imperfect and fragmentary.

The March shows the courage of both Ravetts to acknowledge as much. Fela Ravett indicates that she cannot remember whether the American liberators gave food to those they rescued. And there is that gap in memory between marching and waking up in a hospital: "I don't remember what happened to me then." Perhaps the audience member who questioned Fela's lucidity was basing her evaluation partly on these self-avowed memory lapses. But I would prefer to follow Dori Laub's lead in remaining attuned to the buzz of forgetting. She forgets because what she lived through was "unbelievable," because when she remembers she "start[s] feeling bad," because she doesn't *want* to remember, because it was a long time ago and now she is deathly ill, and because, of course, one of the effects of trauma is forgetting. These aspects of memory, and not Fela's lucidity or lack of it, are at issue in *The March*.

'TAK FOR ALT'

Judy Meisel in *Tak for Alt: Survival of a Human Spirit* is a much more willing narrator than is Fela Ravett. In fact, the film project was initiated by Meisel's own suggestion to the filmmakers Laura Bialis, Broderick Fox, and Sarah Levy that they make her story. In this, and in its use of archival footage, personal photographs, and the device of filming Meisel's return to Europe, *Tak for Alt* would seem to have more in common with *The Last Days*. What we see and hear in the film is Judy Meisel's whole life story as she recollects and narrates it eloquently in interviews shot in the United States and in the European countries where she spent the war years.[59] We are given present-day footage of the village of Jasvene, Lithuania, the Kovno ghetto, Stutthof concentration camp in Poland where Meisel's mother was killed in the gas chamber and where she and her sister Rachel were incarcerated, and the cities of Gdansk and Copenhagen, the latter being the place where the sisters found refuge as the war ended. As is evident from the comparison with *The Last Days,* none of this is unusual in the Holocaust documentary cycle, where straightforward testimony and news-style reporting are now common.

Yet the film does elasticize the doggedly realist conventions of the Holocaust documentary by introducing reenactment and experimental camera, optical, and digital video techniques—the defining attributes of trauma cinema. Along with shots of Meisel's return to her past walks, we get the brief reenactments of scenes from her childhood alluded to in chapter 1: namely, her mother braiding challah dough and lighting the Sabbath candles. As indicated previously, I have heard protests against these sequences: employing actors to replay past scenes is inappropriate when the events under depiction are historical, world-shattering, and subject to denial. But is it necessarily true that fictive strategies taint the legitimacy of represented testimony?

Of course, I continue to argue to the contrary. The challah and Sabbath sequences are reenacted in an experimental manner and interspersed throughout the film. I count three reappearances of bread and candles in the film. But no master shot of the whole scene is ever provided. In the first sequence, for example, we are given five shots of short duration, each of which shows a close-up of a fragment of the scene: hands striking a match and lighting candles (two shots), lighted wicks, a baked challah loaf from which a hand is seen to pull a small share (two shots). Shot and edited as it is, the material serves to evoke the fragile and selective nature of memory; the way that shards of memory come unbidden to traumatized people.

At least two other sequences qualify as "reenacted" in the sense of involving props and events created or borrowed to evoke specific past occurrences while at the same time questioning how we know the past. Meisel relates that she and Rachel escaped from the forced march that followed the liquidation of Stutthof when the road was bombed by the Allies. They then followed a light across a field to a house. There they were helped by locals and a Russian prisoner of war. We see a number of photographically negative images of a field—shot with a bobbing camera to evoke the girls' stumbling forward progress—and of the outside of a house. In addition there is a big close-up of the top right quadrant of a clock hanging on a papered wall. Meisel recounts that the prisoner used a horse to make tracks in the snow to lead her and Rachel to a frozen river that they were directed to cross on hands and knees on their way to a convent. We are given a specially processed black-and-white close-up of a horse's neck followed by shots of the horse's hooves plodding deliberately across the ground. The arrival and departure sequences were reenacted and marked as such by the experimental techniques employed.[60] In a later sequence Meisel relates how she and her sister made it to Denmark, where they were taken in by a Danish couple. Meisel explains that the woman, Paula (to whom the film is dedicated), tried everything to get Meisel's hair to grow back. We see a wide pot containing floating egg yolks and a woman's hands—shot again in grainy black and white—as Meisel recounts how Paula covered Judy's head with a poultice of the yolks and seated her out on the balcony to encourage hair growth. The image of the floating yolk was borrowed from an archival

Figure 4. Representing the house to which Judy and Rachel fled; *Tak for Alt*.

Figure 5. Fragmented memory; *Tak for Alt*.

documentary to illustrate Meisel's memoires. Like the newly shot footage, it is used to exteriorize mental impressions of real occurrences, impressions that Meisel had formed and carried with her into the present. In all these cases, both the simple existence of the reenacted or found footage and the fact of *how* it is rendered make it a placeholder—but not a substitute—for what can never exist again or even be represented, except through reconstruction of a chosen type.

Interestingly, the black-and-white footage shot by the filmmakers is not confined to these reenacted sequences. It is also used to record Meisel's visits to sites of mourning and recovery. For example, Meisel's visit to her father's grave in Jasvene is shot both in color and in Super-8 black and white, as is footage of a shul in Kovno. Like the reenacted sequences, and precisely because of the latter's existence in the film, these nonreenacted but nostalgic sequences also evoke Meisel's subjective state of mind. We are reminded by the choice of film stock (however justifiably, black-and-white footage tends to connote past times) that the meaningfulness of Meisel's actions in the present (for example, brushing dirt and sticks off her father's headstone) is inextricably tied to her past life in the area as the daughter of a large family. The same could be said of a repeated grainy, black-and-white, handheld, low-to-the-ground shot of the bridge Judy crossed when her family was deported to the Kovno. The shot is of the bridge itself as it looks today. But the deliberately low camera position evokes—simultaneously—what the child Judy must have seen as she crossed the bridge more than fifty years ago.

Returning to the device of the fiction to nonfiction continuum, we might say that this original (rather than archival) black-and-white footage ranges in its use from re-presenting the past through the device of reenactment (we plot this application to the left of the continuum) to offering an image of present time suffused with retrospective meaning (we plot this application to the right of the continuum). In the broad middle of the continuum we find an even more complex use of the original black-and-white footage, one that not only bridges fictional and nonfictional modes but also places in abeyance the distinction between objective, direct cinema documentation and subjective memory. Meisel's account of how the liquidation of Stutthof turned to chaos when the Allied bombs scattered the Nazi guards is accompanied by a powerful combination of images and sounds. What we see, intercut, are handheld shots, created by the filmmakers, of the road leading out of Stutthof, and photos—archival in nature—of a forced march, if not *the* forced march. The road was and is a real road, but it is presented within a sequence that uses odd angles, purposely unsteady camera-work, and rapid cutting to evoke the teenaged Judy's amazement. Such shots are simultaneously document and fiction, imagination in memory made animate. Moreover, these shots of the present-day road are accompanied by shouted commands in German. This is made possible by the filmmakers' engagement of a voice actor. In the context of the film as a whole and because of the pains taken by the filmmakers to juxtapose in an unsettling manner the different modalities of the real, the resulting fabric of past and present, fictive and documentary threads avoids the seamlessness of *The Last Days*. The passage, while emotionally affecting, thus strives to maintain and succeeds in maintaining a certain critical distance from the events it invokes. The film both moves us *and* asks us to reflect on the complicated mise-en-scène of memory.

And what of the nasturtiums, vividly orange in the color footage, that brighten the section of the film concerned with Meisel's internment in Stutthof? These new blooms are gathered to represent what Judy *recalls* remembering while incarcerated in the camp: "Amongst the death I would close my eyes and I would think about nasturtiums which we have in Jasvene. I would smell the nasturtiums and it put me in a total trance. I could feel I was taking an extra breath of life. I would also smell my mother's Friday morning baking challah . . . and the most important thing is, I would hear my mother's voice singing a lullaby to me. To me it meant life; that I went back to my good, happy childhood in Jasvene." What Meisel conjures for the circumstance of filming is a memory of a memory that served to keep her body and spirit alive. And her evocation of sensory memory—the *smell* of nasturtiums and challah, the *sound* of her mother's voice—is enhanced by the soundtrack where a lullaby is heard and by the sensual quality of the roving camerawork.

The utility of forgetting as well as remembering was made all the clearer by recent events. In the hospital for knee-replacement surgery, Judy Meisel was told by her doctors that her bones showed signs of having been shattered. Yes, she confirmed, she had been beaten by a guard at Stutthof, and her leg had been badly injured. She had a continuous memory of this event and had even spoken of it to her filmic biographers. But somehow neither she nor they had identified this memory as being significant enough to include in the film. But then, on morphine because of the surgery and with her leg in a heavy cast, Meisel had been having a series of nightmares, flashbacks, and recurrences—the feeling that she was again living the moment that was in reality past. This suggests two things. First, an injured camp inmate who could not work would almost certainly have been put to death. Meisel's deliberate (or was it unconscious?) substitution of the memory of nasturtiums for that of a beating must have served its highest purpose of saving her life. Second, the nasturtiums in the film are a screen for the unrepresented story of the beating. Now we can read the film text itself as amnesiac because we know about the things to which it refers but does not represent.

This clue to the utility of memory work—disremembering—can lend perspective to our reading of the film's second half. I shall circle back to forgetting by and by. Judy's and Rachel's escape from the line of forced marchers occurs halfway through the film. The film then retraces the path they followed: first they reached the convent to which they had been directed by the inhabitants of the house, then they moved on to a private home, where they worked as mistreated servants; finally, they journeyed by boat to Denmark with their employers. Once in Denmark (after the boat was torpedoed and the survivors rescued!), they parted ways with their mistress and were sheltered by humanitarian agencies and the Danish health care system.

According to Meisel's narration, the time in Denmark not only saved her physical life but also enabled a renewal of spirit. The film's structure encourages this sentiment in viewers as well by concentrating in its last third on the measures taken by the Danes to evacuate their Jewish citizens to Sweden in 1943 and welcome them back in 1945. We are given powerful images of the gentile population, led by King Christian, crowding the harbor to celebrate the return of the evacuees from Sweden. It is tremendously heartening to be presented with evidence that not all occupied countries collaborated in the arrest, deportation, and extermination of their Jewish citizens.

But does this tack carry the film into the justifiably suspect category of the "feel-good" Hollywoodian Holocaust history? Some commentators on *Schindler's List* have noted the way the narrative focus on Schindler's Jews dims our cognizance of widespread well-managed genocide by encouraging identification with a rescuer-hero and a small band-as-protagonist. We are greatly relieved when Schindler's Jews are plucked back out of Auschwitz, where their train mistakenly has been directed, and we are detoured around the Jews (the "extras" in the acting pool) who are fated to remain. The film's ending continues the celebration of heroic individualism (Oskar Schindler is portrayed as being devastated because he did not help more people) and survival over Shoah.

I would argue that *Tak for Alt* engages several strategies to qualify its survival story. The film emphasizes that while individuals can make a difference, that difference is generally made in the context of collective action. The film includes a passage in which Meisel herself talks about the impossibility of transcendent individualism as a means of liberation. Why did she and her sister survive? It was luck, she explains, *mazel* in Yiddish. "People say, well you're a survivor. You're very very brave. You're very very strong." "All the people I was with in Stutthof, in the ghetto, everybody was brave, everybody wanted to live," she asserts emphatically. "It was just not their luck." Moreover, the film is structured so that it begins and ends with the history of collective action for change through the civil rights movement. Meisel got involved in the movement when an African American family was being harassed for moving into an all-white neighborhood in Folcroft, Pennsylvania. Meisel explains that she immediately made the connection between the attacks on the Bakers and Kristallnacht, and she went to the Bakers' house with a batch of freshly baked cookies. The very first images of the film (after the credit sequence) are archival images documenting this local struggle in which Meisel was a direct participant. Near its end, the film returns to the topic of the American civil rights movement, and we see footage of Martin Luther King, whom Meisel says she had the privilege of meeting, and the 1963 March on Washington. Thus, when we subsequently see footage of Meisel asking an audience of students who is responsible for the Holocaust, the answer that she gives them, that "*the world* is responsible," evokes a vision of collective action for justice rather than a vision of atomized individuals.

But it is the film's portrayal of the Danes' humane treatment of their Jewish fellow citizens that seals its commitment to showing individual action always within a larger context of cooperation for the general good. Also sealed by the handling of the sequence is the film's commitment to making direct links between individual experience and public history. Elsewhere in the film Meisel narrates personal experiences that may be *and often are* corroborated by other means. For example, her evocative description of the "stench of death" at Stutthof is directly confirmed by historian Stanislaw Swigon, who leads Meisel and the filmmakers to the sites where corpses were burned on pyres. But since Meisel herself was not a Danish evacuee, the film takes the surprising step of interjecting an alternate witness. Instead of sufficing with Meisel's story of how Paula took the sisters down to the harbor to see the return of the Jews, the filmmakers have chosen to include an evacuee (Danish Jew Bella Kaznelson) and two authorities on the subject (Axel Christensen, Danish resistance saboteur and archivist of the Danish Resistance Museum; and Rabbi Bent Melchior, former rabbi of Copenhagen). In a kind of documentary within the documentary, Kaznelson relates how she traveled to the harbor at Elsinore to find a fisherman to take her and her fiancé across to Sweden, and how that same fisherman returned for another twenty-five members of Kaznelson's family. This amazing story is illustrated through footage (culled from a Danish documentary entitled *The Five Years*) of various fishing boats, with particular focus on the cargo areas where the escaping Jews hid. It is also illustrated by more abstract shots of lights over glittering waters and a small boat in a dark expanse, which are accompanied by a portion of the Peter Rogers Melnick score reminiscent of Philip Glass's eerie work in *The Thin Blue Line* (Morris, 1988). The sequence illustrates, therefore, the film's dual commitment to careful historiography and to the affective power of poetic imagery and music.

In Stutthof, Judy Meisel chose to comfort herself with the memory of nasturtiums. Fifty years later, the filmmakers too chose nasturtiums over a beating and so enacted a kind of expedient, cinematic amnesia. However, because the film highlights the foibles and the indeterminate and selective aspects of memory and representation both, its concentration on the magnanimity of the Danes may be read as more than a flight to feel-good sentiment. It may be read as a reflexive *choice* to focus on this particular national outcome among many other less heartening ones that are disremembered. In other words, sadder alternatives remain suspended—floating in the mix—while Meisel's more positive experience is galvanized for the sake of the "survival of the human spirit."

I began this chapter by critiquing the tendency toward pseudoempiricism that characterizes some well-known testimony-based archival projects. Recording and preserving eyewitness accounts is crucial to the historiography of catastrophic events. But convergent means of corroboration must also be employed. Moreover, the seemingly productive and anti-elitist collection and acceptance of survivor testimony loses legitimacy when it ignores the vicissitudes of memory. Corroboration at its most useful is not an antidote to mistaken memory but rather its complement. We know more about the history of given events—and about history itself—if we know which ones make memory quail and if we can make out the trace of memory in the cinematic cloud chamber.

The March presents us with just that. The film is as much about what Fela Ravett *avoids* saying over the twenty-two minutes of the film—and about *why* she needs to avoid those words—as it is about what happened to her on the march. *Tak for Alt* is much more forthcoming about exactly what happened. In fact, it is productively corroborative in its presentation of historical details and evidence. But the film's recourse to imaginative techniques ensures that it too will be about intangible affect and the "limits of representation," including historiography.

SIX

Disremembering the Holocaust

Everything's for You,
Second Generation Video,
and *Mr. Death*

Everything's for You (Abraham Ravett, 1989) is not exactly about its interview subject, the filmmaker's father, to whom the film is dedicated:

In Memory
Chaim R. Ravett
1905–1979

True, the film concentrates on the elder Ravett and contains passages in which he is seen being peppered with questions by his son. When an end credit informs us that portions of the piece were filmed between 1974 and 1977, we take that as a reference to those particular sequences: Chaim Ravett outdoors in a natty jacket and sunglasses, inside before a window with his chin in his hand, seated shirtless against a white wall, and shirtless, again, in bed. It is also true that some facts about Ravett's past are key: he had a wife and two children who were killed in the Holocaust. However, the film is more autobiographical than biographical. Other portions, filmed between 1984 and 1989, feature Abraham Ravett himself along with his mother, his wife, his daughter, and, especially, his son, Chaim Muller-Ravett. And, of course, Abraham has produced, directed, written, and edited the film—his meditation on his considerably fraught relationship with Chaim and on what he himself has become as a mature man and father. The central question of the film is, What is Abraham's heritage as a postwar son, as his father's sole surviving offspring, and as a man who is not satisfied with what he knows of his late father?

All biographical documentaries are in some sense also autobiographical with respect to their makers. But matters of degree are crucial. Although *The March* (Abraham Ravett, 1999) and *Everything's for You* are both films about a parent and about the filmmaker-son's relationship to that individual, the balance of the two is quite different. *The March* is more about the experiences of Fela Ravett than *Everything's for You* is about the experiences of Chaim. In the latter film, as Michael Renov has written, "there can be no question of 'knowing' the elder Ravett's experience."[1] But in and through his inquiries, and in and through Abraham Ravett's filmwork, we do come to know something about the son and something about the potentialities of post-Holocaust representation.

POSTMEMORY AND SECOND-GENERATION FILM AND VIDEO

Over the last twenty years in the United States and Israel especially there has been a growing awareness of the "second generation," a generation of the sons and daughters of Holocaust survivors. These are children for whom the Holocaust has had a formative effect, for although they themselves were born after the war, many were raised by parents who could not speak about their experiences and who had sustained irreparable psychological and physical damage. Dina Wardi explains that the children of survivors represented, on one hand, the miracle of their parents' survival. But, on the other hand, they served as reminders of and compensation for all of the relatives who had perished, including often their parents' own parents, spouses, siblings, and even other children. Parental expectations were therefore extreme, and some of these children became what Wardi calls the "memorial candles" of the Holocaust.[2] The Israeli film scholar Yosefa Loshitzky quotes Wardi in describing how these children " 'have been given the lifework of establishing intergenerational continuity.' As the successors of the survivors, behind whom are 'ruin and death and infinite emotional emptiness,' it is the obligation and privilege of the second generation 'to maintain the nation, to re-establish the vanished family and to fill the enormous physical and emotional void left by the Holocaust' in their survivor parents' 'surroundings and hearts.' "[3]

I choose to quote Loshitzky for several reasons. As the daughter of a mother who escaped to the Soviet Union before the war but whose remaining family was decimated, Loshitzky describes how her mother would react when she, Loshitzky, misbehaved as a child: "Whenever my mother was upset with me she would turn off the lights in our tiny Tel Aviv apartment, sit in the armchair in my parents' bedroom and start crying and complaining in a monotonous, almost ritualized manner, 'Why didn't they [the Nazis] take me to Treblinka? Why didn't I die at Treblinka?'" Loshitzky explains with great self-awareness how her mother's "feelings of guilt for being the only survivor of her family infiltrated [Loshitzky's own] young Sabra consciousness and were grafted onto [her] feelings of guilt for being a 'bad girl' who upset her mother."[4] It is not so much the moving details of Loshitzky's life that are crucial for this discussion as what these personal experiences led her to discern: namely, the significance of the relationship of memory to intergenerational dynamics and "the power and mediation of the movie camera" to create "a linkage between a crisis in the child-parent relationship and the parents' silence."[5]

The ideas of another daughter of Holocaust survivors, Marianne Hirsch, have been most influential in the discussion of intergenerational memory. "Postmemory," the key concept developed by Hirsch, "characterizes the experience of those who grow up dominated by narratives that preceded their birth, whose own belated stories are evacuated by the stories of the previous generation shattered by traumatic events that can be neither understood nor recreated." Postmemory, therefore, is "distinguished from memory by generational distance and from history by deep personal connection." It is "a powerful and very particular form of memory precisely because its connection to its object or source is mediated not through recollection but through an imaginative investment and creation."[6]

As a film about the crisis in mutual understanding between Abraham Ravett and his survivor-father, *Everything's for You* is emphatically second-generational. And, as a film deeply involved with original strategies of "imaginative investment and creation," *Everything's for You* effectively illustrates and extends the possibilities of cinematic postmemory.

The film's handling of father-son interviews foregrounds the problem of "generational distance" and the problem of the "belatedness" of the filmmaker's life experience. Contentwise, the film contains two main father-son conversations, both of which underline how the generation gap that always exists between parents and children is here exacerbated by the terrible facts of the father's past and by his status as an immigrant. The first conversation, held with much prompting on the part of the son, who addresses his

Figure 6. Chaim Ravett; *Everything's for You.*
Still photograph courtesy of Abraham Ravett.

questions from behind the camera, begins the film and sets out the central tragedy of Chaim's life:

ABRAHAM: What about your family . . . the family that you had before the war? . . . What did you have, you had a child?

CHAIM: (speaking in Yiddish-accented English) Children, two childrens.

ABRAHAM: A boy and a girl?

CHAIM: A boy and a girl.

ABRAHAM: How old were they?

CHAIM: The girl . . . what old? . . . I think 11 years and the boy was 8 years.

ABRAHAM: When was the last time you . . . ?

CHAIM: I was with my family in the Lodz ghetto till '45.

This conversation has been edited so that it breaks here to be continued later in the film:

ABRAHAM: That was the last time you saw your family?

CHAIM: Yeah. This was in 1944. They kill anyway right away the wife and the children.

In a conventional Holocaust documentary one understands that such stories are retold on film for posterity so that the world will not forget. But here, it is not only the father's past that matters but the linkage (to borrow Loshitzky's word) between what the father retells and the difficulty of communication between the two men.

In the second main conversation of the film, the filmmaker/son, harking back a few years, reminds his father of the time that he, Abraham, met a gentile girl whom he really liked. His father responds by saying that he should seek a nice Jewish girl instead. Abraham challenges his father's insensitivity to his feelings and makes fun of his father's inadvertent use of the masculine noun when his father suggests that he find a nice *boy*. Presumably knowing that his father would be even more disturbed if his love object were a person of the same sex, but likely knowing that his father has merely made a grammatical error, Abraham pounces, exclaiming, "A boy or a girl?!" His father covers his mistake with a smile. He does not rise to the bait. Later in the film another passage suggests why Abraham's small victory cannot be sustained. Chaim tells a story of how their gentile neighbors tipped off the Nazis to the hiding place of his mother, who had sought to escape evacuation by hiding in an oven. This is why one cannot trust non-Jews. "Now, can I have a feeling towards goyim?" Chaim asks rhetorically. "Never in my life." The two conversations, taken together, demonstrate perfectly how the father-son relationship in the present is deeply informed by the father's hapless moral superiority for having suffered in the past.

That the father was in many respects lost to the son even when he was alive is also underlined through the use of an unusual interview technique. Periodically, would-be interview sequences turn into retrospective musing on the part of the son when what we *see* is footage of Chaim shot before 1979 while what we *hear* are the words of Abraham recorded after his father's death. In Yiddish Abraham asks, "Pop, where are you? Now that I need to talk to you, where are you? Abba, where are you now? I want to talk with you." The meditative monological nature of the queries is further emphasized through the repetition of various phrases ("where are you?" in this case) that are doubly repetitive for being translated to English subtitles as well as being spoken. From a literal perspective we can understand Abraham's queries as a filmic mourning ritual practiced after the death of his father. However, the eerie match between the silence of the posthumously embodied father and his taciturn demeanor in the simultaneous sound sequences suggests that the son did not make much headway in establishing communication even while the father was still alive. The death of the father is represented, therefore, as a double loss. It ends not only the relationship that was but also the relationship that could have been if not for the emotional distance that Chaim maintained.

Another clue to Chaim's limitations as a parent comes from the animated drawings interspersed throughout the film. Three different scenarios unfold in cartoon logic, with objects changing shape and turning into other objects. In the first we see the figure of a man beating a boy with what looks like a towel. A female figure appears and says, in Yiddish, "Henyek, control yourself." The sequence continues later with childlike figures outside a door. As one of the figures runs in and out of the doorway, the key to the lock breaks. Over black we see the following subtitles: "I broke the lock, Pop. Why did you hit me so hard? Tell me why." The second animated sequence features a line of people waiting outside a door. Two figures jump the queue and go right in, one pulling the other, and titles read: "Do you remember, Pop? Do you remember that you couldn't wait like others . . . ? How should I have known what it meant to you? You never told me. . . .

Tell me how." In the third animated sequence, drawings improvise on a sentence the father is heard being made to repeat by his filmmaker son: "If you knew what one potato meant to me, then you would understand." A small man in a hat carrying a potato is accompanied by a much taller man whose face is rendered with eyes alone and no nose or mouth.

Like the interview sequences in which sound and image are nonsimultaneous, these sequences apparently subject past actions to current questioning. If, as a child, Abraham could not voice his questions, as if he had no mouth from which the sounds could emanate, now, as an adult physically larger than his father, he may formulate the questions. But no matter how often they are repeated, they are still out of synch with their would-be interlocutor.

Experimental techniques employed in these sequences both multiply the channels of communication and introduce noise that limits their effectivity. The animated drawings are often duplicated within the film frame so that, for example, we see two separate images of a man beating a boy, one on top of the other. In addition we see Abraham's questions written out in the form of subtitles, and we hear Abraham's mother saying her lines. But the images flash as if their frequency of projection is out of synch with the frequency of the camera that has captured them. And, in any case, all the duplications and rephrasings in the world will still fail to reincarnate a father-son relationship that was what the real relationship was not: intimately gentle and communicative.

Besides the posthumous "interviews" and cartoon drawings, less figurative techniques are used to manifest Abraham's memory of his father as a means of coming to terms with his absence. Close-ups of Chaim's social security card, watch, tailoring scissors (being placed on a wooden surface by a child's hand), and twenty dollar bills folded and nested into one another are presented without direct explanation (i.e., "these were pop's scissors"). But we are given to understand that they are Chaim's remains, the fetish objects that "gather their peculiar power by virtue of a prior contact with some originary object" and "translate experience through space and time in a material medium."[7] To possess something that his father touched and used is to achieve a physical closeness that was not perhaps matched at the time on an emotional level. Abraham apparently watched his father sewing garments, probably saw him using the scissors, but now he queries, "Why didn't you want me to sew?" Photographed by Abraham's camera, these objects become double fetishes in Laura Marks's sense of the term. For Marks there is a "fetishlike/fossil-like quality . . . at work in film: film bears

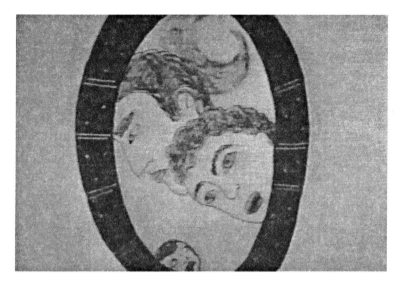

Figure 7. Animating family; *Everything's for You*. Cell animation drawing by Emily Hubley.

the trace of another material object on its surface."[8] Thus these objects become filmic fetishes of fetishes. But of course, as such, they only encode the alienation that they brokenly promise to bridge.

What can we make, then, of the collected photographic relics that appear in the film? The film includes archival footage of the Lodz ghetto, at least one photograph of what appear to be ghetto children or young adults, and several photos of Chaim as a young man, his murdered wife, and his children. In a traditional Holocaust documentary such materials would be used in a reassuring manner to shore up the film's historiographic validity. We command the past because we hold its telling residue. Here are Jews in the Lodz ghetto exactly as explained in the testimony of X. Or, here is a picture of X in the Lodz ghetto as explained in the subtitle provided. In *Everything's for You*, such bits of photographic evidence attest, contrarily, to all we do not know and/or to what we do know but cannot quite comprehend or accept. The film does not indicate clearly whether Chaim and his family are among the people in the group photograph or in the moving footage. We scrutinize the faces in anticipation of a familiar but more youthful visage. But our researches are inconclusive. Either way, this lack of knowledge perpetuates uncertainty. And this uncertainty is compounded by the way the ghetto photo and footage have been handled. The group photograph has been reshot so that the individual faces are presented in close-up and cut together, one after the other, to create a kind of flickering image of an unrecognizable composite. Is one of these faces that of a younger Chaim? Are there other faces here? Does it matter? And, much as in Michelle Citron's home movies, the moving images of the ghetto proceed in slow motion, stopping, starting, repeating. Adding further complications are Abraham's rhetorical questions as they are spoken and written out in subtitles over the Lodz footage: "Is that you, Pop?" "What did your children do, Pop?" "What did you do on the day they transported you out of the ghetto?" "What did your children wear?" "What did your wife say?"

The three photographs of Chaim and his dead wife and children would seem to satisfy Abraham's search for a telling image of his father. These pictures must be the most tangible remains of the narrative that preceded Abraham's birth but affects his life profoundly. They are the photographic correspondence to Abraham's postmemory.

The film presents Abraham's scrutiny of these images. He directs his mother to read and translate the Yiddish on the backs of the photos, and we see in close-up the Hebrew letters on the reverse side of one. The photos are dated, and at least one is inscribed, "For remembrance." Chaim held the pen that spilled the ink. Light etched his image and those of his dead family members on the emulsion of the photos within the film; each one, therefore, is a fetish of a fetish of a fetish. As Abraham indicates verbally and in subtitles over a silent image of his father, he found the photos only after his father's death: "Now after all these years I found three photos. Now I see what you looked like. Now I see. Now I see everything." But I quite agree with Michael Renov, who writes, quoting Lyotard, that the passage returns us "to the aporetic character of Holocaust art, to art 'which does not say the unsayable, but says that it cannot say it.'"[9] That this is indeed the case is emphasized by Abraham's words as they continue: "I don't understand it. What were you afraid of? What can I know? I can't know anything." Thus, the film undermines any "Eureka!" experience that might be had in relation to the photos. They are not merely the cinematic referent of the son's postmemory; they are cinematic postmemory itself. The film interposes these photos, and their subjects, between Chaim and Abraham. They are the crux of the (mis)understanding between the father and the filmmaker/son. They represent Chaim's self-imposed foreclosure of the memories for which *Everything's for You* makes a bid.

The subject of postmemory, reintroduced, brings us to those emblematic postmemory texts, Art Spiegelman's *Maus* and *Maus II*.[10] Although they are book-length comics, the volumes are nevertheless extremely close in spirit to *Everything's for You*. Both are autobiographical works by a son of Holocaust survivors, and both draw attention to the inadequacy of realist representation in the face of historical catastrophe. I hope my foregoing discussion of the film will have made it evident that Dominick LaCapra's insight about *Maus* applies as well to *Everything's for You*: "[I]ts characters . . . may be possessed by the past, unable to supplement melancholy with successful forms of mourning and working-through, and caught up in endless repetition. Still, the text's orchestration, which does not offer total mastery but allows for the unsettling reinscription of trauma, may enable the reader to see how the tensely interactive processes of acting-out and working-through might be engaged."[11] What Marianne Hirsch has written about *Maus*'s artist/son applies also to Abraham Ravett: "[M]emory is unbearable and, in his representational choices, Spiegelman tries to convey just how unbearable it is . . . but the grieving Art does not actually *remember* the concentration camp. . . . [H]is is a postmemory"—a postmemory with a photographic referent. *Maus* and *Maus II* each contain a few scattered photos, photos that both satisfy and mystify their author's and our desire for knowledge of the past.

Maus II contains a baby picture of Art Spiegelman's brother, Richieu, who died during the war. This picture is bracketed by the book's double dedication: "For Richieu" written out above the photo, "And for Nadja" (Art Spiegelman's own daughter) below it. As Hirsch tells us, "the volume is dedicated to two children, one dead, the other alive, one who is the object of postmemory, the other who will herself carry on her father's postmemory."[12] Spiegelman and his readers are satisfied, therefore, because we know what Richieu looked like, but we are also mystified because we will never know what Art's relationship with his "ghost-brother," as he puts it, might have been. "I didn't think about him much when I was growing up," the Art Spiegelman character in *Maus II* reflects. "He was mainly a large, blurry photograph hanging in my parents' bedroom. . . . The photo never threw tantrums or got in any kind of trouble. It was an ideal kid, and *I* was a pain in the ass. I couldn't compete."[13] As Andrea Liss writes, "Spiegelman weaves Richieu's portrait into an appropriate realm of otherworldliness, a space outside of everyday experience, and into a past life that Art can barely gain access to, a life that also enframes him. Richieu's photograph both taunts Art's guilt and haunts him with despair. And he tells [his wife] Françoise: 'It's spooky having sibling rivalry with a photograph.'"[14] Thus, *Maus* perpetuates a confusion not only between Richieu and Nadja through the dedication but also between Richieu and Art. In view of this question of sibling rivalry, it is heartbreaking when, at the end of the volume (the character of) the father, Vladek, addresses his son (the character) Art as follows: "Let's stop, please, your tape recorder. I'm tired from talking, *Richieu,* and it's enough stories for now" (emphasis mine).[15]

My point, of course, is that this paradigm of the son with a tape recorder; the son intensely interested in a parent's stories and in a brother who predeceased him prematurely and who appears in a photograph, silent in all innocence, invokes history in the Barthesian sense as the time before one's birth.[16] It is also the structuring paradigm of *Everything's for You.* The sequence in which the three photos of Chaim's first family appear ends with Abraham's voice-over images of old Jewish men: "All the time I'm looking for someone who looks like you." But one might hazard the guess that what he also seeks is the reflection of himself in his father's eyes.

The relationship between father and son as represented in the film is also complicated by the fact that Abraham himself became a father after his father's death, and the film features his relationship with his own children. The film could very well have been dedicated not only to Chaim Ravett but to Sara and Chaim Muller-Ravett, who, like Nadja Spiegelman, will carry their own postmemories of their father's past. As we hear Abraham say to his (late) father: "I have two children now, just like you had."

There is ample evidence in the film that Abraham is deeply involved with the care and nurturing of his children and that their relationship is close. We see Abraham and his young son changing in a locker room and then, later, showering together. We are given daughter Sara Muller-Ravett's illustrated storybook page by page as she is heard reading it aloud. Making space for his daughter's budding creative expression is a distinct act of generosity by filmmaker/father Ravett. I am also touched by the sequence in which Abraham tells his little son that it is time for a nap. Seated at the kitchen table, the son protests that he is not tired. But his actions of rubbing his eyes and whining suggest otherwise. What I find most affecting is the sound of his sister's voice saying, "[Y]ou're acting like it; I see it right in your eyes." This is obviously a family in which people are attuned to one another, where they are able to read each others' faces to discern moods, needs, thoughts, and feelings. And perhaps more importantly, this is a family where people care to do so. Over a sequence in which two children (I assume they are Abraham's) play in the snow, we hear Abraham speak in Yiddish (translated to English subtitles) to his late father: "It was so hard for you to tell me that you loved me. It was so hard for me to let you know that I loved you."

Abraham reveals his own unclothed body, fully and from the front. In the context of this film about his father's emotional distance, the filmmaker's courage to present his own feelings, and his own body, naked and vulnerable, is particularly striking. The film models how new patterns may be etched into the generational cycle. It must be one of Abraham's children who places her or his grandfather's scissors on the table for the purposes of his or her father's film. Abraham was not taught to sew, but his children are being brought up around film- and videomaking. Here the children of the third generation are initiated into action and discourse; indeed, they are paramount.

But just as Chaim Ravett reserved his secrets, his counsel, and his photographs, so Abraham Ravett maintains his own areas of reticence. I have indicated that at times we see an image of Chaim senior while we hear words that his filmmaker/son recorded after his father's death. This temporal, and mortal, dissonance is something that dawns on us as we watch the film. We glean that the father has passed away from Abraham Ravett's use of the past tense, from the fact that his own son is named Chaim (in Jewish tradition children are not named after the living),[17] and, more directly, from Abraham's statement that he found the three photos of his father with his first family only "after all these years." Nevertheless, the complete chronology of the filmmaking process in relation to Chaim's death remains ambiguous and incomplete, at least until the end of the film, when we are finally given the commemorative epigraph with which I began this chapter and the dates of the periods of filming: 1974–77 and 1984–89. With this placement, the film asks us to reflect back on what we had discerned before we had all the facts. Just as Abraham thought deeply about his relationship with his deceased father, so we think back on a film that we have already watched through to the end.

Also revelatory of Ravett's interest in foregrounding the limits of intrafamilial knowledge and the limits of autobiography is his handling of his film *Thirty Years Later* (1978). Abraham Ravett has mentioned this film to me, explaining that the film "weaves a tapestry of events between the present and the past, between self and family, between a desire to know and the limits of what can be revealed."[18] It is included in the filmography/videography on his Web site. But Ravett has elected to keep the film out of distribution. On his site, generated by Hampshire College, where Ravett is a professor of film and photography, the film is described as follows: "(1978), 43 min., color, sound, documentary film. Utilizing a diary format, the camera is used to record the emotional and psychological impact of the Holocaust on two survivors and the influence this experience has had on their relationship with the filmmaker, their only remaining child."[19] Some people have seen this film, and parts of it are included in *Everything's for You*. It is not that the film is completely unavailable but rather that Ravett prefers that it not be seen. I respect that decision and I do not press. I ponder this situation in which a filmmaker as forthcoming as Ravett, willing to expose his despair over the emotional distance his father maintained, dedicated to changing that pattern with his own children, nevertheless holds back. This reticence about or disbelief in full disclosure suggests an affecting empathy for the father's position. In making films about "the limits of what can be revealed," Ravett communicates the pain felt by the person who does not get to know everything (himself as a second-generation survivor), the psychological necessity to keep some things private, and the expressive potential of the film medium.

Like *Tak for Alt* (Laura Bialis, Broderick Fox, and Sarah Levy, 1999) and, to an even greater extent, Ravett's *Everything's for You*, Joshua Hirsch's *Second Generation Video* (1995) makes manifest Hayden White's insight that the Holocaust is representable, only not in realist terms.[20] *Second Generation Video* overtly broaches the problem of memory's frailty. "Sunday, May 15, 1994," intones camp survivor James Hirsch. "The 50th anniversary of our deportation." In Poland, at Auschwitz-Birkenau with his longtime friend Kassy, James Hirsch reflects as follows: "At Birkenau Kassy and I were trying to figure out the ramp because I remember as the train came in that we disembarked from the train on the left side facing the locomotive and Kassy remembered differently. And then when we went through the selection I remember we went in through a sort of barbed wire gate and then we went to the left between rows of wire. And Kassy remembered something else. Well, I mean, there's nobody we can ask." In and of itself it is immaterial whether Hirsch and Kassy disembarked to the right or to the left. But one man is surely mistaken in the detail while being right about the gist of his internment.

If memory is intrinsically intangible for the rememberer, how much more discarnate must it be for the rememberer's child? Our adult child narrator in this video broaches several examples in which the film image is revealed to be different from or to have a different meaning than what was initially apparent. For example, the narrator realizes that the very striking image of emaciated corpses being bulldozed into a pit at Auschwitz must have been filmed after the liberation of the camp; the action was not, as he had assumed unconsciously, one of the Nazis' bizarre tortures. Or when he sees for the first time an amateur film depicting his father at the French orphanage to which the father, James Hirsch, was brought as a young man after liberation from Buchenwald, he remarks on the surprising inadequacy of the images. A multiple-generation video copy, alternately frozen and animated in its presentation (our narrator tells of having viewed it over and over again, stopping and starting), this film within a video is not offered as a guarantor of reality; rather, it serves, like certain home movie passages in *Capturing the Friedmans* (Andrew Jarecki, 2003), to mark the distance between past action and present historical comprehension. As our narrator says, "[T]he images became for me just another mystery."

This point, that we can and must use documentary practice to intervene in assumptions about the transparency of representational forms, including but not limited to photographic representation, is also made through the use of a woman narrator to speak the first-person autobiographical narration of videomaker Joshua Hirsch. Thus we are distanced not only from the physical residue of the past but from discourses of subjectivity as well. Joshua Hirsch may be researching his father's history in part to gain insight into own identity as his father's son. But such insights proceed, the film suggests, not from the consolidation of the strands of identity, but from the realization that the fabric of identity is loosely woven at best.

In neither *Everything's for You* nor *Second Generation Video* do three extra chimneys materialize. But in these documentaries enactment, reenactment, experimental shot selection, and the acknowledgment of mistaken memory compose the cinematic repertoire for representing fantasy construction in memory. Not even photographs are self-evident. How different such probing representations are from the conventional treatments of Holocaust testimony exemplified by *The Last Days* (James Moll, 1998). The vagaries of *Everything's for You* and *Second Generation Video* are more apt to broach the challenges of critical memory than are the pseudocertainties of conventional Holocaust representation.

HOLOCAUST TOURISM THROUGH GENERATIONS

As I have discussed in the previous chapter, interviewees in conventional and unconventional Holocaust documentaries very often speak from the comfort of their present-day homes. Their accounts are interspersed with photographs and archival footage of the European towns, cities, and countrysides from which they were evicted. In conventional Holocaust films, the archival material is used in such a way that the voiced recollections, however fragile or durable, are made to seem sufficient to the historical project. In experimental films, such connections and would-be sufficiencies are undermined. But both paradigms rely on an established relationship between living room testimony and aged footage.

Shoah (Claude Lanzmann, 1985) made its great impression by avoiding archival footage altogether and by fusing testimony and *paysage* into a widely imitated hybrid: the testimony filmed *in situ*. Images of survivors, returned by Lanzmann to their past walks, reincarnated the landscape from which they had been wiped away, thus enacting events that became a part of history, and audiovisually recorded history at that.

The psychological aspect of enactment is also significant. Hiking forest paths or driving through town centers, survivors remember and report details that they had forgotten or avoided mentioning. Thus, they serve as narrators for this filmic passage down a treacherous memory lane. Filmmaker Laura Bialis reports that until they were on location filming *Tak for Alt,* Judy Meisel had never once mentioned to her filmic biographers the existence of the Danish woman Paula who, with her husband Sven, took Judy and Rachel into their homes and nursed Judy back from the brink of death, and to whom the film is dedicated.[21]

First-generation Holocaust survivors tour and testify to trigger memory. For these individuals and their home/theater companions, the features of the landscape, both those that remain (the rails to Auschwitz, the church in Chelmo) and those that have grown out of the remains (like the well-fertilized Lithuanian forest in *Shoah*), form the basis of experience and memory. The fantasy of speaking stones is realized in a certain sense.

But this significant paradigm undergoes a shift with successive generations. For second-generation survivors whose experiences are once removed from the wartime mortal struggles of their parents, postmemory is the basis from which they begin. Whereas the parents tour to remind themselves and others what once was (however incomprehensible that reality may have been at the time), their offspring tour *to identify a physical point of reference for a preexisting state of mind.*

Of course, as I have argued all along, even with the first generation there is a constant doubt (and my preference is for films in which the doubt is foregrounded) as to whether one has properly identified the exact bridge where a child crossed on her way to the ghetto, or whether a man turned to the left or to the right during the camp selection, or whether the filmic representation of such events is ever adequate to their material *and imaginative* registers. Such questions are only exacerbated in the second and successive generations, who, because they experience a fading of the referent and the referee, also experience a greater need and a greater challenge to symbolize the past for posterity or for history. How will the grandchildren and great-grandchildren of survivors remember the camps after the ravages of time and the passing of their former inmates? Ulrich Baer suggests that Holocaust debates about the "limits of representation" are being overridden by the question of what will become of Holocaust history when the last survivors and witnesses pass away.[22]

Already it is the case that the living survivors were young people during the war, getting younger all the time. And those who would hear the survivors' stories are not only the children but now also the grandchildren of survivors. As this third cohort enjoys its full generational complement of relatives, it grows more distant from survivor and eyewitness accounts.[23]

Dina Wardi identifies another form of distance when she writes movingly of her personal history as an Israeli of Italian birth and heritage whose parents participated in the Italian relief before escaping to Israel at the end of the thirties with her, their baby daughter. Although not technically a child of survivors, Wardi was exposed, as an infant and young child, to the accounts and anxieties of those who were caught in the war. And, although all of her family members survived, with the exception of a distant cousin, Wardi writes that she, "like every member of European Jewry of that period," is a child of survivors, if not in fact, then "in potential."[24] I wish to acknowledge the importance of Wardi's avowed, continuing, and inclusive connection to the events of the Holocaust. I think it is important for us to feel connected *without an actual familial link.* And if no genetic connection is necessary, then it also seems possible that gentiles could share with Jews the sense of being the children of survivors "in potential." Wardi's connected disconnection seems useful in two ways: as a means of lateral inclusion encompassing Jews and non-Jews of the period and as a means of vertical inclusion down through the generations. As the survivors age and pass away, all of us, as the grandchildren and great-grandchildren of survivors "in potential," will carry their memory. Our status increasingly and in generations to come will be marked less by an inherent, tangible, and personal connection to the Holocaust than by an abstract, imaginative one.

Perhaps somewhat paradoxically, we will also have the concrete remains. The abstract and the concrete, without the survivor-witness guarantor. How shall we proceed? While some may welcome this forced turn from messy, contradictory memories and their often pained and insistent authors, I would submit that the fallen stones and used bricks of the camps possess their own polymorphic composition. Not even the ruins of the crematoria at Birkenau are historiographically self-evident. The great challenge, therefore, is that some assembly is required to understand landscapes as well as apparent memories. The problem is multifold. First of all, many concentration camps and other tangible relics—shorn human hair in bulk has been a subject of debate—are razed, ruined, or decaying. Some were destroyed or partially destroyed by the Nazis as they began to lose the war or by the surrounding inhabitants who foraged for scrap brick and wire. Many have been reconstructed as museums and/or memorials. It is certainly understandable that there would be debate over exactly how these physical artifacts once operated organically to achieve the aims of genocide. But more important for our purposes here is the intractable fact that not even landscapes fall outside the epistemological imperative of symbolization. Ground zero itself is discursive; the stones do speak, and that is precisely the problem, for speech implies symbolization and interpretation.

Ulrich Baer has proposed landscape photography by two artists as material evidence in the quandary. He queries, "How can the younger generations be taught that the Holocaust poses a problem for representation except by representing it . . . how can its shattering effects on all categories of thought and known modes of transmission be conveyed except by turning it into a circumscribed and thus finally graspable object of inquiry?"[25] He answers that the landscape photographs, by Dirk Reinartz and Mikael Levin, of seemingly innocent clearings in the woods that are in fact the former sites of concentration camps offer viewers a chance to find "our bearings in reference to a place that is absorbing yet unstable." They furnish "a position from which to address the knowledge that continues to prove excessive, destabilizing."[26] These photographs look to me very like the shots of the forest around Auschwitz filmed for Errol Morris's *Mr. Death* (1999) and presented with a poetic narration that alludes to the unseen elements of the image. "Every year human remains are found; bones, teeth, the earth doesn't give up." I would suggest that the younger (but perhaps already not so young) generations of film- and videomakers, like Bauer's photographers, are also finding new and oblique modes of landscape representation. How can *they* be taught the problems of Holocaust representation? They are teaching themselves by doing. Films and videos by those who have come after, including the work of Abraham Ravett and Joshua Hirsch, demonstrate that "graspable" representations need not be circumscribed or "already known" (read: realistic).

Films and videos by or about the distanced second or third generations convey the Holocaust's "shattering effect on all categories of thought and known modes of transmission" with varying degrees of recourse to the "graspable object." Like their representational predecessors, some texts cleave to the real while others achieve greater understanding of truths about the Holocaust by redefining both what we seek to know and how we pursue that knowledge.

Sorrow: The Nazi Legacy (Gregor Nowinski, 1993) falls into the first category. A documentary made in 1993, the film follows the journey of six Swedish young people ("two from an *ordinary* Swedish Christian family background, two had one Swedish parent and one non-Swedish parent, and two from a Jewish background" [emphasis mine]), on their educational visit to the city of Oswieçim, Poland (Auschwitz under National Socialism), and the Auschwitz concentration camp. There they are exposed to the history of the area and the conditions of the camp. And there they meet Ruth Elias, a camp survivor turned docent, who accompanies the teenagers through the Auschwitz barracks. Stopping at a bench in one of the barracks, Elias points to the spot where she gave birth with the help of an inmate midwife but without the benefit of rags, soap, or water of any kind. Elias tells how Dr. Mengele allowed her to carry her pregnancy to term and give birth to an infant girl, only to withhold all food and let the child starve to death as one of the medical tortures parading as scientific experiments for which Mengele is known. The teenagers are obviously moved, some of them to tears. Later they are visited by the adult son of Hans Frank, the governor-general of Nazi-occupied Poland. The son, Niklas Frank, deplores his father's motivations as a clear example of the banality of evil, for he attributes his father's choices and actions as a war criminal (actions for which he was executed by hanging) to the latter's desire for a luxury car and other expensive material goods.

It is gratifying to see young people willing to subject themselves to such a rigorous Holocaust education. They certainly went the distance in their effort to understand. But I am disturbed by the hint of implication (1) that there is no real understanding to be had out of sight of the referent and (2) that the referent is self-evident. Can we not gain knowledge and be moved from afar and/or in the absence of survivors and eyewitnesses? And is the knowledge we gain really so unequivocal? I fear that the film and others like it, by their prioritization of site-specific learning, imply to a certain extent that, no, we cannot and that, yes, it is. But the results will be paradoxical. If we place all our trust in an ostensibly transparent physical realm, then how can we help but see ourselves as losing understanding with the passing of a generation and the ruination (or necessary reconstruction) of the camps?

Errol Morris's *Mr. Death: The Rise and Fall of Fred A. Leuchter, Jr.* intervenes agilely in this quandary. The film clearly establishes the existence of the Holocaust, contrary to the views of its protagonist, Fred Leuchter, an engineer specializing in human execution machines who has turned Holocaust denier (hence the double reference of the appellation "Mr. Death"). But it does so almost in passing, on the way to a less obvious exploration of human motivation, self-delusion, truth, and the roles of evidence and documentary representation. The brilliance of the film lies, therefore, in the fact that it possesses a rhetorical dimension grounded in tangible proof and, at the same time, analytical with regard to the epistemology of the physical. The film scouts out the *vicissitudes* of concrete evidence, including literally those of the rock samples chiseled from the walls and floor of a Nazi death camp. Such materials are not self-evident as historiographical building blocks. They too must be read.

Mr. Death manages its multidimensional investigation in large part by deeply considering and vetting somebody else's fact-finding practice. Leuchter was converted to the denier camp after he was hired by the prominent revisionist Ernst Zündel and company to confirm—well, actually to deny—the use of gas as a method of mass murder at Birkenau, the killing complex located about a mile and a half from the Auschwitz barracks. Zündel was in the throes of a legal battle against a Canadian charge of Holocaust denial and was therefore seeking evidence to back his claims. At his expense, Leuchter traveled to Poland (on his honeymoon) in February 1988 on a four-day inspection tour that included Auschwitz-Birkenau and Majdanek, another former concentration camp near Lublin. At Birkenau's Krema II and another building that had been used for the delousing of inmates' clothing, Leuchter clandestinely gathered samples by using a hammer and chisel to dig out small chunks of the stone walls and floors, thus defacing what is now a museum visited by a steady flow of pilgrims who recite prayers in the chambers, burn candles, and leave behind offerings in the form of small wooden tablets inscribed with the names of the dead. Leuchter then submitted his specimens to a Massachusetts laboratory for blind testing and wrote a twenty-page report announcing the results of the tests and of his investigations as a whole: cyanide was identified in significant quantity in the fragments from the delousing chamber, but no significant residue of cyanide was found in the samples from the crematoria. Furthermore—according to Leuchter, that is—the crematoria had no exhaust vents, were not explosion-proof, and were not leak-proof; therefore, nobody was gassed in Krema II. Or, as the deniers are fond of saying,

"Only lice were gassed in Auschwitz," which is, as Mark Singer explains in his *New Yorker* article, "a slur that echoed, not coincidentally, Hitler's characterization of Jews as a plague of vermin."[27]

Through direct-address interviews and voice-over narration in *Mr. Death,* Leuchter goes to great pains to assert his scientific expertise, both as an engineer of execution machines and as a consultant in the examination of the Nazi physical plant. "What really makes you competent," he opines, speaking of his former career, "is that you have the necessary background. You do the investigation, you find out what the problem is, you solve it." Throughout, his manner and vocabulary are those of the scientific researcher. With regard to his latter career, he speaks of making "detailed scale drawings" and of "obtaining samples" from "proper locations for condensation of cyanide gas."

What Leuchter perceives as the scientific basis of his method is ostensibly shored up by Zündel and company's production of a video record of his activities at Auschwitz, portions of which are incorporated into Morris's film. "Good morning, my name is Fred Leuchter. I'm an engineer from Boston in the U.S.," announces Leuchter at the beginning of the video, gesturing toward the sign at the entrance to the camp (this is just the sort of video that *The Blair Witch Project* spoofs). He observes the meteorological conditions and indicates the date as a preface to what will unfold: "I'm here on this snowy morning, here at Auschwitz in Poland, and the date is February 28th and it's approximately 10:30am, and I'm here to examine this alleged gas chamber." In later sequences of the videotape footage we will see Leuchter working with his draftsman, Howard Miller, extending a measuring tape to determine the exterior dimensions of the gas chamber and chipping concrete. "It would be nice if I could obtain a floor sample which I will seek in a lower spot." And, self-reflexively, to the videographer, "I guess you're getting me." Leuchter gestures up and to his right, stating, "Sample from the roof." After this experience as a video subject, Leuchter would incorporate video documentation into his working method, as we learn from *Mr. Death*'s inclusion of videotape footage from 1989 showing Leuchter rebuilding Tennessee's electric chair, which had been delivered to his home and carried downstairs to his basement workshop.

All of this was history by the time Errol Morris arrived on the scene. But it was not good science or good historiography. *Mr. Death* fully rebuts Leuchter's claims and those of the deniers, picking apart their pseudoscientific and pseudohistorical conclusions and showing them to be sorely deluded, in the case of Leuchter, and vastly self-interested and

Figure 8. Fred Leuchter obtaining rock samples; *Mr. Death*.

hate-mongering, in the case of Zündel and his group. In fact, Morris has been explicit in interviews about the effort he expended filming additional interviews and other material to add to the film after a screening of an early cut at Harvard University. As he explained to journalist Mark Singer, "It seemed that the audience had no place to stand outside Fred . . . . [W]hen the film was over there were people in the room who wondered whether the Holocaust had really happened."[28] In the finished version of *Mr. Death*, Cornell-educated chemist James Roth and Dutch-born historian Robert Jan Van Pelt (author of *Auschwitz: 1270 to the Present*) are interviewed on camera. Each of the men critiques Leuchter's methods and conclusions. Roth, the chemist from Alpha Analytical Laboratories who performed the analysis of Leuchter's rock samples, explains that since the laboratory did not know what it was dealing with, the proper tests were not done. Whereas cyanide traces should have been sought on the surface of the rock, the samples were instead crushed and therefore diluted. "I don't think the samples have any meaning," he states. "That's like analyzing paint on a wall by analyzing the timber that is behind it." Van Pelt, for his part, explains that Auschwitz has "changed three or four times since the camp operated as an extermination camp." This fact makes illegitimate any claim that the current ruined facilities *in and of themselves* reflect the camp's former use. One needs to do archival research to understand the disposition of the camps, asserts Van Pelt, for documents housed at Auschwitz include blueprints of the gas chambers showing how Zyklon B was introduced into the chambers and showing as well their ventilation systems. *Mr. Death* also uses Van Pelt to narrate the presentation of such archival documents as a German order for gas detectors, a March 1943 order for a gas-tight door with a double-paned spy hole, and a memo regarding a *vergasungskelle,* literally "gassing basement," to which a note was added alerting a Nazi co-worker to the slip that had been made in the use of the forbidden word. "The Nazis were the first deniers," Van Pelt explains, following a close-up of the document, "because they denied to themselves that it's happening." Overall, the film contrasts the pathetic inadequacy of Leuchter's brief, unschooled, and clandestine expedition ("I didn't want to get caught," he explains) to Van Pelt's years of serious study and contextual understanding of Auschwitz. Leuchter's findings are thoroughly discredited in *Mr. Death.*

However, the film's unique artistry locates the rebuttal to Leuchter in the body of the film in such a way that it becomes optional to deniers who persist in liking the film. In other words, the film's formal complexity establishes both its mastery as a film *and* its vulnerability as an historiographic text. I happen to believe it is a worthwhile bargain. The film's two-part structure is notable in this regard, as is its significant use of enactment, re-enactment, and acquired footage.

Deniers see the figure where others see the ground. Whereas I, in accordance with the views of Morris and the majority of mainstream critics, have presented the film as one that gives Leuchter a certain say only to refute his claims and reduce him to a pathetic character by the end, deniers see a film in which such refutations exist as sop to mainstream media outlets that would not otherwise allow the presentation of a film so sympathetic to the revisionist cause. None other than Ernst Zündel himself has posted several "ZGrams" about the film to his Internet "Zundelsite." In one of these messages, he describes the thrill he received attending the premiere of the film at the Toronto Film Festival in the "elegant and superbly restored Elgin Theater." There among the Gothic columns of the "tastefully lit theater," he saw his own story, writ large, and much to his liking:

> Next followed an equally startling, brilliantly colored sequence, shot
> by a camera man for a Toronto TV station, of me being hoisted on the
> shoulders of my friends on January 18, 1988 at the beginning of the trial,
> as I unfurl a huge banner reading "The Holocau$t is a Hoax!" holding
> it up for the entire world to see! Next to me stand supporters who hold
> up similar slogans and signs, saying "The Holocaust is a Racket!" "The
> Holocaust is Hate!" etc.
> That image sat there for what seemed like an eternity to me! I was
> utterly stunned by that opening scene [of the film's second part]!

Man, was I pleased! What an opening statement to a story challenging the Holocaust! And not a word had yet been spoken. (Pt. II, 5)[29]

Zündel also appreciated the film's use of footage from Leni Riefenstahl's *Triumph of the Will* (1935), especially the sight of swastikas: "It is hard to describe what I felt as I saw it all fill the screen. It is a famous series of sequences of Adolf Hitler, winging his way to Nuremberg like in some ride of the Valkyries, high above the clouds over Germany. Then the clouds break and reveal the old medieval town of Nuremberg from a birds-eye's (sic) view, with a swastika flag slowly moving in the breeze as it hangs there languidly from a tall church tower below, as if some god had filmed it!" (Pt. II, 5). The interviews with Roth, Van Pelt, and another individual, Shelly Shapiro, to whom Morris gives the title "Zionist Activist," are not lost on Zündel, but he downplays their significance, seeing them as being among the film's "politically correct concessions." Without such concessions, he explains, "films such as this one are doomed at the box office, if they ever make it to the silver screen at all. . . . [O]ne can sense that Morris put these sequences in to get his documentary past the censors and to secure the distribution for his film in the perfunctory way he presents them, clearly announcing in stark white text 'Zionist Activist' before they appear on the screen. His heart or his artistic hand are obviously not in these perfunctory nods to the Holocaust lobby" (Pt. II., 5). Or, as another revisionist, Michael A. Hoffman, has written in a post to his Web site, "*Mr. Death* is not the usual Hollywood take on revisionism. Morris has given the masses a dollop of the genuine article, instead of fetishizing and burlesquing revisionist views through scripted dialogue via actor-mouthpieces."[30]

Zündel has a particular stake in the film because he was instrumental in its having taken the shape it did. It was Zündel who released to Morris the video footage of Leuchter at Auschwitz, and Zündel is one of the revisionists, along with British revisionist historian David Irving, who is interviewed in the film. Zündel therefore boasts that he was "responsible for the film itself having come into being, even though I was not the producer and did not have to pay a dime for its production." He consented to participate because Leuchter's results had not produced the hoped for "breakthrough into mainstream consciousness" of Holocaust denial (Pt. I, 4) and because Morris and his associate Michael Williams convinced Zündel that they would let Leuchter and Zündel himself tell their side of the story. Zündel, who feels unjustly beleaguered by the suit against him for Holocaust denial and by his "enemies and a hostile media" (Pt. I, 4), had been impressed with the success of *The Thin Blue Line* (1988) in helping another underdog "who was falsely accused and railroaded and was on death row in Texas to get a new, fair trial—a trial after which the man was found innocent!" (Pt. I, 3). Working with Morris, who is Jewish and whose family lost some of its members in the Holocaust, Zündel was conscious of the irony that through *Mr. Death* "the direction of at least part of history was now going to be determined by this artistic non-historian—to boot, a member of the tribe!" (Pt. I, 7).

I am taken aback by Zündel's ability to read against the grain. One sees in this instance why Deborah Lipstadt and Pierre Vidal-Naquet, among other historians, take issue with new historical, deconstructionist, and/or other theoretically informed reading practices. And I see how the film lends itself to Zündel's reading by using the direct interview footage with Leuchter and/or his voice-over narration as a structural element and by avoiding the topic of Holocaust denial until the second part of the film.

The film seems to divide neatly between its first and second parts (which, timewise, amount to a first third and a second two-thirds). During the first part, Leuchter is presented as a quirky guy with an unusual career (in execution machines), an unusual past (accompanying his dad to work at the Massachusetts Correctional Institute), and a somewhat endearing forty-cup-a-day coffee addiction. Audiences are shocked to learn of Leuchter's subsequent line of work. As Mark Singer colorfully describes, "[I]t feels as if one had dashed to the lobby for popcorn, then dashed back into the wrong theatre, where, whoa! a movie about Holocaust denial was being screened."[31] Since in the first part we have already "bonded" with Leuchter as our central protagonist, in the second part we seem to have the option of either accompanying him down the path that chose him or stepping back to examine how he could have been lured in that direction.

Actually, I would argue that in spite of the powerful urge to identify with main characters writ large on the cinema screen, however wrongheaded they may be, the selection and ordering of interview material join with the rebuttal rhetoric in the film's second part to militate against full immersion in Leuchter's perspective. Within the first part of the film, Leuchter himself identifies the flaw in the logic of his various employers who deem him capable of engineering work on one execution machine on the basis of his work on a completely different one. To the stylized visual accompaniment of fluids being forced through glass tubes, we hear Leuchter point out the limitations of a deputy commissioner's reasoning in providing him with a contract to engineer a lethal injection machine on the basis of his experience

Figure 9. Another view of Leuchter; *Mr. Death.*

with electrocution devices: "Now what lethal injection has to do with electrocution is beyond me. Simply because I'm capable of building an electric chair doesn't mean I'm capable of building a lethal injection machine. They're two totally different concepts." While watching Leuchter inspecting a gallows site, we hear him explain, "The reasoning here is that I've built helmets for electric chairs, so now I can build lethal injection machines. I now build lethal injection machines, so I'm now competent to build a gallows. And since I'm building gallows, I'm now competent to work on gas chambers because I've done all the other three." Leuchter has got a point. He himself has articulated, and Morris has elected to include near the start of the film, the very argument that can be used, retrospectively, to discredit Leuchter's so-called expertise as the authenticator of the use or nonuse of Auschwitz's basement as a killing chamber. If, in the next breath, Leuchter turns back around to justify his credentials, the thought that they are specious has nevertheless been expressed.

A proviso is in order. I have just suggested that our fixation on Leuchter as our cinema protagonist is undermined, especially in retrospect, by interview material used early in the film. Through our very acceptance of Leuchter's own words, which just happen to represent his self-critique, we come to suspect his professional incompetence for the Eastern European job. This conundrum is quintessential Errol Morris. His well-established interview style is one in which subjects are allowed to speak with little intervention from him and in speaking at length very often end up contradicting themselves. As Mark Singer observed in 1989, "An Errol Morris movie features real people talking uninterrupted, mainly about literal objects or events, only occasionally about feelings or ideas: trafficking in entertaining truths as well as in equally entertaining transparent prevarications."[32] Or, as Singer confirmed in 1999, "Morris asks as few questions as possible, and lets the truth flow along with alternating currents of benign disingenuousness, malignant prevarication, and potentially tragic false belief."[33] This is especially the fate of interview subjects with whom Morris disagrees, which disagreement becomes apparent not necessarily in the interview itself but in the given film taken as a whole. For example, a salesman interviewed in *The Thin Blue Line* brags about his photographic memory in one moment but takes contradictory stabs at the truth in another. In the context of the rest of the film, it becomes clear that the man made up his story in the first place for material gain. In other words, interviewees in a Morris documentary are often given enough rope to hang themselves, and they do so in full view of cinema audiences. This has never been clearer than in the execution-themed *Mr. Death.*

The fascinating paradox of Morris's documentaries is that while interview subjects are allowed tremendous freedom to speak for and to be themselves, they are also thoroughly controlled by Morris as director. For his film *A Brief History of Time* (1991), about astrophysicist Stephen Hawking, not only did Morris take his usual care with shot composition in framing his interview subjects, including Hawking himself along with his family and friends, but he also duplicated rooms from their homes and Hawking's office on a shooting stage. And all that was done for a film in which Morris felt no need to contradict his subjects. In *The Thin Blue Line,* the self-contradictions of the supposed eyewitnesses who testified at Randall Adams's trial for the murder of a Dallas police officer are highlighted by the presence of intercut shots that undermine their credibility. For example, Emily Miller's interview is interrupted with footage from a cheesy, fictional detective film, while salesman Michael Randell's interview is interrupted with Morris's recreations of the nighttime shooting. These recreations, highly fragmented in style and occurring elsewhere in the film as well as in this particular passage, are used to depict the words of various alleged witnesses, with one important exception. Nowhere does the film depict what Randall Adams testifies to from his prison cell and what Morris believes: that sixteen-year-old David Harris, alone in his car after dropping Adams at his motel, shot and killed Officer Wood. The truth of that testimony would later be upheld and Adams would be freed after his conviction was set aside, thanks in part to Morris's film.[34] The point is that the numerous recreations of the events immediately before, during, and after the killing in *The Thin Blue Line* portray the falsehoods or false memories of the alleged witnesses and David Harris himself, but no one reenactment depicts what actually occurred. Hence the distinction I make here between a "recreation" and a "reenactment."

In *Mr. Death,* Morris continues his exploration of the relationship between truth and cinematic strategies for representing traumatic past events, or, as he himself has put it in a 1989 television interview with Bill Moyers, between "style and the real world." In the later film, enactment is generously used, as during the first part, when abstract cinematography[35] depicts Leuchter, in spaces meticulously art directed by Ted Bafaloukos (are these sets or locations?), pulling levers and pushing buttons as he demonstrates for Morris the operations of various execution machines. Reenactment is also generously used, this time to point to truths about a situation. Genuine actuality footage, on the other hand, is exposed as disingenuous. Specifically, Morris appropriates the videotape of Leuchter's trip and intercuts it with enacted and reenacted footage of his own, thereby discrediting both Leuchter's scientific pretensions and his assumption that cinema verité is homologous with truth.

The film builds its argument in a multistep process. Leuchter's assumption goes something like this: the video shows me taking a sample from the ceiling, therefore I am scientific, therefore I am right that there were no gas chambers at Auschwitz. Van Pelt disproves Leuchter's findings by first studying his video and retracing Leuchter's steps as depicted in the video. Morris, for his part, films Van Pelt on the latter's fact-finding journey, creating an alternate travelogue of Auschwitz. As Van Pelt explains:

> Holocaust denial for me is so revolting and the way for me not to immediately become sick of having to deal with Leuchter was by saying, OK, I'm going to map his journey. I have a job to do, and my job, my first job is to try to understand where this guy was, at what time; to take that tape and to record every camera angle where it was, what piece of wall they were looking at, where they took the samples. It was important to be able to follow that trail very precisely. I wanted to see how he had done it.

Through his own emplotment of Leuchter's positionality, Van Pelt offers a critique of Leuchter's method and conclusions: "Leuchter's a victim of the myth of Sherlock Holmes. A crime has been committed. You go to the site of the crime and with a magnifying glass you find a hair or you find a speck of dirt on the shoe. Leuchter thinks that is the way reality can be reconstructed. But he is no Sherlock Holmes."

By intermixing footage of Leuchter's video with footage of Van Pelt on location at Auschwitz (enacted footage, that is), Morris offers another level of critique of Leuchter's method and conclusions. The film thus contextualizes and supersedes Leuchter's earlier video. Several juxtapositions illustrate. After Leuchter's on-camera introduction to his video, Morris gives us the image of Leuchter entering the gas chamber and Leuchter's voice-over narration: "I'm here to examine this alleged gas chamber." A moment later, we see the same passageway leading to the gas chamber, but now we hear Van Pelt's voice, introduced for the first time in the film, explaining why Zündel needed Leuchter to prove the (nonexistent) truth of Zündel's claims. Several shots of the gas chamber door appear, each closer than the next and linked by dissolves. It is as if *we* are entering the chamber through its familiar door, which now is painted red, but the story is completely different. The sequence proceeds in alternation between Leuchter's video and Morris's return visit with Van Pelt. Now, instead of Leuchter's arm waving in the direction of the ceiling, we follow what we take to be Van Pelt's hand gesturing from a paper diagram across to the wall of one of the delousing chambers as the soundtrack continues with the latter's narration of his reinvestigation of Leuchter's pseudoinvestigation. Another choice Morris makes is to use Van Pelt's voice over Leuchter's video. At one point we see Leuchter walking through the ruins. He turns to look back at someone or something and the film catches a slack-jawed expression. At that very instant Morris uses Van Pelt's voice exclaiming incredulously, "And to have a fool come in, coming completely unprepared; it's sacrilege."

Van Pelt takes the opposite approach to Leuchter with respect to concrete evidence. When we see him walk through the above-ground ruins of the camp, we hear his above-mentioned assertion of the changes that Auschwitz has undergone since the end of the war. While a split-screen effect causes one black-and-white photo of victims and then another to share place with a color photo of modern-day Auschwitz (shades of *Night and Fog*), we hear Van Pelt's view of the physical terrain: "There's no way that when you go to the crematorium you really can understand what it was to be led there as a victim; to have to undress and be let into the gas chamber." To the contrary, "when you are in the building archive," and only then, is it "possible to *re*imagine what the place was like during the war."

Van Pelt is also a skeptic when it comes to the ostensible transparency of video images as a window on truth. Although Van Pelt makes use of Leuchter's video, assuming that what we see in it are the actions Leuchter really performed, he is no more convinced than Morris that Leuchter's conclusions follow. At one point we hear Van Pelt's voice: "OK, let's go slightly back." To the familiar squeak of that electronic process, we see the tape rewind. Leuchter has just pulled himself up from a hole in the ground above the gas chamber. Rewinding sends him down again, backwards. Then, for the second time we see the same images of Leuchter traipsing through the underground chamber, but now with Van Pelt's voice-over: "Krematorium II is the most lethal building at Auschwitz. Within twenty-five thousand square feet of this one room, more people lost their life than any other place on this planet. Five hundred thousand people were killed. If you would draw a map of human suffering, if you would create a geography of atrocity, this would be the absolute center."

One additional path criss-crosses this topography, and that is the path pounded out by the steps Morris has taken to reenact Leuchter's journey into the heart of Auschwitz. Like Van Pelt, who followed the directions of Leuchter's video map, Morris traveled to Poland and descended to the sunken chambers. There, like Leuchter and Van Pelt before him, and with the help of both, he made his own cinematographic map of the inside of absolute horror. Morris has imitated Leuchter's video, and his imitated sequences are intercut with it in the film. In a way, Morris's cinematic spelunking cleaves to verisimilitude. Morris's company includes Van Pelt himself, who poses for Morris in the delousing chamber that he and Leuchter previously visited on separate occasions. It also includes one of the film's producers, David Collins, wearing the very same brown sheepherder's jacket that Leuchter wore on his expedition and lent to Morris for the latter's shoot. Nevertheless, Morris's material is, in his own word, "contrived."[36] Lighting and camera exposures are adjusted at one point so that the figures moving about the chamber are shot in silhouette. At other points, as when Van Pelt gestures from the diagram to the wall, the use of big close-ups and odd angles abstracts the scene from the past actions to which it refers. A slow dolly shot moves toward the spy hole in the gas chamber door until the edges of the hole disappear, leaving only the view through transparent glass. A reverse angle frames a green eye (Van Pelt's?) in the spy hole's circular frame. This section is very much in keeping with the extreme stylization of the film's dramatic opening, in which Leuchter seems almost to float in his electric chair while bolts of static electricity crackle around him. Eerie choral music as well as instrumental music by Caleb Sampson adds to the feeling of being moved and yet removed. Some images are so abstract that one cannot be sure they were actually shot on

Figure 10. Chiseling, reenacted; *Mr. Death.*

location. The slow-motion shots of a hammer hitting the head of a chisel and expelling rock fragments may not have been (and probably were not) shot at Auschwitz at all. At one point the film cuts from the video of Leuchter scraping up a handful of pebbles from the bottom of a shallow pool of water on the chamber floor to a film image of concentric ripples created by a stone being dropped into a pool. There would have been no need to shoot this on location. In fact, better control of lighting and art direction could be achieved elsewhere. And are those really Van Pelt's hands we see leafing through documents in the Auschwitz archive?

Morris has indeed contrived these measured interjections into Leuchter's video. But he has not done so to subtract truth from the presence of the killing floor. As I have stated, his film confirms the existence of mass gas executions at Auschwitz. Rather, Morris uses contrivance to develop critical consciousness about past events and about the means of its representation. In this he is deliberate: "Because Fred uses a handheld camera and shoots with available light, his film is somehow authentic, vérité-in-a-nutshell, 'true' cinema. . . . The irony here is that his cinéma vérité is in the service of falsehood. And my contrived material, I like to think, is in the service of underlying truth."[37] Who can protest even if he ends his statement with an impish "[B]ut, of course, I could be wrong"? In Errol Morris one finds a filmmaker explicitly critical of pat associations among truths about the past and of positivistic methods and realist shooting styles.

How are we to absorb the meaning of the traumatic past once those who suffered firsthand are gone? *Everything's for You, Second Generation Video,* and *Mr. Death* all suggest that we should proceed as always, as long as we redefine *always*. Just because eyewitnesses and intact brickworks still exist is no reason to assume that we have a hold of history. Just because we often lack concrete evidence and eyewitnesses is no reason to assume we cannot comprehend history. Whether or not such references are available to students of the past, the testimonies and tangible relics of events are extremely significant materials that must be read. The movie (or video) cameras in each of these three films seize on elements of the visible world and suspend them for our attention: three photographs of a father's former family, a scratched and grainy video, a pitted cellar wall. These are all deeply important objects. We hover close to them, hoping against hope that their auras will speak. And then we research, we compare and coordinate, we quail at the limitations and inconsistencies, and we write. Some of us write with film, and so we should. The three films discussed in this chapter draw abundant attention to the inevitable relationship between disremembering and intergenerational dynamics and to the role of film and video as agents of the historiographic action.

Conclusion

Trauma Cinema is an apologia for the role played by mistaken memory in understanding catastrophic past events. Mistaken memory, I conclude, is especially legible in relation to concrete evidence. Yet the book also comprehends physical things as a form of evidence that may be mistaken. This epistemological conundrum–the book's thesis—is that these two ways of coming to know the past may be conjoined to good effect in history writing and film- and videomaking.

The films and videos of this study manifest and celebrate an aesthetics of disremembering. In trauma cinema, the material world is everywhere represented—in the haunts of James Ronald Whitney's family ("It started with our grandparents a long long time ago. I decided to go back home . . ."), in the Friedmans' basement, in the reassembled bricks of Auschwitz-Birkenau. Photographs and home movies make the past portable, bearing it into the present in youthful images of Michelle Citron, Odette Springer, and the deceased half-siblings of Abraham Ravett. First-person accounts of persistent survivorship by Lynn Hershman and Judy Meisel inspire empathy and the flush of understanding.

But trauma cinema refuses the traditional self-satisfaction of documentary historiography, going beyond sober cognizance of the real and also beyond self-reflexivity. Trauma cinema's project does not end either with a barrage of facts or with the notion that demystifying documentary's means of production brings us to unadulterated truth. Nor does it end by asserting the impossibility of knowledge, the notion that traumatic historiography "does not say the unsayable, but says that it cannot say it."[1]

Rather, trauma cinema, as presented in this study, figures an alternative form of saying and knowing that conveys the fantasy elements of memory and the historiographic frailty of physical properties through an aesthetic that is fragmentary, sensory, and abstract. Physical evidence as it appears in trauma cinema is changeable and subject to interpretation; photographic evidence is telling but inconclusive; and testimony is marked as subjective by the prominence of the autobiographical impulse. Borrowing the mise-en-scène of psychological trauma and tending toward the use of (auto)biographical elements, the films and videos studied here elicit recurrent memory through home movies, photographs, and repetitive truncated images. They also render the dissociative features of subjectivity through conflicting testimonies and evoke psychological reenactment or recurrence through its documentary counterpart. Audiences of trauma films and videos are invited to engage with the contingent truths that emerge through the necessarily imperfect historiography of these works.

Films on many other subjects besides incest and the Holocaust share the traumatic aesthetic theorized in the preceding pages. While I have chosen to write about films on these two particular themes, I hope that my theoretical approach to a significant category of trauma cinema is more broadly applicable. Indeed, the qualities of productive abstraction that I have identified in the documentaries studied here are increasingly common not only in unusual texts and independent venues but also in mainstream products.

Two examples will serve to open out the frame of reference: *Beneath the Veil* (created and reported by Saira Shah and produced and directed by Cassian Harrison, 2001), about the lives and deaths of women in Afghanistan under Taliban rule and during the U.S. attack, and *9/11* (James Hanlon, Gedeon Naudet, and Jules Naudet, 2002), whose subject is evident from the title. Both are news documentaries that reached large audiences and were repeatedly televised. Both expand the conventional repertoire of strategies for reporting monumental events into the realm characterized in the foregoing pages. The use of image repetition, slow-motion photography, handheld camerawork, canted angles, first-person narration, family pictures, a mosaic of perspectives, and, above all, a sense that what is being represented is extraordinarily memorable at the same time that it is partly unfathomable marks these two documentaries as trauma cinema.

The British journalist Saira Shah is of Afghan descent. *Beneath the Veil* has an autobiographical framing structure and is compiled using footage from various sources, including new material shot on Shah's trip to Afghanistan and old photographs of Shah's father and of the town of his youth. Also included is archival material shot by the Revolutionary Association of Women of Afghanistan (RAWA) and by Human Rights Watch, and some gruesomely poetic footage of murdered corpses in the falling snow that was lent by a wedding photographer whose camera was put to a strange and horrible use.

One of the film's two main accomplishments is to trace the repressive realities of women's lives—and the lives of men as well—under the Taliban. At one point near the start we see the swirling fabric of a burka falling over Shah as she leaves her professional crew and goes undercover with RAWA to investigate a secret girls' school and follow women carrying on normal activities made illegal under the Taliban. These latter sequences are presumably shot by women from the group. Elsewhere, Shah provides commentary over hidden camera shots of soldiers detaining Shah and her crew and confiscating their cameras and film. Footage captured clandestinely by RAWA provides a disturbing historical backdrop for Shah and the Afghani women's actions. Presented in slow motion, images of heavily veiled women being forced to their knees and executed in front of a stadium crowd shock television spectators at a grateful remove.

This slow-motion footage is key to the film's other outstanding accomplishment besides its informational value: to reach spectators on an emotional level by bending film language to the form of traumatic memory. Here, as in the films discussed in the body of this book, there is no dissonance between historiography and expressive antirealistic cinematographic or videographic techniques. Just as Michelle Citron in *Daughter Rite* (1979) has step-printed and repeated her family's home movies to make strange their patriarchal patterns, so *Beneath the Veil* denaturalizes killing as a spectator sport by slowing it down and importing it into the context of the film's indictment of Taliban atrocities.

Reenactment is also featured. At one point some men speak about how their village was occupied by Taliban soldiers who rounded up and massacred fellow villagers. Handheld camerawork, black-and-white stock, and special digital processing, as in *Tak for Alt* (Laura Bialis, Broderick Fox, and Sarah Levy, 1999), mimic the passage of soldiers through the rooms of a house on their way to a killing spree. A bit later villagers use their body positions along with hand and arm motions to show the Western journalists what happened and where.

Interviews are used dissociatively as in *Shoah* (Claude Lanzmann, 1985) and *Just, Melvin* (James Ronald Whitney, 2000). A Taliban foreign minister complains to Shah, only somewhat in jest, that if the West objects to the use of the sports stadium as a killing floor they should send money for a separate facility. These words are made to seem doubly vile and disingenuous by their placement shortly after a harrowing interview with three young girls whose mother was shot by Taliban soldiers in the presence of the youngest girl for protesting the soldiers' occupation of the family home. Besides illustrating that people's words are not always truthful, the film also registers the unsaid. The soldiers remained in the house for two days after the murder of the girls' mother; the girls, we learn, have been crying for weeks. Shah tells us that they will not speak about what was done to them by soldiers during those two days. Our hearts ache for these children, whose robes of bright red, aqua, and orange contrast dramatically with the tears that spill from their burka-framed eyes.

Saira Shah carried her father's photograph with her on her journey, along with a photograph of the pleasure garden that was the jewel of his boyhood town. The garden's central fountain remains, without the flow of water. Manmade war has withered the gardens and scorched the earth and its people. As with the Holocaust films discussed here, in which survivors, their children, and their fellow travelers return to former walks in the wake of crises, there is great contrast between what was and what is. Only, in this case, trouble rages on.

9/11 began innocently as a direct cinema documentary about New York City firemen. The structure planned by brothers Jules and Gedeon Naudet was to follow a rookie fireman through his probationary period on the job. But the firehouse selected was a few blocks from the World Trade Center and it was the summer of 2001. The documentary that resulted was made in retrospect. Narrated by the filmmakers, it is about the sweet, heroic story that could have been and the world-changing events that intervened. The documentary contains some extraordinary footage of the attacks and of people's horrified responses. Gazing at the smoke, debris, casualties, and chaos, or fleeing the scene, the witnesses and survivors are captured in their common humanity. Direct cinema footage of ground zero seems specially processed, but it is really the world itself that has been transformed by a scrim of grayish-white dust and ash.

As in the immediate news coverage, the destruction of the towers is shown in shot after shot to powerful effect in this documentary. But it is another instance of repetition that truly encapsulates the melding of public and private, verisimilitude and imagination, and death and survival through which trauma cinema disremembers the catastrophic past. When he heard the rumble signaling the collapse of one of the towers, Gedeon Naudet began to run. The camera he was holding bobbed up and down shooting stray fleeing figures, emergency vehicles, rocks rolling like tumbleweeds in the wind, and a car tire seen from under the fender. In the documentary we see Gedeon at a later point in time describing how a man jumped on top of him, and we see a strange shot through a lens pitted by pebbles and obscured by lack of light and by a manila card or envelope blown up against it. The man, as it turns out, was Chief Pfiefer, protecting Gedeon with his body. The partially illegible shot is repeated near the end of the film with music accompaniment.

I too am taken with this image. It is what nobody saw but what the lens captured when circumstances forced its operator to turn away from the crumbling tower and run for his life. Its denotative meaning is vague, but, partly because of this, it connotes a sensory shock that could barely be grasped at the time. Televised later, the image is catastrophe's afterburn, the means through which we and Gedeon disremember the traumatic past.

The circle widens. Beautiful, terrible, and strange, the texts discussed here, and others that are appearing every day, take up events defined by their intensity and by their ability to sound our capacity to respond. These films and videos suspend facts and fantasies, documents and memories, and fictions and nonfictions in liquid history. As representational objects, they are by definition a generation removed from the catastrophes they depict, and their audiences may be a generation removed from the original sufferers. But in and through this remove, trauma films and videos model a new and empathetic historiography after the demands of a world where audiovisual culture is extensive and people at odds live in close proximity to one another.

I find these films and videos useful and satisfying. They speak to the very human desire to work and worry an injurious past. The past is never wholly accessible, nor is it ever really over. Evidence disintegrates and memory quails at the historiographic gateway. But in the process of coming to terms with what was, through a kind of productive disremembering, we may find a measure of peace.

1. This evocative phrase comes from Dina Wardi, *Memorial Candles: Children of the Holocaust,* trans. Naomi Goldblum (New York: Routledge, 1992). Wardi's work is discussed in chapter 6.

2. For example, Vivian Sobchack refers to this Smithsonian controversy in her discussion of the "new self-consciousness about history." See Vivian Sobchack, "Introduction: History Happens," in *The Persistence of History: Cinema, Television, and the Modern Event,* ed. Vivian Sobchack (New York: Routledge, 1996), 3. See also the essays in Laura Hein, ed., "Remembering the Bomb: The Fiftieth Anniversary in the United States and Japan," Special Issue, *Bulletin of Concerned Asian Scholars* 27, no. 2 (April–June 1995).

3. Binjamin Wilkomirski, *Fragments: Memories of a Wartime Childhood,* trans. Carol Brown Janeway (New York: Schocken Books, 1996). See the review of the controversy surrounding the book in Philip Gourevitch, "The Memory Thief," *New Yorker,* 14 June 1999, 48–68, and Stefan Mächler, *The Wilkomirski Affair: A Study in Biographical Truth,* trans. John E. Woods (New York: Schocken Books, 2001).

4. It is noteworthy that, in contrast to the way in which women's reports of childhood molestation by their fathers were strenuously attacked, popular discourses in the spring of 2002, and a year later as I write this, have accepted as generally truthful men's allegations of childhood molestation by Catholic priests.

5. Michael Frisch, "The Memory of History," chap. 2 in *A Shared Authority:*

Essays on the Craft and Meaning of Oral and Public History (Albany: SUNY Press, 1990), 15–16.

6. David Lowenthal, *The Past Is a Foreign Country* (Cambridge: Cambridge University Press, 1985), 19. The quoted phrases represent ideas Lowenthal describes but does not subscribe to.

7. Saul Friedlander, "Trauma, Transference and 'Working Through' in Writing the History of the *Shoah*," *History and Memory* 4 (1992): 52. See also Saul Friedlander, introduction to *Probing the Limits of Representation: Nazism and the "Final Solution,"* ed. Saul Friedlander (Cambridge, Mass.: Harvard University Press, 1992). Deborah Lipstadt, in *Denying the Holocaust: The Growing Assault on Truth and Memory* (New York: Plume, 1993), discusses how under deconstructionist methodology "experience was relative and nothing was fixed" and how such methodology thereby "created an atmosphere of permissiveness toward questioning the meaning of historical events and made it hard for its proponents to assert that there was anything 'off limits' for this skeptical approach" (18).

8. *False memory* is the name given to recovered memories of childhood sexual assault (especially incestuous assault) by those who deny their validity. The False Memory Syndrome Foundation was established to support parents (mainly fathers) accused by their children (mainly daughters) of perpetrating sexual assault against them and to publicize "false memory syndrome" as an explanation for these children's beliefs.

9. Hayden White, "Historical Emplotment and the Problem of Truth," in Friedlander, *Probing the Limits,* and "The Modernist Event," in Sobchack, *Persistence of History.*

10. Frisch, "The Memory of History," 16; Friedlander, "Trauma, Transference," 52–53.

11. Thanks are due here to Julia Lesage for suggesting this way of putting what I was trying to say.

12. David Thelen, "Memory and American History," *Journal of American History* 75, no. 4 (March 1989): 1127.

13. Friedlander, "Trauma, Transference," 53. Frisch, in "The Memory of History," also acknowledges public history's relationship to "the process of memory" (15–16). In addition, see Dominick LaCapra's *History and Memory after Auschwitz* (Ithaca, N.Y.: Cornell University Press, 1998), Friedlander's *Probing the Limits of Representation,* and Hayden White's magisterial *Metahistory: The Historical Imagination in Nineteenth-Century Europe* (Baltimore: Johns Hopkins University Press, 1973).

14. For one excellent discussion of the Historians' Debate, see LaCapra, *History and Memory,* especially chap. 2, "Revisiting the Historians' Debate: Mourning and Genocide."

15. Shoshana Felman, *The Juridical Unconscious: Trials and Traumas in the Twentieth Century* (Cambridge, Mass: Harvard University Press, 2002), 2.

16. See Joshua Hirsch's account of the German program to destroy all witnesses and his discussion of the two minutes of 8mm film shot by Reinhard Wiener of the execution of Jews in Latvia in 1941. Hirsch, "Introduction to Film, Trauma, and the Holocaust," chap. 1 in *Afterimage: Film, Trauma, and the Holocaust* (Philadelphia: Temple University Press, 2004). Hirsch was given the information that this film is unique by a representative of the U.S. Holocaust Memorial Museum's film department. See Hirsch, *Afterimage*, 164 n. 1.

17. See Dori Laub, "An Event without a Witness: Truth, Testimony, and Survival," chap. 3, and Felman, "The Return of the Voice: Claude Lanzmann's *Shoah*," chap. 7, both in Shoshana Felman and Dori Laub, *Testimony: Crises of Witnessing in Literature, Psychoanalysis, and History,* (New York: Routledge, 1992).

1. CATASTROPHE, REPRESENTATION

1. Elizabeth Waites, *Trauma and Survival: Post-Traumatic and Dissociative Disorders in Women* (New York: W. W. Norton, 1993), 28. Waites cites Lenore Terr, *Too Scared to Cry: Psychic Trauma in Childhood* (New York: HarperCollins, 1990), and C. M. Fair, *Memory and Central Nervous Organization* (New York: Paragon House, 1988). I have previously discussed PTSD, the so-called memory wars, and the work of Elizabeth Waites in Janet Walker, "The Vicissitudes of Traumatic Memory and the Postmodern History Film," in *Trauma and Cinema: Cross-Cultural Explorations,* ed. E. Ann Kaplan and Ban Wang (Hong Kong: Hong Kong University Press, 2004), and I am partially drawing from that essay.

2. Lenore Terr, "True Memories of Childhood Trauma: Flaws, Absences, and Returns," in *The Recovered Memory/False Memory Debate,* ed. Kathy Pezdek and William P. Banks (San Diego: Academic Press, 1996); Daniel Schacter, *Searching for Memory: The Brain, the Mind, and the Past* (New York: Basic Books, 1996), 9 and chap. 4, "Reflections in a Curved Mirror: Memory Distortion."

3. Janet Walker, "The Traumatic Paradox: Documentary Films, Historical Fictions, and Cataclysmic Past Events," *Signs* 22, no. 4 (Summer 1997): 803–25; revised as "The Traumatic Paradox: Autobiographical Documentary and the Psychology of Memory," in *Contested Pasts: The Politics of Memory,* ed. Katharine Hodgkin and Susannah Radstone (New York: Routledge, 2003). The concept that traumatic memory is paradoxical in relation to accepted standards of evidence evaluation is gleaned from Judith Herman, *Trauma and Recovery* (New York: Basic Books, 1992), and Waites, *Trauma and Survival.*

4. Dori Laub, "Bearing Witness, or the Vicissitudes of Listening," in Felman and Laub, *Testimony,* 59.

5. Ibid., 59–60, 62–63. I have used this example and some of the same wording in Walker, "Vicissitudes of Traumatic Memory."

6. Lenore Terr, *Unchained Memories: True Stories of Traumatic Memories, Lost and Found* (New York: Basic Books, 1994).

7. Quoted in Maura Dolan, "Credibility under Attack in Repressed Memory Case," *Los Angeles Times,* 21 February 1996, A3. Franklin-Lipsker, who was referred to by the hyphenated name by 1995, is particularly vulnerable to this attack because she has made it public that she has recovered memories of two other murders perpetrated by her father, but the validity of these memories has not been borne out by investigators.

8. The quoted passage is from Robert Schwarz and Stephen Gilligan, "The Devil Is in the Details: Fact and Fiction in the Recovered Memory Debate," *Family Therapy Networker,* March/April 1995, 22, describing the work of Lenore Terr.

9. Waites, *Trauma and Survival,* 36.

10. Terr, *Unchained Memories,* 35.

11. See Waites, *Trauma and Survival,* especially chap. 1, "Psychobiology and Post-Traumatic Pathology."

12. I find it telling that Jean Laplanche and J.-B. Pontalis, in *The Language of Psycho-Analysis,* trans. Donald Nicholson-Smith (New York: W. W. Norton, 1973), use the phrase "pathogenic infantile scenes" to describe what Freud calls sexual "seduction" or "premature sexual experience" and what feminists call "childhood sexual molestation" or "assault."

13. Sigmund Freud, "The Aetiology of Hysteria" (1896), in *The Standard Edition of the Complete Psychological Works of Sigmund Freud,* ed. and trans. James Strachey (London: Hogarth Press, 1962), 3:203.

14. Sigmund Freud, "An Autobiographical Study" (1925), in Strachey, *Standard Edition,* 20:34.

15. Diane Waldman and Janet Walker, "John Huston's *Freud* and Textual Repression: A Psychoanalytic Feminist Reading," in *Close Viewings: An Anthology of New Film Criticism,* ed. Peter Lehman (Tallahassee: Florida State University Press, 1990), 284; Florence Rush, *The Best Kept Secret: Sexual Abuse of Children* (Englewood Cliffs, N.J.: Prentice Hall, 1980); Jeffrey Masson, *The Assault on Truth: Freud's Suppression of the Seduction Theory* (New York: Penguin, 1984).

16. Herman, *Trauma and Recovery,* 14.

17. Ibid., 34.

18. Ibid., 38.

19. Juliet Mitchell, *Psychoanalysis and Feminism: Freud, Reich, Laing and Women* (New York: Vintage, 1975); Juliet Mitchell, Introduction I to *Feminine Sexuality: Jacques Lacan and the École Freudienne,* ed. Juliet Mitchell and Jacqueline Rose, trans. Jacqueline Rose (New York: Macmillan, 1982); Jacqueline Rose, Introduction II to Mitchell and Rose, *Feminine Sexuality.*

20. Waldman and Walker, "John Huston's *Freud,*" 285. In support of our claims, we cite Sigmund Freud, "Introductory Lectures on Psychoanalysis" (1916), in Strachey, *Standard Edition,* 3:168; footnote written in 1924 to "The

Neuro-Psychoses of Defence" (1896), in Strachey, *Standard Edition,* 20:33–34; "An Autobiographical Study" (1925), in Strachey, *Standard Edition,* 20:120; "Female Sexuality" (1931), in Strachey, *Standard Edition,* 21:238; and "Feminin-ity," in *New Introductory Lectures on Psychoanalysis,* trans. W. J. H. Sprott (New York: W. W. Norton, 1933), 22:120. These examples are cited in Masson, *Assault on Truth,* 195–200; the latter two are cited in Jane Gallop, *The Daughter's Seduc-tion: Feminism and Psychoanalysis* (Ithaca, N.Y.: Cornell University Press, 1982).

21. Laplanche and Pontalis, *Language of Psycho-Analysis,* 314. The origin and significance of the term's alternate spellings are discussed in the commentary by Laplanche and Pontalis. Although the authors prefer the German-derived *phan-tasy,* I will continue with conventional American spelling, still hoping to retain all of the complexities inherent in the term.

22. Ibid., 315.

23. This concept of "propping" is taken from Jean Laplanche's discussion in *Life and Death in Psychoanalysis,* trans. Jeffrey Mehlman (Baltimore: Johns Hop-kins University Press, 1976).

24. Katharine Hodgkin and Susannah Radstone, "Remembering Suffering: Trauma and History," in Hodgkin and Radstone, *Contested Pasts,* 97. I am grate-ful to Katharine Hodgkin and Susannah Radstone for corresponding about these ideas during the editing of my own chapter in their volume. Indeed, I am grateful to them for including my essay, considering that our views are not quite the same.

25. Jacqueline Rose, "An Interview with Jacqueline Rose," interview by Maire Jaanus and Michael Payne, in *Why War? Psychoanalysis, Politics, and the Return to Melanie Klein* (Cambridge, Mass.: Blackwell, 1993), 234–35. For a discussion of perpetrator narratives, see Elizabeth Mertz and Kimberly A. Lonsway, "The Power of Denial: Individual and Cultural Constructions of Child Sexual Abuse," *Northwestern Law Review* 92, no. 4 (Summer 1998): "[I]t is fairly common [to] find child molesters attempting to evade responsibility by arguing that the child actually instigated the abuse—that the child was in some way seductive or promiscuous and actually caused the perpetrator to act" (1429). See also Louise Armstrong, *Rocking the Cradle of Sexual Politics: What Happened When Women Said Incest* (Reading, Mass.: Addison-Wesley, 1994).

26. Waites, *Trauma and Survival;* Susan L. Reviere, *Memory of Childhood Trauma: A Clinician's Guide to the Literature* (New York: Guilford Press, 1996); Janice Haaken, *Pillar of Salt: Gender, Memory, and the Perils of Looking Back* (New Brunswick, N.J.: Rutgers University Press, 1998), Terr, *Unchained Memories.*

27. Waites, *Trauma and Survival,* 5–6.

28. Ibid., 34.

29. Haaken, *Pillar of Salt,* 62–63. She attributes the phrase to Richard Ull-man and Doris Brothers, *The Shattered Self: A Psychoanalytic Study of Trauma* (Hillsdale, N.J.: Analytic Press, 1988).

30. American Psychiatric Association, *Diagnostic and Statistical Manual of Mental Disorders,* 4th ed. (Washington, D.C.: American Psychiatric Association, 1994), 424; hereafter cited as *DSM-IV.*

31. As is likely evident from the context of my discussion, the term *propping* is used to describe a relationship between fantasy and reality that does indeed exist although that relationship is not one of mirroring.

32. John F. Kihlstrom, "Exhumed Memory," in *Truth in Memory,* ed. Steven Jay Lynn and Kevin M. McConkey (New York: Guilford Press, 1998), 18.

33. Frederick Crews, *The Memory Wars: Freud's Legacy in Dispute* (New York: New York Review of Books, 1995).

34. Schwarz and Gilligan, "Devil Is in the Details," 37: "By the end of 1994, more than 300 articles on 'false memory' had appeared in magazines and newspapers," including Daniel Goleman, "Childhood Trauma: Memory or Invention," *New York Times,* 21 July 1992, B6; "Buried Memories, Broken Families," a six-day front-page series, published in the *San Francisco Examiner* in April 1993; Leon Jaroff and Jeanne McDowell, "Lies of the Mind," *Time,* 29 November 1993, 52. See also John Hochman, " 'Recovered' Memory's Real Victims," *Los Angeles Times,* 18 November 1993, opinion page, B7; Fred Frankel, "Discovering New Memories in Psychotherapy: Childhood Revisited, Fantasy, or Both?" *New England Journal of Medicine* 333, no. 9 (31 August 1995): 591–94; "Dispatch from the Memory War," *Psychology Today,* May–June 1996, 6ff.; Janice Haaken, "The Debate over Recovered Memory of Sexual Abuse: A Feminist-Psychoanalytic Perspective," *Psychiatry: Interpersonal and Biological Processes* 58, no. 2 (May 1995): 189–98; and James H. Andrews, "Dredging the Past: Recovered Memory or False Memory?" *Christian Science Monitor,* 25 July 1994, 13; Max McCarthy, "The Accusation," *Detroit Free Press Magazine,* 8 January 1995, 11–13; Ethan Watters, "Doors of Memory," *Mother Jones,* January/February 1993, 24–29, 76–77; Sharon Begly, "Some Memories May Be More Imagined Than Real," *Detroit Free Press,* 30 September 1994.

35. False Memory Syndrome Foundation stationery, back page. Cited in Rosaria Champagne, *The Politics of Survivorship: Incest, Women's Literature, and Feminist Theory* (New York: New York University Press, 1996), 170. The False Memory Syndrome Foundation (which had four thousand members, 48 chapters, and an annual budget of $700,000 by the mid-1990s) has mounted a vast advocacy campaign that includes not only advertising and a newsletter but also the planting of "news reports." For example, the *Detroit Free Press Magazine* story provides the toll-free number for the False Memory Syndrome Foundation after the author's blurb.

36. Elizabeth Loftus and Katherine Ketcham, *The Myth of Repressed Memory: False Memories and Allegations of Sexual Abuse* (New York: St. Martin's Press, 1994); Richard Ofshe and Ethan Watters, *Making Monsters: False Memories, Psychotherapy and Sexual Hysteria* (New York: Charles Scribner's Sons, 1994); and

Mark Pendergrast, *Victims of Memory: Incest Accusations and Shattered Lives* (Hinesburg, Vt.: Upper Access Books, 1995).

37. Walter Goodman, "Growth Industry: Helping Recall Sexual Abuse," review of *Divided Memories, New York Times,* 4 April 1995, B6.

38. The majority of incest survivors remember the incest all along. Of those who do have severe amnesia for childhood abuse, the great majority are able to find outside corroboration in the form of admission by perpetrators, hospital and doctors' office records, photographs, or sibling corroboration.

39. Herman, *Trauma and Recovery,* 9.

40. As the feminist psychologist Ann Scott writes, "It is [the] capacity to bear uncertainty, while allowing for a principled engagement with the actual relations of power in the culture" that a "psychoanalytic perspective can offer and support." Ann Scott, "Screen Memory/False Memory Syndrome," *Feminism and Psychology* 7, no. 1 (February 1997): 20.

41. Friedlander, "Trauma, Transference," 53.

42. David G. Payne and Jason M. Blackwell, "Truth in Memory: Caveat Emptor," in Lynn and McConkey, *Truth in Memory,* 53.

43. It is a good question just how complete Loftus's denial of any phenomenon called repression or repressed memory is. From its title, it should be clear that Loftus and Ketcham's *Myth of Repressed Memory* is deeply skeptical of repressed memory's existence. So-called repression, Loftus opines, quoting herself in a dialogue with Ellen Bass, coauthor of the best-known and best-selling reference work for childhood sexual abuse survivors (Ellen Bass and Laura Davis, *The Courage to Heal: Guide for Women Survivors of Child Sexual Abuse* [New York: Harper and Row, 1988]), is "a magical homunculus in the unconscious mind that periodically ventures out into light of day, grabs hold of a memory, scurries underground, and stores it away in a dark corner of the insensible self, waiting a few decades before digging it up and tossing it back out again" (214). It is not the same as forgetting, she emphasizes. "I don't question memories of abuse that existed all along, because these are as believable as other kinds of memories, positive or negative, from the past. I don't question the fact that memories can come back spontaneously, that details can be forgotten, or even that memories of abuse can be triggered by various cues many years later" (214). What she questions is the possibility that a person can lose memory and also "*all awareness that they have lost it*" (216, italics in original).

Nevertheless, a chapter that Loftus coauthored for an edited volume makes some acknowledgment of the phenomenon of repression: "Does this mean that repression is an invalid concept? Not at all. Even if we were to take the lowest incidence figure (19%) from the four studies . . . and [if we] 'discounted' it for the possibility of infantile amnesia (e.g., throwing out all claims of abuse that occurred during the first 2 years of life on the ground that they cannot be expected to have been recalled, thus including the failure to recall them as evidence that they were repressed inflates the prevalence of repression), ordinary forgetting, and so on, this might still leave a residual of cases that could not be dismissed as artifactual. We believe that the most prudent reading of this literature is that repression may occur, but not as frequently as any of the four studies indicate." Stephen J. Ceci, Mary Lyndia Crotteau Huffman, Elliott Smith, and Elizabeth Loftus, "Repeatedly Thinking about a Non-event: Source Misattributions among Preschoolers," in Pezdek and Banks, *Recovered Memory/False Memory Debate,* 241.

My own readings of Loftus lead me to conclude that in scholarly venues as opposed to popular ones, when coauthoring articles with other memory researchers, and, probably, as time goes on, Loftus shows a greater tendency to acknowledge that repression may exist and be evidenced by a small number of cases.

44. Michael Nash, "Psychotherapy and Reports of Early Sexual Trauma: A Conceptual Framework for Understanding Memory Errors," in Lynn and McConkey, *Truth in Memory,* 91. I have previously discussed Nash's ideas in Walker, "Vicissitudes of Traumatic Memory," and I am partially drawing from that source.

45. Ibid., 91.

46. Scott, "Screen Memory/False Memory Syndrome," 19.

47. Elaine Showalter, *Hystories: Hysterical Epidemics and Modern Media* (New York: Columbia University Press, 1997), 5. I have made the same critique of Showalter's book in some of the same language in Walker, "Vicissitudes of Traumatic Memory."

48. See, for example, Jack O'Sullivan, *Independent* (London), 11 June 1997, cover story, 2; Jackie Wullschlager, *Financial Times,* 7 June 1997, Books section, 8; M. G. Lord, review of *Hysterical Epidemics and Modern Media,* by Elaine Showalter, *Artforum International* 35, no. 10 (Summer 1997): S30; Taner Edis and Amy Sue Bix, "Tales of Hysteria: Review of *Hystories: Hysterical Epidemics and Modern Culture,*" *Skeptical Inquirer: The Magazine for Science and Reason,* September/October 1997, 52; Steve Sailer, "*Hystories: Hysterical Epidemics and Modern Culture,*" *National Review,* 1 September 1997, 48.

49. Showalter, *Hystories,* 156.

50. Armstrong, *Rocking the Cradle,* especially chap. 11, "The Infantilization of Women III: The Demonic Dialogues."

51. See, for example, Nash, "Psychotherapy and Reports," 98–101.

52. Toni Morrison, *Beloved* (New York: Alfred A. Knopf, 1987), 118–19.

53. Deborah Horvitz, "Nameless Ghosts: Possession and Dispossession in *Beloved,*" in *Critical Essays on Toni Morrison's "Beloved,"* ed. Barbara H. Solomon (New York: G. K. Hall, 1998), 101.

54. Morrison, *Beloved,* 35–36.

55. Caroline Rody, "Toni Morrison's *Beloved*: History, 'Rememory,' and a

'Clamor for a Kiss,' " in *Understanding Toni Morrison's "Beloved" and "Sula": Selected Essays and Criticism of the Works by the Nobel Prize-Winning Author*, ed. Solomon O. Iyasere and Marla W. Iyasere (Troy, N.Y.: Whitston Publishing, 2000), 93.

56. Morrison, *Beloved*, 275.

57. Rody, "Toni Morrison's *Beloved*," 106.

58. José Esteban Muñoz, *Disidentifications: Queers of Color and the Performance of Politics* (Minneapolis: University of Minnesota Press, 1999), 3.

59. Ibid., 4.

60. Readers unfamiliar with the foundations of contemporary film theory might refer to the lengthy discussions on the subject of Hollywood classical realism that were carried on in numerous film journals and publications, including, notably, the British film journal *Screen* during the mid- to late 1970s and the U.S. journal *Camera Obscura: A Journal of Feminism and Film Theory* (now *Camera Obscura: Feminism, Culture, and Media Studies*) from the mid-1970s through the mid-1980s. Because of this semantic tradition in film studies I have opted to retain the term *antirealist* for the experimental films under analysis here, even though these texts and their purpose have a great deal in common with the representational system that Michael Rothberg has called "traumatic realism." Michael Rothberg, *Traumatic Realism: The Demands of Holocaust Representation* (Minneapolis: University of Minnesota Press, 2000).

61. White, "Modernist Event," 20.

62. See my discussion of *Saving Private Ryan* in Walker, "Vicissitudes of Traumatic Memory."

63. White, "Modernist Event," 22–23.

64. Ibid., 23.

65. White, "Historical Emplotment," 51–52.

66. I borrow the phrase, even as I reapply the concept, both from David Lowenthal in *Possessed by the Past: The Heritage Crusade and the Spoils of History* (New York: Free Press, 1996) and from Cathy Caruth, who writes in her introduction to *Trauma: Explorations in Memory*, ed. Cathy Caruth (Baltimore: Johns Hopkins University Press, 1995), that "to be traumatized is precisely to be possessed by an image or event" (4–5).

67. Linda Williams, "Mirrors without Memories: Truth, History, and the New Documentary," *Film Quarterly* 46, no. 3 (Spring 1993): 12.

68. Robert Rosenstone, "The Future of the Past: Film and the Beginnings of Postmodern History," in Sobchack, *Persistence of History*, 201–2.

69. Friedlander, "Trauma, Transference," 53.

70. Ibid., 39–59.

71. Laura Marcus, *Auto/biographical Discourses: Theory, Criticism, Practice* (New York: Manchester University Press, 1995), 1.

72. Shari Benstock, ed., *The Private Self: Theory and Practice of Women's Auto-*

biographical Writings (Chapel Hill: University of North Carolina Press, 1988), especially her own chapter, "Authorizing the Autobiographical."

73. See also Sidonie Smith and Julia Watson, eds., *Women, Autobiography, Theory: A Reader* (Madison: University of Wisconsin Press, 1998); Estelle C. Jelinek, ed., *Women's Autobiography: Essays in Criticism* (Bloomington: Indiana University Press, 1980); Bella Brodzki and Celeste Schenck, eds., *Life/Lines: Theorizing Women's Autobiography* (Ithaca, N.Y.: Cornell University Press, 1988); Françoise Lionnet, *Autobiographical Voice: Race, Gender, Self-Portraiture* (Ithaca, N.Y.: Cornell University Press, 1989); Valerie Smith, *Self-Discovery and Authority in African-American Narratives* (Urbana: University of Illinois Press, 1979); Hertha Dawn Wong, *Sending My Heart Back across the Years: Tradition and Innovation in Native American Autobiography* (New York: Oxford University Press, 1992).

74. Leigh Gilmore, "The Mark of Autobiography: Postmodernism, Autobiography, and Genre," in *Autobiography and Postmodernism,* ed. Kathleen Ashley, Leigh Gilmore, and Gerald Peters (Amherst: University of Massachusetts Press, 1994), 7.

75. Stephen Mamber, *Cinema Verite in America: Studies in Uncontrolled Documentary* (Cambridge: MIT Press, 1974), especially his chapter "Direct Cinema and the Crisis Structure."

76. Vivian Sobchack, "Inscribing Ethical Space: Ten Propositions on Death, Representation, and Documentary," *Quarterly Review of Film Studies* 9, no. 4 (Fall 1984): 283–300.

77. Michael Renov, "Introduction: The Truth about Non-fiction," in *Theorizing Documentary,* ed. Michael Renov (New York: Routledge, 1993), 2–3.

78. Bill Nichols, *Representing Reality: Issues and Concepts in Documentary* (Bloomington: Indiana University Press, 1991), xv.

79. *The Maelstrom* (1997), by Hungarian found-footage filmmaker Péter Fórgacs, achingly presents the opposite. Whereas in *Tak for Alt,* Judy Meisel has survived but there are no home movies, the image track of *The Maelstrom* is composed of home movie footage—of a family that was nearly wiped out.

80. See Fred H. Frankel, "The Concept of Flashbacks in Historical Perspective," *International Journal of Clinical and Experimental Hypnosis* 42, no. 4 (October 1994): 321–36. From a survey of the literature, Frankel concludes that war trauma flashbacks and child sexual abuse flashbacks are generally written about as if they were veridical memories (Frankel's article was written in 1993, before the public outcry against women's recovered memories as false memories). But, interestingly, his close analysis of such studies shows that they themselves contain evidence that fantasy elements are a feature of supposedly true memories.

81. Quoted in Gregory L. Vistica, "One Awful Night in Thanh Phong," *New York Times Magazine,* 25 April 2001, 54. Thanks to Juliet Williams for calling this article to my attention and providing me a copy.

2. THE EXCISION OF INCEST

Special thanks are due to Janet Bergstrom for her astute editorial comments on a version of this chapter published in *Endless Night: Cinema and Psychoanalysis, Parallel Histories,* ed. Janet Bergstrom (Berkeley: University of California Press, 1999).

1. Prohibitions against references to incest were so strong in the period that while the depiction of incestuous situations was certainly disallowed by its classification under the category of "sex perversions," the word *incest* itself never appears in the text of the Production Code.

2. My perusal of the various story synopses, treatments, and scripts for the film *Kings Row* has revealed that the incestuous relationship between Dr. Tower and his daughter Cassie was removed between the stage of the synopsis by Harriet Hinsdale dated 17 July 1940, and the stage of the treatment by credited screenwriter Casey Robinson dated 30 August 1940. I could locate no letters or memos detailing the necessity for such an excision, and I would speculate that the need for it was "understood" in light of the Production Code requirements and carried out as a matter of course. See the *Kings Row* file, Warner Bros. Archives, Doheny Library, School of Cinema-Television, University of Southern California, Los Angeles.

3. I have made this point previously in collaboration with Diane Waldman (Waldman and Walker, "John Huston's *Freud* and Textual Repression") and in chap. 6 and the conclusion of my book *Couching Resistance: Women, Film, and Psychoanalytic Psychiatry* (Minneapolis: Minnesota University Press, 1993).

4. Jean-Paul Sartre, *The Freud Scenario,* ed. J.-B. Pontalis, trans. Quintin Hoare (Chicago: University of Chicago Press, 1985).

5. Both screenplays may be consulted in the John Huston Collection at the Margaret Herrick Library of the Academy of Motion Picture Arts and Sciences in Beverly Hills, Calif. I had not consulted these screenplays in my prior writings on the film, but their content reconfirms Waldman's and my thesis that incestuous themes were better represented in script form than they were on film. And, as I shall suggest below, these early script versions are important as texts in and of themselves.

6. This last piece of information is conveyed in John Huston's autobiography, *An Open Book* (New York: Alfred Knopf, 1980).

7. Charles Kaufman and Wolfgang Reinhardt, *Freud,* revised first draft screenplay, 14 April 1961, John Huston Collection, Margaret Herrick Library, Academy of Motion Picture Arts and Sciences, Beverly Hills, Calif.

8. Sigmund Freud and Joseph Breuer, *Studies on Hysteria, 1893–95,* ed. and trans. James Strachey (New York: Basic Books, 1955).

9. Geoffrey M. Shurlock, memorandum, 21 September 1960, Production

Code Administration files, Margaret Herrick Library, Academy of Motion Picture Arts and Sciences, Beverly Hills, Calif. Huston's attempts to authorize his film script in spite of the PCA's reservations via the use of eminent outside consultants are traced in chap. 6 of Walker's *Couching Resistance*.

10. This term is used by Ned Lukacher in his introduction to Marie Balmary's *Psychoanalyzing Psychoanalysis: Freud and the Hidden Fault of the Father*, trans. Ned Lukacher (Baltimore: Johns Hopkins University Press, 1982), xi.

11. In *The Wages of Sin: Censorship and the Fallen Woman Film, 1928–1942* (Madison: University of Wisconsin Press, 1991), Lea Jacobs argues that censorship was not simply a matter of cutting out the objectionable parts of films. Rather, the rules censors developed were "constructive," producing new narrative strategies for the expression of material that was touchy by social standards. In Jacobs's book, as here, female sexuality is a key area of sociocultural contestation.

12. Henry Bellamann, *Kings Row* (New York: Simon and Schuster, 1942), 339–40.

13. Maureen Turim, *Flashbacks in Film: Memory and History* (New York: Routledge, 1989), 1.

14. Joseph Breen to Jack Warner, letter, 24 April 1941, Warner Bros. Archives, Doheny Library, School of Cinema-Television, University of Southern California, Los Angeles.

15. Edith Hamilton, *Mythology* (New York: Mentor Books, 1940), 202.

16. Ibid., 242, 243.

17. Lesley Brill makes the good point that a narrative detail foretells the narrative conclusion, delivered via the character Freud, that no father-daughter incest occurred in Cecily's case: Cecily is first introduced to Freud after a false pregnancy in which "another physician had examined her and informed Breuer and Freud that she was not pregnant 'nor could she be.'" Lesley Brill, "*Freud* (1961)," in *John Huston's Filmmaking* (Cambridge: Cambridge University Press, 1997), 182.

18. Aspects of these sequences are also discussed in Waldman and Walker, "John Huston's *Freud*," and in Walker, *Couching Resistance*.

19. Sigmund Freud to Wilhelm Fliess, letter, 31 May 1897, in Freud, *The Standard Edition of the Complete Psychological Works of Sigmund Freud*, ed. and trans. James Strachey (London: Hogarth Press, 1953–74), 1:206. This letter is also reproduced in a slightly different translation in *The Complete Letters of Sigmund Freud to Wilhelm Fliess, 1887–1904*, ed. and trans. Jeffrey Moussaieff Masson (Cambridge, Mass.: Harvard University Press, 1985), 249. There the phrase reads, "[M]y wish to catch a *Pater* as the originator of neurosis and thus [the dream] puts an end to my ever recurring doubts."

20. Charles Bernheimer, "Introduction: Part I," in *In Dora's Case: Freud, Hysteria, Feminism*, ed. Charles Bernheimer and Claire Kahane (New York: Columbia University Press, 1985), 39.

21. Sigmund Freud, "From the History of an Infantile Neurosis (1918)," in *Three Case Histories*, trans. by Philip Rieff (New York: Collier Books, 1963), 236.

22. Ibid., 243.

23. Phyllis Greenacre, "The Influence of Infantile Trauma on Genetic Patterns (1967; *Journal of the American Psychoanalytic Association)*," in *Emotional Growth: Psychoanalytic Studies of the Gifted and a Great Variety of Other Individuals*, vol. 1 (New York: International Universities Press, 1971). Although the publication date of the particular article cited here is 1967, thus postdating the production of the film *Freud,* the clinical research with patients that is the basis of the article went on before, during, and after the period of the film's preparation. I cannot say whether the (male) psychiatric consultants to the film *Freud* knew about Greenacre's findings. But I do think a more honest film might have been prepared with the benefit of those ideas. In any case, the main point here is to illuminate the film's ideological approach to psychoanalysis with reference to alternative views.

24. Ibid., 276.

25. Ibid., 277–78.

26. Ibid., 281–83.

27. Ibid., 276.

28. Laplanche and Pontalis, *Language of Psycho-Analysis*, 391–94.

29. Ibid., 393.

30. American Psychiatric Association, *DSM-IV,* "Dissociative Disorders."

31. Waites, *Trauma and Survival,* 6.

32. Edward J. Frischholz, "The Relationship among Dissociation, Hypnosis, and Child Abuse in the Development of Multiple Personality Disorder," in *Childhood Antecedents of Multiple Personality,* ed. Richard P. Kluft (Washington, D.C.: American Psychiatric Press, 1987), 108.

33. Frank W. Putnam, Jr., "Dissociation as a Response to Extreme Trauma," in Kluft, *Childhood Antecedents,* 73.

34. Groverman Blake, " 'Kings Row' Comes to Capitol Screen—Film Taken from Henry Bellaman (sic) Book," *Cincinnati Times-Star,* 6 April 1942.

35. The script of the trailer may be found in the *Kings Row* "Publicity and Press Clippings" file in the Warner Bros. Archives, Doheny Library, School of Cinema-Television, University of Southern California, Los Angeles.

36. Balmary, *Psychoanalyzing Psychoanalysis,* 162.

37. Sartre, *The Freud Scenario,* 241.

38. Geoffrey Shurlock's and John A. Vizzard's instructions to replace Magda and her father with a "prototype father and child" are communicated in a memorandum from John Huston's publicist William Gordon to John Huston, 11 August 1961, John Huston collection, Margaret Herrick Library, Academy of Motion Picture Arts and Sciences, Beverly Hills, Calif.

In the final shooting script of *Freud,* dated 10 February 1962, one flashback does actually depict a "young and beautiful Magda," but she merely walks along the edge of a lake. When it comes time for the suggestive actions to be depicted, the father undressing the daughter is not Magda's father, but his hands tremble, "Like," Magda recounts, "like my father's did long, long ago when I was a little girl and supposed to go swimming. My own father."

3. INCEST ON TELEVISION

1. Sandra Butler, *Conspiracy of Silence: The Trauma of Incest* (New York: Bantam, 1978); Rush, *Best Kept Secret;* Judith L. Herman, *Father-Daughter Incest* (1981; reprint, with a new afterword, Cambridge, Mass.: Harvard University Press, 2000); David Finkelhor, *Sexually Victimized Children* (New York: Free Press, 1979), and *Child Sexual Abuse: New Theory and Research* (New York: Free Press, 1984); Diana E. H. Russell, *The Secret Trauma: Incest in the Lives of Girls and Women* (1986; rev. ed. with a new introduction, New York: Basic Books, 1999).

2. Lynn Sacco, "Incest Survivors and Feminist Activism: An Historical Examination of the Relationships between the Recovery Movement and Social Challenges" (master's thesis, State University of New York at Buffalo, 1996), 60.

3. Carolyn Swift indicates that 50 to 80 percent of child sexual assault cases go unreported in "Sexual Assault of Children and Adolescents," testimony prepared for the Subcommittee on Science and Technology of the U.S. House of Representatives, 11 January 1978, cited in Rush, *Best Kept Secret,* 198 n. 10. See also Robert A. Prentky, Raymond A. Knight, and Austin F. S. Lee, "Child Sexual Molestation: Research Issues," National Institute of Justice Research Report, U.S. Department of Justice, June 1997, www.ncjrs.org.

4. See Howard N. Snyder, "Sexual Assault of Young Children as Reported to Law Enforcement: Victim, Incident, and Offender Characteristics," statistical report using data from the National Incident-Based Reporting System, National Center for Juvenile Justice, July 2000, NCJJ 182990, www.ojp.usdoj.gov/bjs/pub/pdf/saycrle.pdf, and Prentky, Knight, and Lee, "Child Sexual Molestation."

5. Rush gives the figures of 80 to 90 percent, while Snyder indicates in "Sexual Assault" that 96 percent of all offenders are male. See also Prentky, Knight, and Lee, "Child Sexual Molestation," and Julia Whealin, "Child Sexual Abuse: A National Center for PTSD Fact Sheet," National Center for PTSD, White River Junction, Vt., May 2003, www.ncptsd.org/facts/specific/fs.

6. See Herman, *Father-Daughter Incest* (14), for a comparative discussion of boy and girl victims in the five studies from 1940 to 1978. Butler, in *Conspiracy of Silence,* reports that 97 percent of perpetrators are male while 87 percent of victims are girls. The NCJJ figures in Snyder, "Sexual Assault," indicate that 86 percent of victims of sexual assault of all ages are female. Broken down by the age of the victim, the findings are as follows: 69 percent of victims under the age of six are female; 73 percent under the age of twelve are female; and 82 percent of all

juveniles are female. The female proportion of sexual assault victims reached 90 percent at age thirteen and 95 percent at age nineteen. However, according to evidence coming to light at the time of this writing, abuse perpetrated by Catholic clergy—that is, extrafamilial abuse—was perpetrated mainly against boys.

7. Lynn Sacco, *A Noisy Silence: A History of Father-Daughter Incest in the United States* (Baltimore: Johns Hopkins University Press, forthcoming). Sacco provides a superb historical analysis of society's long-standing difficulty acknowledging crimes against children that take place in families. She demonstrates in detail that once science could link infectious bacteria, including gonorrhea, with intrafamilial sexual contact and therefore locate incest in every racial and socioeconomic group, including middle-class whites, otherwise intelligent professionals reverted to patently illogical explanations for infection that served to deny the widespread reality of incest.

8. Butler, *Conspiracy of Silence,* 17. Snyder, "Sexual Assault," indicates that 77 percent of sexual assaults of juvenile victims occurred in a residence—that of the victim, the offender, or another individual—while 49 percent of the offenders of victims under age six were family members. Adults were the offenders in 60 percent of the cases involving youths under the age of twelve.

9. Herman, *Father-Daughter Incest,* 10–21.

10. Finkelhor, *Sexually Victimized Children,* 68–71.

11. Herman, *Father-Daughter Incest,* 17, 18.

12. Alfred Kinsey et al., *Sexual Behavior in the Human Female* (Philadelphia: W. B. Saunders, 1953), 121, quoted in Herman, *Father-Daughter Incest,* 18.

13. Kinsey et al., *Sexual Behavior,* 20–21, quoted in Herman, *Father-Daughter Incest,* 17.

14. For example, see Rayline A. De Vine, "Sexual Abuse of Children: An Overview of the Problem," in *Sexual Abuse of Children: Selected Readings,* ed. Barbara M. Jones et al. (Washington, D.C.: U.S. Department of Health and Human Services, 1980); and Allan R. De Jong, Arturo R. Hervada, and Gary A. Emmett, "Epidemiologic Variations in Childhood Sexual Abuse," *Child Abuse and Neglect* 7, no. 2 (1983): 155–62. These articles are cited in a 1995 law review article aiming to present the definitive word on sexual abuse statistics and repressed memory: Joy Lazo, "Comment: True or False: Expert Testimony on Repressed Memory," *Loyola of Los Angeles Law Review* 28 (Summer 1995): 1345ff., Lexis-Nexis Academic, http://web.lexis-nexis.com/universe/document?_m = 23a8e962c6c5 fd36235c4e3430814b73&_docnum = 1&wchp = dGLbVtzSkVA&_md5 = 36ca66 c0d22673bd54b8607e3708ba20.

15. Butler, *Conspiracy of Silence,* 4–5.

16. Ibid., 5.

17. Ibid.

18. In *Best Kept Secret,* published in 1980 but stemming from a paper she delivered on 17 April 1971 at a conference on rape, Florence Rush writes that "[a]dult

sex with children presents an increasing serious health problem. Cases of rectal fissures, lesions, poor sphincter control, lacerated vaginas, foreign bodies in the anus and vagina, perforated anal and vaginal walls, death by asphyxiation, chronic choking from gonorrheal tonsillitis, are most always related to adult sexual contacts with children" (6). She cites "Sexual Abuse of Children Common, Study Finds," *Record* (Bergen County, N.J.), 15 November 1977, and Harold I. Lief, comp., "Medical Symptoms of Sexual Abuse in Children," in *Medical Aspects of Human Sexuality: 750 Questions Answered by 500 Authorities* (Baltimore: Williams and Wilkins, 1975), 139.

19. James Ryan, "Child Sex Abuse: A Victim Reveals the Pain," *Arizona Republic,* 26 September 1993, Television section, 4.

20. Trey Paul, "'Shattered Trust' Deals Carefully with Real-Life Story of Child Abuse," *Buffalo News,* 26 September 1993, TV Topics. Paul is referring to the three 1993 made-for-television movies about Amy Fisher, a teenager who shot the wife of her lover, Joey Buttafuoco, in the face, and another 1993 television movie about the 1992 storming of the Branch Davidian compound in Waco, Texas.

21. Ray Loynd, "'Shattered Trust': A Fierce Look at Incest," *Los Angeles Times,* 27 September 1993, Calendar section, F11.

22. Ibid.

23. Walker, *Couching Resistance.* I do argue, however, that the adaptive model of psychiatry is not the only one depicted in Hollywood classical films about women and psychiatry. Once psychological issues are broached, complications ensue, and such films often contain a genuinely subversive strain critical of conventional social relations. Unfortunately, Hollywood films depicting women psychiatrists may be, paradoxically, some of the least subversive.

24. Flora Rheta Schreiber, *Sybil* (Chicago: Henry Regnery, 1973).

25. Clinical findings have indicated that etiology of multiple personality disorder is, in the majority of cases, childhood sexual abuse. See for example, Kluft, *Childhood Antecedents.*

26. Armstrong, "The Great Incest Massacre I," chap. 6 in *Rocking the Cradle.*

27. Gregory G. Gordon, "Adult Survivors of Childhood Sexual Abuse and the Statute of Limitations: The Need for Consistent Application of the Delayed Discovery Rule," *Pepperdine Law Review* 20 (May 1993): 1359ff., Lexis-Nexis Academic, http://web.lexis-nexis.com/universe/document?_m = 9fe71ece75079e667f 8a15ed914218ec&_docnum = 1&wchp = dGLbVIz-zSkVb&_md5 = d52a5837197 fa9ed54809767e7adbc63.

28. Ibid., 10 (online text), citing 264 Cal. Rptr. 639 (Ct. App. 1989).

29. Jeannyne Thornton, "Family Violence Emerges from the Shadows," *USA Today,* 23 January 1984.

30. Herman, *Trauma and Recovery,* 175. Herman is reporting from a presentation by F. Snider at a meeting of the Boston Area Trauma Study Group (1986).

31. The substitution of the mother molester for the father figure, and of instruments for the penis, is very much in keeping with television producers' reluctance, similar to that of film producers, to represent father-daughter incest prior to the 1990s. Of course, the television movie is relying on events and characters related in the biography *Sybil,* but it is revealing of cultural practices that it was this particular story that got published and this particular published book that was acquired for movie adaptation. The implication in the film is that Sybil's mother also suffered from multiple personality disorder or at least delusions about the wrath of God, perhaps due to abuse at the hands of her own father. She is described by the town physician as having been "nervous."

32. As I indicated in chapter 1 of this book, Schwarz and Gilligan ("Devil Is in the Details," 37) reported that "by the end of 1994, more than 300 articles on 'false memory' had appeared in magazines and newspapers."

33. Russell, *Secret Trauma,* xx. Russell cites Kenneth S. Pope, "Science as Careful Questioning: Are Claims of a False Memory Syndrome Epidemic Based on Empirical Evidence?" *American Psychologist* 52 (September 1997): 997–1006.

34. Judith Herman indicates that "[s]exual abuse of children is common (best estimates: at least one girl in three, one boy in ten). It is not overreported but vastly underreported (best estimates: under 10 percent of all cases come to the attention of child-protective agencies or police)." Quoted from Judith Herman, "The Abuses of Memory," *Mother Jones,* March/April 1993, 3–4, as the epigraph of Rosaria Champagne, "Oprah Winfrey's *Scared Silent* and the Spectatorship of Incest," *Discourse* 17, no. 2 (Winter 1994–95): 123–38. Champagne's essay is reprinted as chap. 6 of *Politics of Survivorship.*

35. Champagne, "Oprah Winfrey's *Scared Silent,*" 126.

36. Ibid.

37. Sacco in particular has developed a fascinating in-depth analysis of the "strategies and tactics" of the FMSF. See Sacco, "The False Memory Syndrome Foundation: Its Strategies and Tactics," chap. 3 in "Not Talking about 'It': A History of Incest in the United States, 1890–1940" (Ph.D. diss., University of Southern California, Los Angeles, 2001).

38. Diana Russell *(Secret Trauma,* xxxix) cites a case in which a twelve-year-old girl in Phoenix, Arizona, asserted repeatedly that she was being abused by her grandfather. It was only when she brought a cup of her grandfather's semen to the police that she was finally believed.

39. Champagne, "Oprah Winfrey's *Scared Silent,*" 128.

40. Linda Meyer Williams, "Adult Memories of Child Sexual Abuse: Placing Sexual Assault in Long-Term Perspective," paper presented at the World Conference of the International Society for Traumatic Studies, "Trauma and Tragedy: The Origins, Management and Prevention of Traumatic Stress in Today's World," Amsterdam, 1992. See also Linda Meyer Williams, "Recall of Childhood Trauma: A Prospective Study of Women's Memories of Child Sexual Abuse,"

Journal of Consulting and Clinical Psychology 62, no. 6 (1994): 1167–76, and "Recovered Memories of Abuse in Women with Documented Child Sexual Victimization Histories," *Journal of Traumatic Stress* 8 (1995): 649–74. These studies are cited in Michelle Citron, *Home Movies and Other Necessary Fictions* (Minneapolis: Minnesota University Press, 1999).

41. The higher percentages are cited by the following studies: Judith L. Herman and Emily Schatzow, "Recovery and Verification of Memories of Childhood Sexual Trauma," *Psychoanalytic Psychology* 4, no. 1 (1987): 1–14 (reports 67 percent of women as amnesiac for childhood sexual abuse), and J. N. Briere, "Amnesia in Adults Molested as Children," paper presented at the annual meeting of the American Psychological Association, New Orleans, 1989 (reports 60 percent of the clinical sample as having experienced amnesia), both cited in Catherine Cameron, "Comparing Amnesic and Nonamnesic Survivors of Childhood Sexual Abuse: A Longitudinal Study," in Pezdek and Banks, *Recovered Memory/False Memory Debate.*

42. Williams, "Recovered Memories," cited in Citron, *Home Movies.*

43. Herman, *Father-Daughter Incest,* 237. She cites D. Jones and J. M. McGraw, "Reliable and Fictitious Accounts of Sexual Abuse to Children," *Journal of Interpersonal Violence* 2 (1987): 27–45.

44. See Tom Feran, "'Frontline' Airs 'the Holy War' on Child Abuse," *Plain Dealer,* 4 April 1995, Arts and Living section, p. 11E; and Robert P. Laurence, "'Frontline' Examines Repressed Memory," *San Diego Union-Tribune,* 10 April 1995.

45. Ed Siegel, "The Good News at PBS," *Boston Globe,* 15 October 1995, Arts and Film section, 57, quoted in Sacco, "Not Talking about 'It.'"

46. Tamar Lewin, "Judge Upsets Murder Conviction Focused on 'Repressed Memory,'" *New York Times,* 5 April 1995, 18.

47. See Cynthia Grant Brown and Elizabeth Mertz, "A Dangerous Direction: Legal Intervention in Sexual Abuse Survivor Therapy," *Harvard Law Review* 109 (January 1996): 549. In this article the authors question popular discourses that dispute the validity of repressed and recovered memories and criticize a court's decision to allow a father to recover "third party" damages from his daughter's therapists.

48. The social perception that false memory is a problem of epidemic proportions is belied by studies reporting that (1) most child abuse victims *remember* their attacks rather than repressing the memories of them and (2) of those who do repress and recover abuse memories the majority are able to find or get corroborating evidence of them. This means that unconfirmed reports of childhood sexual abuse make up only a fraction of cases of childhood sexual abuse. See, for example, Herman and Schatzow, "Recovery and Verification."

49. Ian Hacking, *Rewriting the Soul: Multiple Personality and the Sciences of Memory* (Princeton, N.J.: Princeton University Press, 1995), 249.

50. Ibid., 245–49.

51. Ibid., 258.

52. Ibid., 259.

53. Waites, *Trauma and Survival,* 27.

54. Armstrong, *Rocking the Cradle,* 251.

55. Letter signed, "Cynthia Knudson, Falmouth, Massachusetts."

56. Armstrong, *Rocking the Cradle,* 246–59. In this connection, Diana Russell notes in *Secret Trauma* that "no corroboratory evidence of satanic ritual abuse was ever found in connection with [the McMartin Preschool and the other like] day care cases" (xx), citing Mary DeYoung, "The Devil Goes to Day Care: McMartin and the Making of a Moral Panic," *Journal of American Culture* 20, no. 1 (1997): 19–25.

57. Williams, "Mirrors without Memories," 15.

58. Ibid., 18. Williams cites Shoshana Felman, "A l'age du temoinage: *Shoah* de Claude Lanzmann," in *Au sujet de* Shoah: *Le film de Claude Lanzmann,* series ed. Michel Deguy (Paris: Editions Belin, 1990). I also suggest Felman, "The Return of the Voice, Claude Lanzmann's *Shoah,*" in Felman and Laub, *Testimony.*

4. STRANGE BEDFELLOWS

1. Michelle Citron, "Fleeing from Documentary: Autobiographical Film/ Video and the 'Ethics of Responsibility,'" in *Feminism and Documentary,* ed. Diane Waldman and Janet Walker (Minneapolis: Minnesota University Press, 1999); and Citron, *Home Movies.*

2. For example, see Linda Williams and B. Ruby Rich, "The Right of Re-Vision: Michelle Citron's *Daughter Rite,*" vol. 2 of *Movies and Methods,* ed. Bill Nichols (Berkeley: University of California Press, 1985); Jane Feuer, "'Daughter Rite': Living with Our Pain and Love," in *Films for Women,* ed. Charlotte Brunsdon (London: British Film Institute, 1986); and E. Ann Kaplan, "Mothers and Daughters in Two Recent Women's Films: Mulvey/Wollen's *Riddles of the Sphinx* (1976) and Michelle Citron's *Daughter-Rite* (1978)," in *Women and Film: Both Sides of the Camera* (New York: Methuen, 1983). See also references to *Daughter Rite* in Annette Kuhn, *Women's Pictures: Feminism and Cinema* (London: Routledge and Kegan Paul, 1982); Alan Rosenthal, ed., *New Challenges for Documentary* (Berkeley: University of California Press, 1988); and Nichols, *Representing Reality.*

3. Citron, "Fleeing from Documentary," 282.

4. Citron, *Home Movies,* 21.

5. Ibid., 22.

6. Williams, "Mirrors without Memories," 12.

7. P. Adams Sitney, "Autobiography in Avant-Garde Film," *Millennium Film Journal* 1, no. 1 (Winter 1977): 60–63, quoted in David James, "Lynn Hershman:

The Subject of Autobiography," in *Resolutions: Contemporary Video Practices,* ed. Michael Renov and Erika Suderburg (Minneapolis: University of Minnesota Press, 1996), 125.

8. Kuhn, *Women's Pictures,* 162.

9. Citron, *Home Movies,* 24.

10. Citron, "Fleeing from Documentary," 273.

11. Citron, *Home Movies,* 154.

12. I would like to acknowledge a debt to Cynthia Felando for bringing this film to my attention.

13. Writer-director Catherine Cyran, who is interviewed on camera in *Some Nudity Required,* cites a Berkeley professor as having discussed with her the fact that B movie women characters are always killed off if they have sex and/or are seen to be sexual. Perhaps that professor is Carol Clover, author of *Men, Women, and Chain Saws: Gender in Modern Horror Film* (Princeton, N.J.: Princeton University Press, 1992).

14. But Dan Leopard reveals that even if he was not in the room, he was Lynn Hershman's cameraperson. The cameraperson, he reminds us, is a structuring absence that is pivotal to Hershman's ability to speak to her video audience while paradoxically asserting her solitude. "Any work of art," he reminds us, "is a field of competition among auteurs." Dan Leopard, "I Was Lynn Hershman's Cameraperson, or The Interplay of Authorship in the Field of Competitive Production," paper presented at the annual meeting of the Society for Cinema Studies, Denver, Colorado, 23–26 May 2002.

15. James, "Lynn Hershman," 124. Although James is referring to the specificity of video as opposed to cinema when he writes, "Only in the multiple, dispersed yet interconnected practices that constitute television as a whole can an adequately extensive, flexible, and nuanced metaphor for the self now be found" (124), he acknowledges that "correlatives for Hershman's innovations lie in avant-garde film of the late sixties and early seventies as much as in video" (125). My own view is that the video medium's cheapness relative to film and its facilitation of special effects do indeed encourage an aesthetic of self-discovery where the self may be understood as fragmented. But this is not to say that film excludes such investigations, and in fact the filmic mode where they have historically taken place is the feminist autobiographical experimental documentary.

16. Julia Lesage, "Women's Fragmented Consciousness in Feminist Experimental Autobiographical Video," in Waldman and Walker, *Feminism and Documentary.* I am grateful to Julia not only for her insightful essay on Hershman's work but also for sending me an entire, thick clippings file on Hershman's life and works.

17. Ibid., 329.

18. This recycling of material relates to another of Hershman's practices mentioned by Lesage and James, which is to reedit the tapes after they have been

finished and shown (Lesage, "Women's Fragmented Consciousness," 336 n. 8; James, "Lynn Hershman," 126).

19. James, "Lynn Hershman," 126.

20. See Robert Atkins, "Who Is Roberta Breitmore? And What Is She Doing in the Arts?" *San Francisco Bay Guardian*, 4 May 1978, 35.

21. Lynn Hershman, "Retrospective Notes: Roberta Breitmore, 1971–1979, San Diego, Ferrara Italy, San Francisco. A Private Performance Based in Real Time and Real Life," undated typescript.

22. The exceptions to this rule are the handful of shots of Hershman in *Binge* that are recorded silent instead of with synchronous sound.

23. See note 18 above.

24. Felman, "The Return of the Voice," in Felman and Laub, *Testimony*, 211.

25. Ibid., 219.

26. Patricia Erens, "*Shoah*," *Film Quarterly* 39, no. 4 (1986): 29.

27. Williams, "Mirrors without Memories," 17.

28. Felman, "Return of the Voice," 255.

29. Ibid., 267.

30. Williams, "Mirrors without Memories," 18.

31. American Psychiatric Association, *DSM-IV*, 428.

32. Jesse Friedman, "Free Jesse,"www.freejesse.net (accessed 12 August 2003).

33. Nick Poppy, "One Family's Elusive Truth: Andrew Jarecki's *Capturing the Friedmans*," indieWIRE, www.indiewire.com/people/people_030530jarecki .html.

34. Williams, "Mirrors without Memories," 15.

35. The film relates that Arnold and his brother slept in the same bed together in the same room with their divorced mother. She would bring her boyfriends there for sexual relations. I wonder if Arnold was abused by one of these men.

36. Hacking, *Rewriting the Soul*, 249.

37. The place of the middle brother, Seth, in the family's history remains enigmatic. We see him in the family archives, but he declined to be interviewed for the film.

5. 'THE LAST DAYS' IS NOT 'SHOAH'

1. Shoah Visual History Foundation, "Who We Are: Frequently Asked Questions," www.vhf.org/vhfmain-2.htm.

2. Douglas Greenberg, "Return with Me Now to Those Days of Yesteryear," paper presented at the panel "How Technology Presents Opportunities for Making History Education More Immediate," hosted by the Gevirtz School of Education, University of California, Santa Barbara, 23 February 2001.

3. As stated by Steven Spielberg in a direct address to the camera at the beginning of *The Last Days* (James Moll, 1998).

4. See Lipstadt, *Denying the Holocaust,* and *Mr. Death* (Errol Morris, 1999).

5. See Rothberg, *Traumatic Realism,* 219, and Rothberg, "'Touch an Event to Begin': Americanizing the Holocaust," chap. 6 of *Traumatic Realism.* For a history of Holocaust memory in America, see Peter Novick, "Holocaust Memory in America," in *The Art of Memory: Holocaust Memorials in History,* ed. James E. Young (New York: Prestel, 1994).

6. Harold Marcuse addressed these comments to Greenberg after the latter's presentation, "Return with Me Now," at the panel "How Technology Presents Opportunities for Making History Education More Immediate," hosted by the Gevirtz School of Education, University of California, Santa Barbara, 23 February 2001.

7. "Complete unanimity among historians regarding an event of such magnitude would itself be highly suspicious," writes Lipstadt *(Denying the Holocaust,* 61).

8. Lawrence Langer, *Holocaust Testimonies: The Ruins of Memory* (New Haven, Conn.: Yale University Press, 1991).

9. James Young, "Holocaust Video and Cinemagraphic Testimony: Documenting the Witness," chap. 9 in *Writing and Rewriting the Holocaust: Narrative and the Consequences of Interpretation* (Bloomington: Indiana University Press, 1988).

10. See Deborah Lefkowitz, "On Silence and Other Disruptions," in Waldman and Walker, *Feminism and Documentary.*

11. Daniel Eisenberg, *"Displaced Persons:* Dan Eisenberg Interviewed by Alf Bold," *Millennium Film Journal* 27 (Winter 1993–94): 48–63, http://mfj-online .org/journalPages/MFJ27/ABoldDEisenb.html.

12. Theodor W. Adorno, *Prisms,* trans. Samuel and Shierry Weber (1967; reprint, Cambridge: MIT Press, 1988). For discussions of Adorno's "aperçu," in Gertrud Koch's word, as it has been applied to the possibility of Holocaust art, literature, poetry, and film, see Gertrud Koch, "The Aesthetic Transformation of the Image of the Unimaginable: Notes on Claude Lanzmann's *Shoah,*" *October* 48 (Spring 1989): 15–24. See also Koch, "The Angel of Forgetfulness and the Black Box of Facticity: Trauma and Memory in Claude Lanzman's *Shoah,*" *History and Memory* 3, no. 1 (1991): 119–36; LaCapra, *History and Memory;* and Rothberg, *Traumatic Realism.*

13. See Miriam Bratu Hansen, *"Schindler's List* Is Not *Shoah*: Second Commandment, Popular Modernism, and Public Memory," in *Spielberg's Holocaust: Critical Perspectives on Schindler's List,* ed. Yosefa Loshitzky (Bloomington: Indiana University Press, 1997).

14. Koch, "Aesthetic Transformation," 15.

15. Theodor W. Adorno, *Negative Dialectics,* trans. E. B. Ashton (New York: Seabury, 1973), 362, quoted in Koch, "Aesthetic Transformation," 15.

16. LaCapra, *History and Memory,* 181.

17. Hansen, in *"Schindler's List,"* discusses the film's popular and critical

reception, enumerating the first three elements on my list of responses to the film. The mention of the skating routines I owe to Rothberg's discussion in *Traumatic Realism*. The book of critical essays referred to is Loshitszky's *Spielberg's Holocaust*.

18. Loshitzky, "Holocaust Others: Spielberg's *Schindler's List* versus Lanzmann's *Shoah*," in Loshitzky, *Spielberg's Holocaust*.

19. Hansen, "*Schindler's List*," 79.

20. Ibid., 84–85.

21. Loshitzky, "Holocaust Others," 107. Loshitzky draws the Lanzmann quotation from André Colombat, *The Holocaust in French Film* (Metuchen, N.J.: Scarecrow Press, 1993), 313.

22. Loshitzky, "Holocaust Others," 109.

23. Hansen, "*Schindler's List*," 84–85.

24. I am referring here to the fifteen-minute infomercial for the Survivors of the Shoah Visual History Foundation included on the videocassette of the television documentary *Survivors of the Holocaust* (Allan Holzman, 1996).

25. Erens, "*Shoah*"; Shoshana Felman, "The Return of Voice: Claude Lanzmann's *Shoah*," in Felman and Laub, *Testimony*; Friedlander, "Trauma, Transference"; Hirsch, *Afterimage*; Koch, "Aesthetic Transformation" and "Angel of Forgetfulness"; LaCapra, *History and Memory*; Michael Roth, "*Shoah* as Shivah," chap. 13 in *The Ironist's Cage: Memory, Trauma, and the Construction of History* (New York: Columbia University Press, 1995); Rothberg, *Traumatic Realism*; and Williams, "Mirrors without Memories."

26. Joshua Hirsch, "Introduction to Film, Trauma, and the Holocaust," chap. 1 in "Afterimage: Film, Trauma, and the Holocaust" (Ph.D. diss., University of California, Los Angeles, 2001), 22.

27. Erens, "*Shoah*," 28.

28. Ibid., 31.

29. LaCapra, *History and Memory*, 104 (emphasis mine).

30. See also Dominick LaCapra, "Trauma, Absence, Loss," *Critical Inquiry* 25 (Summer 1999): 696–727, for LaCapra's continuing discussion of his distinction between mourning and melancholia as historiographic devices.

31. LaCapra, *History and Memory*, 111.

32. Ibid., 113.

33. Rothberg, *Traumatic Realism*, 238.

34. Ibid., 236.

35. Joshua Hirsch, "*Shoah* and the Posttraumatic Documentary after Cinema Verite," chap. 3 in *Afterimage*, 84.

36. Rothberg, in *Traumatic Realism*, indicates that Felman overlooks "*how* historical understanding is being stalked" in *Shoah* because she overemphasizes "the word" (236). But I would argue that Rothberg's criticism is more true of LaCapra than it is of Felman.

37. Hirsch, *Afterimage*, 63. See also Rothberg, *Traumatic Realism*; Koch, "Angel of Forgetfulness"; Williams, "Mirrors without Memories;" Nichols, *Blurred Boundaries: Questions of Meaning in Contemporary Culture* (Blooming-ton: Indiana University Press, 1994); and Walker, "Traumatic Paradox."

38. LaCapra, in *History and Memory*, partially accepts Lanzmann's own con-tention that the film is not historical but a work of art. "In Lanzmann," writes LaCapra, "art poses provocative questions to history. To some extent I shall reverse the procedure and have history pose questions to art" (98).

39. Claude Lanzmann, "Holocauste, le représentation impossible," *Le Monde*, 3 March 1994, "Arts et Spectacles," VII, quoted and translated by Rothberg, *Trau-matic Realism*, 233.

40. Erens, "*Shoah*," 29.

41. LaCapra, *History and Memory*, 128 n. 28.

42. I am thinking, for example, of *The Children Were Watching, Crisis: Behind a Presidential Commitment*, and other Drew Associates films of the 1960s.

43. The discussion of the use of *enactment* appears in chapter 4.

44. Thus I disagree with, or at least would qualify, LaCapra's statement that "*Shoah* is not strictly a documentary film in that scenes in it are carefully con-structed" (*History and Memory*, 96).

45. Felman, "Return of the Voice," 267.

46. Williams, "Mirrors without Memories," 17.

47. Rothberg, *Traumatic Realism*, 235–36.

48. Ibid., 237.

49. Ibid., 234.

50. Hansen, "*Schindler's List*," 98. Hansen cites Alison Landsberg, "Prosthetic Memory: The Logics and Politics of Memory in Modern American Culture" (Ph.D. diss., University of Chicago, 1996), especially chap. 4.

51. This film is discussed in Hirsch, "Introduction to Film," and in Joshua Hirsch, "Posttraumatic Film and the Holocaust Documentary," *Film and History* 32, no. 1 (2002): 9–21. Hirsch, on the basis of what he learned from a rep-resentative of the film department of the U.S. Holocaust Memorial Museum, states that this film is unique as the only "known piece of motion picture footage" depicting the extermination during the Holocaust of more than ten mil-lion people (*Afterimage*, 1, 164 n. 1).

52. Michael Frisch, "Oral History, Documentary, and the Mystification of Power: A Critique of *Vietnam: A Television History*," chap. 7 in *A Shared Author-ity*, 160.

53. Cathy Caruth, "Unclaimed Experience: Trauma and the Possibility of History," *Yale French Studies* 79 (1991): 187. This essay is reprinted as "Unclaimed Experience: Trauma and the Possibility of History (Freud, *Moses and Monothe-ism*)," chap. 1 in *Unclaimed Experience: Trauma, Narrative, and History* (Balti-more: Johns Hopkins University Press, 1996).

54. Nichols, *Representing Reality*, 44–48. See also Citron's discussion of Nichols's categories and her application of them to her own filmmaking practice in "Fleeing from Documentary."

55. Citron, "Fleeing from Documentary."

56. I thank Diane Waldman for drawing my attention to the difference between Fela's lively narration here when thinking about her grandson and her reluctant narration of the story of the march.

57. The film was screened on 19 August 2001 at the Denver Jewish Film Festival as a part of an "Image and Identity" series sponsored by the National Foundation for Jewish Culture.

58. Quoted in Koch, "Angel of Forgetfulness," 19.

59. I have previously discussed *Tak for Alt* and am partially drawing from my essay "The Vicissitudes of Traumatic Memory."

60. Filmmaker Laura Bialis was kind enough to share with me that the house we see is not the actual house where the events in Meisel's life took place. Rather, the exterior shots are of a house in the Jasvene shtetl and the interior shots were taken in the home of a righteous gentile in Jasvene.

6. DISREMEMBERING THE HOLOCAUST

1. Michael Renov, "The Address to the Other: Ethical Discourse in *Everything's for You* (1989)," chap. 10 in *The Subject of Documentary* (Minneapolis: Minnesota University Press, 2004), 162.

2. Wardi, *Memorial Candles.*

3. Yosefa Loshitzky, "Hybrid Victims: Second-Generation Israelis Screen the Holocaust," in *Visual Culture and the Holocaust,* ed. Barbie Zelizer (New Brunswick, N.J.: Rutgers University Press, 2001), 154. Loshitzky is quoting Wardi, *Memorial Candles,* 35.

4. Yosefa Loshitzky, *Identity Politics on the Israeli Screen* (Austin: University of Texas Press, 2001), 23.

5. Ibid., 29.

6. Marianne Hirsch, *Family Frames: Photography, Narrative, and Postmemory* (Cambridge, Mass.: Harvard University Press, 1997), 22.

7. Laura Marks, "Fetishes and Fossils: Notes on Documentary and Materiality," in Waldman and Walker, *Feminism and Documentary,* 224.

8. Ibid., 228.

9. Renov, "Address to the Other," 161. Jean-François Lyotard, *Heidegger and "the Jews,"* trans. Andreas Michel and Mark S. Roberts (Minneapolis: University of Minnesota Press, 1990), 47.

10. Art Spiegelmann, *Maus: A Survivor's Tale* (New York: Pantheon Books, 1986), and *Maus II: A Survivor's Tale: And Here My Troubles Began* (New York: Pantheon Books, 1991).

11. LaCapra, *History and Memory*, 149.

12. Hirsch, *Family Frames*, 32, 36.

13. Spiegelman, *Maus II*, 15. These lines are also quoted in Andrea Liss, *Trespassing through Shadows: Memory, Photography, and the Holocaust* (Minneapolis: Minnesota University Press, 1998), 58; and in Hirsch, *Family Frames*, 37.

14. Spiegelman, *Maus II*, 15, quoted in Liss, *Trespassing through Shadows*, 58.

15. Spiegelman, *Maus II*, 136, quoted in Liss, *Trespassing through Shadows*, 58, and in Hirsch, *Family Frames*, 37.

16. Roland Barthes, *Camera Lucida: Reflections on Photography* (New York: Hill and Wang, 1981).

17. Michael Renov also notes this point about Jewish naming tradition in *The Subject of Documentary* ("Address to the Other," 165).

18. Abraham Ravett, conversation with filmmaker, Denver, Colo., 19 August 2001; Abraham Ravett, e-mail correspondence with filmmaker, 31 July 2004.

19. Abraham Ravett, "The Films of Abraham Ravett," http://helios.hampshire .edu/~arPF/, specifically http://helios.hampshire.edu/~arPF/previous.html#Thirty (accessed 7 August 2003).

20. White, "Historical Emplotment" and "Modernist Event."

21. Laura Bialis, conversation with filmmaker, Santa Barbara, Calif., 11 November 2001.

22. Ulrich Baer, "To Give Memory a Place: Holocaust Photography and the Landscape Tradition," *Representations* 69 (Winter 2000): 44, reworked and republished as "To Give Memory a Place: Contemporary Holocaust Photography and the Landscape Tradition," chap. 2 in *Spectral Evidence: The Photography of Trauma* (Cambridge, Mass.: MIT Press, 2002). Page citations are to the *Representations* article.

23. See the particularly insightful discussion of the desire to transcend this distance in Daniel Mendelsohn's "What Happened to Uncle Shmiel?" *New York Times Magazine*, 14 July 2002, cover story.

24. Wardi, *Memorial Candles*, 5.

25. Baer, "To Give Memory a Place," 44.

26. Ibid., 47.

27. Mark Singer, "The Friendly Executioner: How Did an Electric-Chair Repairman Come to Deny the Holocaust? And Other Odd Questions." *New Yorker*, 1 February 1999, 35–36. This fine article is an excellent source of facts about Leuchter and the making of *Mr. Death*.

28. Errol Morris, quoted in Singer, "Friendly Executioner," 37.

29. Ernst Zündel, Zundelsite Zgram, 6 October 1999 and 7 October 1999, www.revisionists.com/leuchter/mr_death/zgram_october6–99_zundel_review1 .htm and www.revisionists.com/leuchter/mr_death/zgram_october7–99_zundel_ review2.htm (accessed 22 April 2001).

30. Michael A. Hoffman II, "The Hoffman Wire," www.revisionists.com/

leuchter/mr_death/the_hoffman_wire_on_leuchter.html, p. 2 (accessed 22 April 2001). Hoffman, who is a Holocaust denier, posts his credentials as "former reporter for the New York Bureau of the Associated Press," editor of the *Revisionist History* newsletter, and founder and president of the Campaign for Radical Truth in History.

31. Singer, "Friendly Executioner," 34.

32. Mark Singer, "Profiles: Errol Morris," *New Yorker,* 6 February 1989, 38.

33. Singer, "Friendly Executioner," 34.

34. Zündel is mistaken in his statement that Adams was retried. He was merely released after more than a decade in prison, much of that on Death Row.

35. The cinematographer is Peter Donahue; Robert Richardson, known for his Oscar-winning work with Oliver Stone, received credit for additional photography.

36. Morris, quoted in Singer, "The Friendly Executioner," 38.

37. Ibid.

CONCLUSION

1. Jean-François Lyotard, *Heidegger and "the Jews,"* trans. Andreas Michel and Mark S. Roberts (Minneapolis: University of Minnesota Press, 1990), 47.

BIBLIOGRAPHY

Adorno, Theodor W. *Negative Dialectics.* Translated by E. B. Ashton. New York: Seabury, 1973.

———. *Prisms.* Translated by Samuel and Shierry Weber. 1967. Reprint, Cambridge, Mass.: MIT Press, 1988.

American Psychiatric Association. *Diagnostic and Statistical Manual of Mental Disorders.* 4th ed. Washington, D.C.: American Psychiatric Association, 1994.

Antze, Paul, and Michael Lambek, eds. *Tense Past: Cultural Essays in Trauma and Memory.* New York: Routledge, 1996.

Armstrong, Louise. *Rocking the Cradle of Sexual Politics: What Happened When Women Said Incest.* Reading, Mass.: Addison-Wesley, 1994.

Avisar, Ilan. *Screening the Holocaust: Cinema's Images of the Unimaginable.* Bloomington: Indiana University Press, 1988.

Baer, Ulrich. "To Give Memory a Place: Holocaust Photography and the Landscape Tradition." *Representations* 69 (Winter 2000): 38–62. Reworked and republished as "To Give Memory a Place: Contemporary Holocaust Photography and the Landscape Tradition," chap. 2 in *Spectral Evidence: The Photography of Trauma* (Cambridge, Mass.: MIT Press, 2002).

Bal, Mieke, Jonathan Crew, and Leo Spitzer, eds. *Acts of Memory: Cultural Recall in the Present.* Hanover, Mass.: University Press of New England, 1999.

Balmary, Marie. *Psychoanalyzing Psychoanalysis: Freud and the Hidden Fault of the Father.* Trans. Ned Lukacher. Baltimore: Johns Hopkins University Press, 1982.

Barta, Tony, ed. *Screening the Past: Film and the Representation of History.* Westport, Conn.: Praeger, 1998.

Barthes, Roland. *Camera Lucida: Reflections on Photography.* New York: Hill and Wang, 1981.

Bass, Ellen, and Laura Davis. *The Courage to Heal: Guide for Women Survivors of Child Sexual Abuse.* New York: Harper and Row, 1988.

Bellamann, Henry. *Kings Row.* New York: Simon and Schuster, 1942.

Benstock, Shari, ed. *The Private Self: Theory and Practice of Women's Autobiographical Writings.* Chapel Hill: University of North Carolina Press, 1988.

Bergstrom, Janet, ed. *Endless Night: Cinema and Psychoanalysis, Parallel Histories.* Berkeley: University of California Press, 1999.

Bernheimer, Charles. "Introduction: Part I." In *In Dora's Case: Freud, Hysteria, Feminism,* edited by Charles Bernheimer and Claire Kahane. New York: Columbia University Press, 1985.

Breen, Joseph. Letter to Jack Warner. 24 April 1941. Warner Bros. Archives. Doheny Library, School of Cinema-Television, University of Southern California, Los Angeles.

Briere, J. N. "Amnesia in Adults Molested as Children." Paper presented at the annual meeting of the American Psychological Association, New Orleans, 1989.

Brill, Lesley. *"Freud* (1961)." In *John Huston's Filmmaking.* Cambridge: Cambridge University Press, 1997.

Brodzki, Bella, and Celeste Schenck, eds. *Life/Lines: Theorizing Women's Autobiography.* Ithaca, N.Y.: Cornell University Press, 1988.

Brown, Cynthia Grant, and Elizabeth Mertz. "A Dangerous Direction: Legal Intervention in Sexual Abuse Survivor Therapy." *Harvard Law Review* 109 (January 1996): 551–639.

Butler, Sandra. *Conspiracy of Silence: The Trauma of Incest.* New York: Bantam, 1978.

Cameron, Catherine. "Comparing Amnesic and Nonamnesic Survivors of Childhood Sexual Abuse: A Longitudinal Study." In *The Recovered Memory/ False Memory Debate,* edited by Kathy Pezdek and William P. Banks. San Diego: Academic Press, 1996.

Caruth, Cathy, ed. *Trauma: Explorations in Memory.* Baltimore: Johns Hopkins University Press, 1995.

———. "Unclaimed Experience: Trauma and the Possibility of History." *Yale French Studies* 79 (1991): 181–92. Reprinted as "Unclaimed Experience: Trauma and the Possibility of History (Freud, *Moses and Monotheism*)," chap. 1 in *Unclaimed Experience: Trauma, Narrative, and History* (Baltimore: Johns Hopkins University Press, 1996).

Ceci, Stephen J., Mary Lyndia Crotteau Huffman, Elliott Smith, and Elizabeth Loftus. "Repeatedly Thinking about a Non-event: Source Misattributions among Preschoolers." In *The Recovered Memory/False Memory Debate,* edited by Kathy Pezdek and William P. Banks. San Diego: Academic Press, 1996. Originally published in *Consciousness and Cognition* 3 (1994): 388–407.

Champagne, Rosaria. "Oprah Winfrey's *Scared Silent* and the Spectatorship of Incest." *Discourse* 17, no. 2 (Winter 1994–95): 123–38.

———. *The Politics of Survivorship: Incest, Women's Literature, and Feminist Theory.* New York: New York University Press, 1996.

Citron, Michelle. "Fleeing from Documentary: Autobiographical Film/Video and the 'Ethics of Responsibility.'" In *Feminism and Documentary,* edited by Diane Waldman and Janet Walker. Minneapolis: Minnesota University Press, 1999.

———. *Home Movies and Other Necessary Fictions.* Minneapolis: Minnesota University Press, 1999.

Cohen, Stanley. *States of Denial: Knowing about Atrocities and Suffering.* Cambridge: Polity Press, 2001.

Colombat, André. *The Holocaust in French Film.* Metuchen, N.J.: Scarecrow Press, 1993.

Crews, Frederick. *The Memory Wars: Freud's Legacy in Dispute.* New York: New York Review of Books, 1995.

De Jong, Allan R., Arturo R. Hervada, and Gary A. Emmett. "Epidemiologic Variations in Childhood Sexual Abuse." *Child Abuse and Neglect* 7, no. 2 (1983): 155–62.

De Vine, Rayline A. "Sexual Abuse of Children: An Overview of the Problem." In *Sexual Abuse of Children: Selected Readings,* edited by Barbara M. Jones et al. Washington, D.C.: U.S. Department of Health and Human Services, 1980.

Doneson, Judith E. *The Holocaust in American Film.* Philadelphia: Jewish Publication Society, 1987.

Eisenberg, Daniel. "Displaced Persons: Daniel Eisenberg Interviewed by Alf Bold." *Millennium Film Journal* 27 (Winter 1993–94). http://mfj-online.org/journalPages/MFJ27/ABoldDEisenb.html.

Erens, Patricia. "*Shoah.*" *Film Quarterly* 39, no. 4 (1986): 28.

Fair, C. M. *Memory and Central Nervous Organization.* New York: Paragon House, 1988.

Farrell, Kirby. *Post-Traumatic Culture: Injury and Interpretation in the Nineties.* Baltimore: Johns Hopkins University Press, 1998.

Felman, Shoshana. *The Juridical Unconscious: Trials and Traumas in the Twentieth Century.* Cambridge, Mass.: Harvard University Press, 2002.

Felman, Shoshana, and Dori Laub. *Testimony: Crises of Witnessing in Literature, Psychoanalysis, and History.* New York: Routledge, 1992.

Feuer, Jane. "'Daughter Rite': Living with Our Pain and Love." In *Films for Women,* edited by Charlotte Brunsdon. London: British Film Institute, 1986.

Finkelhor, David. *Child Sexual Abuse: New Theory and Research.* New York: Free Press, 1984.

————. *Sexually Victimized Children.* New York: Free Press, 1979.

Frankel, Fred H. "The Concept of Flashbacks in Historical Perspective." *International Journal of Clinical and Experimental Hypnosis* 42, no. 4 (October 1994): 321–36.

————. "Discovering New Memories in Psychotherapy: Childhood Revisited, Fantasy, or Both?" *New England Journal of Medicine* 333, no. 9 (31 August 1995): 591–94.

Freud, Sigmund. "An Autobiographical Study (1925)." In *The Standard Edition of the Complete Psychological Works of Sigmund Freud,* vol. 20, edited and translated by James Strachey. London: Hogarth Press, 1962.

————. *The Complete Letters of Sigmund Freud to Wilhelm Fliess, 1887–1904.* Edited and translated by Jeffrey Moussaieff Masson. Cambridge, Mass.: Harvard University Press, 1985.

————. "Female Sexuality (1931)." In *The Standard Edition of the Complete Psychological Works of Sigmund Freud,* vol. 21, edited and translated by James Strachey. London: Hogarth Press, 1962.

————. "From the History of an Infantile Neurosis (1918)." In *Three Case Histories,* translated by Philip Rieff. New York: Collier Books, 1963.

————. "Introductory Lectures on Psychoanalysis (1916)." In *The Standard Edition of the Complete Psychological Works of Sigmund Freud,* vol. 3, edited and translated by James Strachey. London: Hogarth Press, 1962.

————. "The Neuro-Psychoses of Defense (1896)." In *The Standard Edition of the Complete Psychological Works of Sigmund Freud,* vol. 3, edited and translated by James Strachey. London: Hogarth Press, 1962.

————. *New Introductory Lectures on Psychoanalysis.* Vol. 22. Translated by W. J. H. Sprott. New York: W. W. Norton, 1933.

Freud, Sigmund, and Joseph Breuer. *Studies on Hysteria, 1893–95.* Translated and edited by James Strachey. New York: Basic Books, 1955.

Friedlander, Saul, ed. *Probing the Limits of Representation: Nazism and the "Final Solution."* Cambridge, Mass.: Harvard University Press, 1992.

————. "Trauma, Transference and 'Working Through' in Writing the History of the *Shoah.*" *History and Memory* 4 (1992): 39–59.

Friedman, Jesse. "Free Jesse." www.freejesse.net. Accessed 12 August 2003.

Frisch, Michael. *A Shared Authority: Essays on the Craft and Meaning of Oral and Public History.* Albany: SUNY Press, 1990.

Frischholz, Edward J. "The Relationship among Dissociation, Hypnosis, and Child Abuse in the Development of Multiple Personality Disorder." In *Childhood Antecedents of Multiple Personality,* edited by Richard P. Kluft. Washington, D.C.: American Psychiatric Press, 1987.

Gallop, Jane. *The Daughter's Seduction: Feminism and Psychoanalysis.* Ithaca, N.Y.: Cornell University Press, 1982.

Gilmore, Leigh. "The Mark of Autobiography: Postmodernism, Autobiography, and Genre." In *Autobiography and Postmodernism,* edited by Kathleen Ashley, Leigh Gilmore, and Gerald Peters. Amherst: University of Massachusetts Press, 1994.

Gordon, Gregory G. "Adult Survivors of Childhood Sexual Abuse and the Statute of Limitations: The Need for Consistent Application of the Delayed Discovery Rule." *Pepperdine Law Review* 20 (May 1993): 1359ff. Lexis-Nexis Academic. http://web.lexis-nexis.com/universe/document?m = 9fe71ece7507 9e667f8a15ed914218ec&docnum = 1&wchp = dGLbVlz-zSkVb&md5 = d52a5 837197fa9ed54809767e7adbc63.

Gordon, William. Memorandum to John Huston, 11 August 1961. John Huston collection, Margaret Herrick Library, Academy of Motion Picture Arts and Sciences, Beverly Hills, Calif.

Gourevitch, Philip. "The Memory Thief." *New Yorker,* 14 June 1999, 48–68.

Greenacre, Phyllis. "The Influence of Infantile Trauma on Genetic Patterns (1967; *Journal of the American Psychoanalytic Association*)." In *Emotional Growth: Psychoanalytic Studies of the Gifted and a Great Variety of Other Individuals,* vol. 1. New York: International Universities Press, 1971.

Greenberg, Douglas. "Return with Me Now to Those Days of Yesteryear." Paper presentation at the How Technology Presents Opportunities for Making History Education More Immediate panel, hosted by the Gevirtz School of Education, University of California, Santa Barbara, 23 February 2001.

Haaken, Janice. "The Debate over Recovered Memory of Sexual Abuse: A Feminist-Psychoanalytic Perspective." *Psychiatry: Interpersonal and Biological Processes* 58, no. 2 (May 1995): 189–98.

———. *Pillar of Salt: Gender, Memory, and the Perils of Looking Back.* New Brunswick, N.J.: Rutgers University Press, 1998.

Hacking, Ian. *Rewriting the Soul: Multiple Personality and the Sciences of Memory.* Princeton, N.J.: Princeton University Press, 1995.

Hamilton, Edith. *Mythology.* New York: Mentor Books, 1940.

Hansen, Miriam Bratu. "*Schindler's List* Is Not *Shoah:* Second Commandment, Popular Modernism, and Public Memory." In *Spielberg's Holocaust: Critical Perspectives on Schindler's List,* edited by Yosefa Loshitzky. Bloomington: Indiana University Press, 1997.

Hartman, Geoffrey H., ed. *Holocaust Remembrance: The Shapes of Memory.* Cambridge, Mass.: Blackwell Publishers, 1994.

Hass, Aaron. *The Aftermath: Living with the Holocaust.* Cambridge: Cambridge University Press, 1995.

Haver, William. *The Body of This Death: Historicity and Sociality in the Time of AIDS.* Stanford, Calif.: Stanford University Press, 1996.

Hein, Laura, ed. "Remembering the Bomb: The Fiftieth Anniversary in the United States and Japan." Special Issue. *Bulletin of Concerned Asian Scholars* 27, no. 2 (April–June 1995).

Herman, Judith L. *Father-Daughter Incest.* 1981. Reprint, with a new afterword, Cambridge, Mass.: Harvard University Press, 2000.

———. *Trauma and Recovery.* New York: Basic Books, 1992.

Herman, Judith L., and Emily Schatzow. "Recovery and Verification of Memories of Childhood Sexual Trauma." *Psychoanalytic Psychology* 4, no. 1 (1987): 1–14.

Hershman, Lynn. "Retrospective Notes: Roberta Breitmore, 1971–1979, San Diego, Ferrara Italy, San Francisco. A Private Performance Based in Real Time and Real Life." Undated typescript.

Hirsch, Joshua. *Afterimage: Film, Trauma, and the Holocaust.* Philadelphia: Temple University Press, 2004.

———. "Posttraumatic Cinema and the Holocaust Documentary." *Film and History* 32, no. 1 (2002): 9–21.

Hirsch, Marianne. *Family Frames: Photography, Narrative, and Postmemory.* Cambridge, Mass.: Harvard University Press, 1997.

Hodgkin, Katharine, and Susannah Radstone, eds. *Contested Pasts: The Politics of Memory.* New York: Routledge, 2003.

Hoffman II, Michael A. "The Hoffman Wire." www.revisionists.com/leuchter/mrdeath/thehoffmanwireonleuchter.html. Accessed 22 April 2001.

Horvitz, Deborah. "Nameless Ghosts: Possession and Dispossession in *Beloved.*" In *Critical Essays on Toni Morrison's "Beloved,"* edited by Barbara H. Solomon. New York: G. K. Hall, 1998.

Huston, John. *An Open Book.* New York: Alfred Knopf, 1980.

Insdorf, Annette. *Indelible Shadows: Film and the Holocaust.* New York: Random House, 1983.

Jacobs, Lea. *The Wages of Sin: Censorship and the Fallen Woman Film, 1928–1942.* Madison: University of Wisconsin Press, 1991.

James, David. "Lynn Hershman: The Subject of Autobiography." In *Resolutions: Contemporary Video Practices,* edited by Michael Renov and Erika Suderburg. Minneapolis: University of Minnesota Press, 1996.

Jelinek, Estelle C., ed. *Women's Autobiography: Essays in Criticism.* Bloomington: Indiana University Press, 1980.

Jones, D. and J. M. McGraw. "Reliable and Fictitious Accounts of Sexual Abuse to Children." *Journal of Interpersonal Violence* 2 (1987): 27–45.

Kaplan, E. Ann. "Mothers and Daughters in Two Recent Women's Films: Mulvey/Wollen's *Riddles of the Sphinx* (1976) and Michelle Citron's *Daughter-Rite* (1978)." In *Women and Film: Both Sides of the Camera.* New York: Methuen, 1983.

Kaplan, E. Ann, and Ban Wang, eds. *Trauma and Cinema: Cross-Cultural Explorations.* Hong Kong: Hong Kong University Press, 2004.

Kaufman, Charles, and Wolfgang Reinhardt. *Freud.* Revised first draft screenplay. 14 April 1961. John Huston Collection, Margaret Herrick Library, Academy of Motion Picture Arts and Sciences, Beverly Hills, Calif.

———. *Freud.* First draft screenplay. 26 April 1961. John Huston Collection, Margaret Herrick Library, Academy of Motion Picture Arts and Sciences, Beverly Hills, Calif.

———. *Freud.* Final draft screenplay. 9 August 1961. John Huston Collection, Margaret Herrick Library, Academy of Motion Picture Arts and Sciences, Beverly Hills, Calif.

Kihlstrom, John F. "Exhumed Memory." In *Truth in Memory,* edited by Steven Jay Lynn and Kevin M. McConkey. New York: Guilford Press, 1998.

Kings Row file. Warner Bros. Archives. Doheny Library, School of Cinema-Television, University of Southern California, Los Angeles.

Kinsey, Alfred, Wardell B. Pomeroy, Clyde E. Martin, and Paul H. Gebhard. *Sexual Behavior in the Human Female.* Philadelphia: W. B. Saunders, 1953.

Kluft, Richard P., ed. *Childhood Antecedents of Multiple Personality,* Washington, D.C.: American Psychiatric Press, 1984.

Koch, Gertrud. "The Aesthetic Transformation of the Image of the Unimaginable: Notes on Claude Lanzmann's *Shoah.*" *October* 48 (Spring 1989): 15–24.

———. "The Angel of Forgetfulness and the Black Box of Facticity: Trauma and Memory in Claude Lanzmann's *Shoah.*" *History and Memory* 3, no. 1 (1991): 119–36.

Kuhn, Annette. *Women's Pictures: Feminism and Cinema.* London: Routledge and Kegan Paul, 1982.

LaCapra, Dominick. *History and Memory after Auschwitz.* Ithaca, N.Y.: Cornell University Press, 1998.

———. "Trauma, Absence, Loss." *Critical Inquiry* 25 (Summer 1999): 696–727.

Landsberg, Alison. *Prosthetic Memory: The Transformation of American Remembrance in the Age of Mass Culture.* New York: Columbia University Press, 2004.

Landy, Marcia. *Cinematic Uses of the Past.* Minneapolis: University of Minnesota Press, 1996.

Langer, Lawrence. *Holocaust Testimonies: The Ruins of Memory.* New Haven, Conn.: Yale University Press, 1991.

———. *Preempting the Holocaust.* New Haven, Conn.: Yale University Press, 1998.

Lanzmann, Claude. "Holocauste, le représentation impossible." *Le Monde,* 3 March 1994, "Arts et Spectacles," vii. Quoted and translated by Michael Rothberg in *Traumatic Realism.*

Laplanche, Jean. *Life and Death in Psychoanalysis.* Translated by Jeffrey Mehlman. Baltimore: Johns Hopkins University Press, 1976.

Laplanche, Jean, and J.-B. Pontalis. *The Language of Psycho-Analysis.* Translated by Donald Nicholson-Smith. New York: W. W. Norton, 1973.

Laub, Dori. "An Event without a Witness: Truth, Testimony, and Survival." In Shoshana Felman and Dori Laub, *Testimony: Crises of Witnessing in Literature, Psychoanalysis, and History.* New York: Routledge, 1992.

Lazo, Joy. "Comment: True or False: Expert Testimony on Repressed Memory."

Loyola of Los Angeles Law Review 28 (Summer 1995): 1345ff. Lexis-Nexis Academic. http://web.lexis-nexis.com/universe/document?m = 23a8e962c6c5fd362 35c4e3430814b73&docnum = 1&wchp = dGLbVtz-zSkVA&md5 = 36ca66c0d2 2673bd54b8607e3708ba20.

Lefkowitz, Deborah. "On Silence and Other Disruptions." In *Feminism and Documentary,* edited by Diane Waldman and Janet Walker. Minneapolis: Minnesota University Press, 1999.

Leopard, Dan. "I Was Lynn Hershman's Cameraperson, or The Interplay of Authorship in the Field of Competitive Production." Paper presented at the annual meeting of the Society for Cinema Studies, Denver, Colorado, 23–26 May 2002.

Lesage, Julia. "Women's Fragmented Consciousness in Feminist Experimental Autobiographical Video." In *Feminism and Documentary,* edited by Diane Waldman and Janet Walker. Minneapolis: Minnesota University Press, 1999.

Lewin, Tamar. "Judge Upsets Murder Conviction Focused on 'Repressed Memory.'" *New York Times,* 5 April 1995, 18.

Leys, Ruth. *Trauma: A Genealogy.* Chicago: University of Chicago Press, 2000.

Lief, Harold I., comp. "Medical Symptoms of Sexual Abuse in Children." In *Medical Aspects of Human Sexuality: 750 Questions Answered by 500 Authorities.* Baltimore: Williams and Wilkins, 1975.

Lionnet, Françoise. *Autobiographical Voice: Race, Gender, Self-Portraiture.* Ithaca, N.Y.: Cornell University Press, 1989.

Lipstadt, Deborah. *Denying the Holocaust: The Growing Assault on Truth and Memory.* New York: Plume, 1993.

Liss, Andrea. *Trespassing through Shadows: Memory, Photography, and the Holocaust.* Minneapolis: Minnesota University Press, 1998.

Loftus, Elizabeth, and Katherine Ketcham. *The Myth of Repressed Memory: False Memories and Allegations of Sexual Abuse.* New York: St. Martin's Press, 1994.

Loshitzky, Yosefa. "Holocaust Others: Spielberg's *Schindler's List* versus Lanzmann's *Shoah.*" In *Spielberg's Holocaust: Critical Perspectives on "Schindler's List,"* edited by Yosefa Loshitzky. Bloomington: Indiana University Press, 1997.

———. "Hybrid Victims: Second-Generation Israelis Screen the Holocaust." In *Visual Culture and the Holocaust,* edited by Barbie Zelizer. New Brunswick, N.J.: Rutgers University Press, 2001.

———. *Identity Politics on the Israeli Screen.* Austin: University of Texas Press, 2001.

———, ed. *Spielberg's Holocaust: Critical Perspectives on "Schindler's List."* Bloomington: Indiana University Press, 1997.

Lowenthal, David. *The Past Is a Foreign Country.* Cambridge: Cambridge University Press, 1985.

———. *Possessed by the Past: The Heritage Crusade and the Spoils of History.* New York: Free Press, 1996.

Lukacher, Ned. Introduction to *Psychoanalyzing Psychoanalysis: Freud and the Hidden Fault of the Father,* by Marie Balmary, translated by Ned Lukacher. Baltimore: Johns Hopkins University Press, 1982.

Lynn, Steven Jay, and Kevin M. McConkey, eds. *Truth in Memory.* New York: Guilford Press, 1998.

Lyotard, Jean-Francois. *Heidegger and "the Jews."* Translated by Andreas Michel and Mark S. Roberts. Minneapolis: University of Minnesota Press, 1990.

Mächler, Stefan. *The Wilkomirski Affair: A Study in Biographical Truth.* Translated by John E. Woods. New York: Schocken Books, 2001.

Mamber, Stephen. *Cinema Verite in America: Studies in Uncontrolled Documentary.* Cambridge, Mass.: MIT Press, 1974.

Marcus, Laura. *Auto/biographical Discourses: Theory, Criticism, Practice.* Manchester and New York: Manchester University Press, 1995.

Marcuse, Harold. Verbal response to Douglas Greenberg's presentation, "Return with Me Now to Those Days of Yesteryear," at the panel How Technology Presents Opportunities for Making History Education More Immediate, Gevirtz School of Education, University of California, Santa Barbara, 23 February 2001.

Marks, Laura. "Fetishes and Fossils: Notes on Documentary and Materiality." In *Feminism and Documentary,* edited by Diane Waldman and Janet Walker. Minneapolis: Minnesota University Press, 1999.

Masson, Jeffrey. *The Assault on Truth: Freud's Suppression of the Seduction Theory.* New York: Penguin, 1984.

Mendelsohn, Daniel. "What Happened to Uncle Shmiel?" *New York Times Magazine,* 14 July 2002, cover story.

Mertz, Elizabeth, and Kimberly A. Lonsway. "The Power of Denial: Individual and Cultural Constructions of Child Sexual Abuse." *Northwestern Law Review* 92, no. 4 (Summer 1998): 1415–58.

Mintz, Alan. *Popular Culture and the Shaping of Holocaust Memory.* Seattle: University of Washington Press, 2001.

Mitchell, Juliet. *Psychoanalysis and Feminism: Freud, Reich, Laing and Women.* New York: Vintage, 1975.

Mitchell, Juliet, and Jacqueline Rose, eds. *Feminine Sexuality: Jacques Lacan and the École Freudienne.* New York: Macmillan, 1982.

Morrison, Toni. *Beloved.* New York: Alfred A. Knopf, 1987.

Muñoz, José Esteban. *Disidentifications: Queers of Color and the Performance of Politics.* Minneapolis: University of Minnesota Press, 1999.

Nash, Michael. "Psychotherapy and Reports of Early Sexual Trauma: A Conceptual Framework for Understanding Memory Errors." In *Truth in Memory,* edited by Steven Jay Lynn and Kevin M. McConkey. New York: Guilford Press, 1998.

Nichols, Bill. *Blurred Boundaries: Questions of Meaning in Contemporary Culture.* Bloomington: Indiana University Press, 1994.

———. *Representing Reality: Issues and Concepts in Documentary.* Bloomington: Indiana University Press, 1991.

Novick, Peter. "Holocaust Memory in America." In *The Art of Memory: Holocaust Memorials in History,* edited by James E. Young. New York: Prestel, 1994.

Ofshe, Richard, and Ethan Watters. *Making Monsters: False Memories, Psychotherapy and Sexual Hysteria.* New York: Charles Scribner's Sons, 1994.

Payne, David G., and Jason M. Blackwell. "Truth in Memory: Caveat Emptor." In *Truth in Memory,* edited by Steven Jay Lynn and Kevin M. McConkey. New York: Guilford Press, 1998.

Pendergrast, Mark. *Victims of Memory: Incest Accusations and Shattered Lives.* Hinesburg, Vt.: Upper Access Books, 1995.

Pezdek, Kathy, and William P. Banks, eds. *The Recovered Memory/False Memory Debate.* San Diego: Academic Press, 1996.

Poppy, Nick. "One Family's Elusive Truth: Andrew Jarecki's *Capturing the Friedmans.*" indieWIRE. www.indiewire.com/people/people030530jarecki.html.

Prentky, Robert A., Raymond A. Knight, and Austin F. S. Lee. "Child Sexual Molestation: Research Issues." National Institute of Justice Research Report. U.S. Department of Justice. June 1997. www.ncjrs.org.

Putnam, Frank W. "Dissociation as a Response to Extreme Trauma." In *Childhood Antecedents of Multiple Personality,* edited by Richard P. Kluft. Washington, D.C.: American Psychiatric Press, 1987.

Radstone, Susannah, ed. *Memory and Methodology.* Oxford, England: Berg, 2000.

Radstone, Susannah, and Katharine Hodgkin, eds. *Regimes of Memory.* New York: Routledge, 2003.

Rauch, Angelika. "Post-Traumatic Hermeneutics: Melancholia in the Wake of Trauma." *Diacritics* 28, no. 4 (1998): 111–20.

Renov, Michael. *The Subject of Documentary.* Minneapolis: Minnesota University Press, 2004.

———. "Introduction: The Truth about Non-fiction," in *Theorizing Documentary,* edited by Michael Renov. New York: Routledge, 1993.

Renov, Michael, and Erika Suderburg, eds. *Resolutions: Contemporary Video Practices.* Minneapolis: Minnesota University Press, 1996.

Reviere, Susan L. *Memory of Childhood Trauma: A Clinician's Guide to the Literature.* New York: Guilford Press, 1996.

Rody, Caroline. "Toni Morrison's *Beloved*: History, 'Rememory,' and a 'Clamor for a Kiss.'" In *Understanding Toni Morrison's "Beloved" and "Sula": Selected Essays and Criticism of the Works by the Nobel Prize-Winning Author,* edited by Solomon O. Iyasere and Marla W. Iyasere. Troy, N.Y.: Whitson Publishing, 2000.

Rose, Jacqueline. "An Interview with Jacqueline Rose." Interview by Maire

Jaanus and Michael Payne. In *Why War? Psychoanalysis, Politics, and the Return to Melanie Klein,* 231–55. Cambridge, Mass.: Blackwell, 1993.

Rosenstone, Robert. "The Future of the Past: Film and the Beginnings of Postmodern History." In *The Persistence of History: Cinema, Television, and the Modern Event,* edited by Vivian Sobchack. New York: Routledge, 1996.

Rosenthal, Alan, ed. *New Challenges for Documentary.* Berkeley: University of California Press, 1988.

Roth, Michael. "*Shoah* as Shivah." Chap. 13 in *The Ironist's Cage: Memory, Trauma, and the Construction of History.* New York: Columbia University Press, 1995.

Rothberg, Michael. *Traumatic Realism: The Demands of Holocaust Representation.* Minneapolis: University of Minnesota Press, 2000.

Rush, Florence. *The Best Kept Secret: Sexual Abuse of Children.* Englewood Cliffs, N.J.: Prentice Hall, 1980.

Russell, Diana E. H. *The Secret Trauma: Incest in the Lives of Girls and Women.* 1986. Rev. ed. with a new introduction, New York: Basic Books, 1999.

Sacco, Lynn. "Incest Survivors and Feminist Activism: An Historical Examination of the Relationships between the Recovery Movement and Social Challenges." Master's thesis, State University of New York at Buffalo, 1996.

———. *A Noisy Silence: A History of Father-Daughter Incest in the United States.* Baltimore: Johns Hopkins University Press, forthcoming.

———. "Not Talking about 'It': A History of Incest in the United States, 1890–1940." Ph.D. diss., University of Southern California, Los Angeles, 2001.

Sartre, Jean-Paul. *The Freud Scenario,* edited by J.-B. Pontalis and translated by Quintin Hoare. Chicago: University of Chicago Press, 1985.

Schacter, Daniel. *Searching for Memory: The Brain, the Mind, and the Past.* New York: Basic Books, 1996.

———. *The Seven Sins of Memory: How the Mind Forgets and Remembers.* Boston: Houghton Mifflin, 2001.

Schreiber, Flora Rheta. *Sybil.* Chicago: Henry Regnery, 1973.

Scott, Ann. "Screen Memory/False Memory Syndrome." *Feminism and Psychology* 7, no. 1 (February 1997): 17–21.

Shay, Jonathan. *Achilles in Vietnam.* New York: Atheneum, 1994.

Showalter, Elaine. *Hystories: Hysterical Epidemics and Modern Media.* New York: Columbia University Press, 1997.

Shurlock, Geoffrey M. Memorandum. 21 September 1960. Production Code Administration files, Margaret Herrick Library, Academy of Motion Picture Arts and Sciences, Beverly Hills, Calif.

Singer, Mark. "The Friendly Executioner: How Did an Electric-Chair Repairman Come to Deny the Holocaust? And Other Odd Questions." *New Yorker,* 1 February 1999, 33–39.

———. "Profiles; Errol Morris." *New Yorker,* 6 February 1989, 38–72.

Sitney, P. Adams. "Autobiography in Avant-Garde Film." *Millennium Film Journal* 1, no. 1 (Winter 1977): 60–105.

Smith, Sidonie, and Julia Watson, eds. *Women, Autobiography, Theory: A Reader.* Madison: University of Wisconsin Press, 1998.

Smith, Valerie. *Self-Discovery and Authority in African-American Narratives.* Urbana: University of Illinois Press, 1979.

Snyder, Howard N. "Sexual Assault of Young Children as Reported to Law Enforcement: Victim, Incident, and Offender Characteristics." Statistical report using data from the National Incident-Based Reporting System. National Center for Juvenile Justice, July 2000, NCJJ 182990. www.ojp.usdoj.gov/bjs/pub/pdf/saycrle.pdf.

Sobchack, Vivian. "Inscribing Ethical Space: Ten Propositions on Death, Representation, and Documentary." *Quarterly Review of Film Studies* 9, no. 4 (Fall 1984): 283–300.

———. "Introduction: History Happens." In *The Persistence of History: Cinema, Television, and the Modern Event,* edited by Vivian Sobchack. New York: Routledge, 1996.

———, ed. *The Persistence of History: Cinema, Television, and the Modern Event.* New York: Routledge, 1996.

Spiegelman, Art. *Maus: A Survivor's Tale.* New York: Pantheon Books, 1986.

———. *Maus II: A Survivor's Tale: And Here My Troubles Began.* New York: Pantheon Books, 1991.

Sturken, Marita. *Tangled Memories: The Vietnam War, the AIDS Epidemic, and the Politics of Remembering.* Berkeley: University of California Press, 1997.

Tal, Kalí. *Worlds of Hurt: Reading the Literatures of Trauma.* Cambridge: Cambridge University Press, 1996.

Terr, Lenore. *Too Scared to Cry: Psychic Trauma in Childhood.* New York: HarperCollins, 1990.

———. "True Memories of Childhood Trauma: Flaws, Absences, and Returns." In *The Recovered Memory/False Memory Debate,* edited by Kathy Pezdek and William P. Banks. San Diego: Academic Press, 1996.

———. *Unchained Memories: True Stories of Traumatic Memories, Lost and Found.* New York: Basic Books, 1994.

Thelen, David. "Memory and American History." *Journal of American History* 75, no. 4 (March 1989): 1117–29.

Turim, Maureen. *Flashbacks in Film: Memory and History.* New York: Routledge, 1989.

Turner, Fred. *Echoes of Combat: Trauma, Memory, and the Vietnam War.* Minneapolis: University of Minnesota Press, 1996.

Ullman, Richard, and Doris Brothers. *The Shattered Self: A Psychoanalytic Study of Trauma.* Hillsdale, N.J.: Analytic Press, 1988.

Vistica, Gregory L. "One Awful Night in Thanh Phong." *New York Times Magazine,* 25 April 2001.

Waites, Elizabeth. *Trauma and Survival: Post-Traumatic and Dissociative Disorders in Women.* New York: W. W. Norton, 1993.

Waldman, Diane, and Janet Walker. "John Huston's *Freud* and Textual Repression: A Psychoanalytic Feminist Reading." In *Close Viewings: An Anthology of New Film Criticism,* edited by Peter Lehman. Tallahassee: Florida State University Press, 1990.

———, eds. *Feminism and Documentary.* Minneapolis: Minnesota University Press, 1999.

Walker, Janet. *Couching Resistance: Women, Film, and Psychoanalytic Psychiatry.* Minneapolis: Minnesota University Press, 1993.

———. "Trauma Cinema: False Memories and True Experience." *Screen* 42, no. 2 (Summer 2001): 211–16.

———. "The Traumatic Paradox: Documentary Films, Historical Fictions, and Cataclysmic Past Events." *Signs* 22, no. 4 (Summer 1997): 803–25. Reworked and republished as "The Traumatic Paradox: Autobiographical Documentary and the Psychology of Memory," in *Contested Pasts: The Politics of Memory,* edited by Katharine Hodgkin and Susannah Radstone (New York: Routledge, 2003).

———. "The Vicissitudes of Traumatic Memory and the Postmodern History Film." In *Trauma and Cinema: Cross-Cultural Explorations,* edited by E. Ann Kaplan and Ban Wang. Hong Kong: Hong Kong University Press, 2004.

Wardi, Dina. *Memorial Candles: Children of the Holocaust.* Translated by Naomi Goldblum. New York: Routledge, 1992.

Wealin, Julia. "Child Sexual Abuse: A National Center for PTSD Fact Sheet." National Center for PTSD, White River Junction, Vt. May 2003. www.ncptsd .org/facts/specific/fs.

White, Hayden. "Historical Emplotment and the Problem of Truth." In *Probing the Limits of Representation: Nazism and the "Final Solution,"* edited by Saul Friedlander. Cambridge, Mass.: Harvard University Press, 1992.

———. *Metahistory: The Historical Imagination in Nineteenth-Century Europe.* Baltimore: Johns Hopkins University Press, 1973.

———. "The Modernist Event." In *The Persistence of History: Cinema, Television, and the Modern Event,* edited by Vivian Sobchack. New York: Routledge, 1996.

Williams, Linda. "Mirrors without Memories: Truth, History, and the New Documentary." *Film Quarterly* 46, no. 3 (Spring 1993): 9–21.

Williams, Linda, and B. Ruby Rich. "The Right of Re-Vision: Michelle Citron's *Daughter Rite.*" Vol. 2 of *Movies and Methods,* edited by Bill Nichols. Berkeley: University of California Press, 1985.

Williams, Linda Meyer. "Adult Memories of Child Sexual Abuse: Placing Sexual Assault in Long-Term Perspective." Paper presented at the World Conference of the International Society for Traumatic Studies. Trauma and Tragedy: The Origins, Management and Prevention of Traumatic Stress in Today's World, Amsterdam, 1992.

———. "Recall of Childhood Trauma: A Prospective Study of Women's Memories of Child Sexual Abuse." *Journal of Consulting and Clinical Psychology* 62, no. 6 (1994): 1167–76.

———. "Recovered Memories of Abuse in Women with Documented Child Sexual Victimization Histories," *Journal of Traumatic Stress* 8 (1995): 649–74.

Young, James E. "Holocaust Video and Cinemagraphic Testimony: Documenting the Witness." Chap. 9 in *Writing and Rewriting the Holocaust: Narrative and the Consequences of Interpretation.* Bloomington: Indiana University Press, 1988.

Zelizer, Barbie. *Visual Culture and the Holocaust.* New Brunswick, N.J.: Rutgers University Press, 2001.

Zündel, Ernst. Zündelsite Zgram. 6 October 1999 and 7 October 1999. www .revisionists.com/leuchter/mrdeath/zgramoctober6–99zundelreview1.htm and www.revisionists.com/leuchter/mrdeath/zgramoctober7–99zundelreview2 .htm. Accessed 22 April 2001.

9/11. 2002, 112 min. Directed by James Hanlon, Gedeon Naudet, and Jules
Naudet. Originally aired 10 March 2002 on CBS. CBS Television, Goldfish
Productions, Reveille Productions, and Silverstar Pictures. Widely available on
DVD and VHS at major video rental and sales outlets.

Attic Secrets. 1998, 11 min. Directed by Heidi Bollock. Evergreen State College,
Olympia, Wash. To procure, contact Little Chicken Productions, 8107 Rock-
wood Lane, Austin, Tex., 78757; phone: 512–470–5261. Or contact Heidi
Bollock at hbollock@yahoo.com.

Beneath the Veil. 2001, 60 min. CNN feature documentary. Created and reported
by Saira Shah. Produced and directed by Cassian Harrison. Originally aired
in Britain in June 2001 and cablecast on CNN on 26 August 2001. CNN Productions, Hardcash Productions, and Channel Four Television Group. Visit
the documentary's listing on the CNN Web site at www.cnn.com/CNN/
Programs/presents/index.veil.html.

Capturing the Friedmans. 2003, 107 min. Directed by Andrew Jarecki. HBO
Documentary and Notorious Pictures. Widely available on DVD at major
video rental and sales outlets. Visit the film's official Web site at www
.capturingthefriedmans.com/main.html.

Daughter Rite. 1979, 53 min. Directed by Michelle Citron. Available on VHS
through Women Make Movies at www.wmm.com/catalog/pages/c356.htm.
Visit Michelle Citron's Web site at http://pubweb.acns.nwu.edu/~citron/index
.html.

Displaced Person. 1981, 10 1/2 min. 16 mm. Directed by Daniel Eisenberg. To procure, contact The Film-Makers' Cooperative, c/o Clocktower Gallery, 108

Leonard Street, 13th floor, New York, N.Y., 10013; phone: 212–267–5665; fax: 212–267–5666; e-mail: film6000@aol.com.; Web site: www.film-makerscoop .com/.

Divided Memories. 1995, 240 min. Two-part "Frontline" series. Produced by Ofra Bikel, U.S.A. Part 1 originally aired 4 April 1995 on PBS. Part 2 originally aired 11 April 1995 on PBS. Visit the "Frontline" report archive at www.pbs .org/wgbh/pages/frontline/programs/1995.html.

The Electronic Diary. Video series, 1984–96. Directed by Lynn Hershman Leeson. *Confessions of a Chameleon* (1986), *Binge* (1987), *First Person Plural* (1989), *Re Covered Diary* (1994). To procure, contact Hotwire Productions, 1261 Howard, San Francisco, Calif., 94103; phone: 415–626–9947; fax: 415–626– 9948; e-mail: hotwirelh@aol.com. Visit Lynn Hershman Leeson's Web site at www.lynnhershman.com/.

Everything's for You. 1989, 58 min. 16 mm. Directed by Abraham Ravett. Distributed by Canadian Filmmakers Distribution Center, Canyon Cinema, and The National Center for Jewish Film. Available on VHS from the filmmaker or from his distributors at www.cfmdc.org/, www.canyoncinema.com/rentsale .html, and www.brandeis.edu/jewishfilm/distr.html. Contact Abraham Ravett at aravett@hampshire.edu, or visit his Web site at http://helios.hampshire.edu/ ~arPF/.

Fatal Memories: The Eileen Franklin Story. 1992, 100 min. Directed by Daryl Duke. MGM Television. Originally aired on 9 November 1992 on NBC. Available on VHS at specialty video outlets.

Freud. 1962, 139 min. Directed by John Huston. Universal International Pictures. Available on VHS at specialty video sales outlets.

History and Memory: For Akiko and Takashige. 1991, 32 min. Directed by Rea Tajiri. Available on VHS through Women Make Movies at www.wmm.com/ Catalog/pages/c111.htm, through the Video Data Bank at www.vdb.org/, and through Electronic Arts Intermix at www.eai.org/eai/tape.jsp?itemID=4027.

Intervals of Silence: Being Jewish in Germany. 1990, 58 min. Directed by Deborah Lefkowitz. To procure, contact Deborah Lefkowitz/Lefkowitz Films, P.O. Box 94, Riverside, Calif., 92502; phone: 909–682–0444.

Just, Melvin: Just Evil. 2000, 96 min. Directed by James Ronald Whitney. Production 920. For information on how to procure, visit the film's official Web site at www.justmelvin.com/. Or contact James Ronald Whitney, 666 5th Avenue, Suite 344, New York, N.Y., 10103; phone: 917–319–4957; e-mail: Whitneyjrw@aol.com.

Kings Row. 1942, 127 min. Directed by Sam Wood. Warner Brothers. Available on VHS at specialty video sales outlets.

The Last Days. 1998, 87 min. Directed by James Moll. Ken Lipper/Julie Beallor Production and Shoah Foundation. Widely available on DVD and VHS at major video rental and sales outlets.

Liar, Liar. 1992, 90 min. Directed by Jorge Montesi. Phil Savath and Canadian Broadcasting Corporation, Canada. Originally aired in the United States 22 June 1993. To procure, go to www.cbc.ca/homevideo/Drama/Liar.htm. Or contact the CBC Home Video Products Boutique directly at CBC Boutique, P.O. Box 500, Station A, Toronto, ON, M5W 1E6, Canada; phone: 800–955–7711; fax: 416–205–2139.

The March. 1999, 25 min. 16 mm. Directed by Abraham Ravett. Distributed by Canyon Cinema; Light Cone, Paris; and The National Center for Jewish Film. Available on VHS from the filmmaker or from his distributors at www .canyoncinema.com/rentsale.html and www.brandeis.edu/jewishfilm/distr .html. Contact Abraham Ravett at aravett@hampshire.edu, or visit his Web site at http://helios.hampshire.edu/~arPF/.

Mr. Death: The Rise and Fall of Fred A. Leuchter, Jr. 1999, 91 min. Directed by Errol Morris. Channel Four Films, Fourth Floor Pictures, Independent Film Channel, and Scout Productions. Widely available on DVD and VHS at video rental and sales outlets. Visit Errol Morris's Web site at www.errolmorris.com/.

Scared Silent: Exposing and Ending Child Abuse. 1992, 51 min. Directed by Melissa Jo Peltier. Distributed by ABC, CBS, NBC, and PBS. To procure, contact AIMS Multimedia, 9710 De Soto Avenue, Chatsworth, Calif., 91311; phone: 800–367–2467 (extension 343); fax: 818–341–6700; e-mail: www .aimsmultimedia.com.

Scared Silent: Incest. 1994, 22 min. Directed by Melissa Jo Peltier. MPH Entertainment. To procure, contact AIMS Multimedia, 9710 De Soto Avenue, Chatsworth, Calif., 91311; phone: 800–367–2467 (ext. 306); fax: 818–341–6700; e-mail: www.aimsmultimedia.com. Or contact MPH Entertainment; phone: 818–441–5040.

Second Generation Video. 1995, 24 min. Directed by Joshua Hirsch. Not in regular distribution. To procure, contact The National Center for Jewish Film, Brandeis University, Lown 102, MS053, Waltham, Mass., 02454; phone: 781–899–7044; fax 781–736–2070; e-mail: ncjf@brandeis.edu; Web site: www .brandeis.edu/jewishfilm/distr.html.

Shattered Trust: The Shari Karney Story. 1993, 94 min. Directed by Bill Corcoran. Produced by John Danylkiw. Originally aired 27 September 1993 on NBC. Not in regular distribution.

Shoah. 1985, 544 min. Directed by Claude Lanzmann. Historia, Les Films Aleph, Ministère de la Culture de la Republique Française, France. Widely available on DVD and VHS at major video rental and sales outlets.

Some Nudity Required. 1998, 82 min. Directed by Odette Springer, co-directed by Johanna Demetrakas. Only Child Production. Available on VHS at major video sales outlets.

Sorrow: The Nazi Legacy. 1993, 33 min. Directed by Gregor Nowinski. Ergo Media. Available on VHS at specialty video sales outlets.

Sybil. 1976, 198 min. Directed by Daniel Petrie. Lorimar Productions. Originally aired 14–15 November 1976 on ABC. Available on VHS at specialty video sales outlets.

Tak for Alt: Survival of a Human Spirit. 1999, 61 min. Directed by Laura Bialis, Broderick Fox, and Sarah Levy. Sirena Films. Available on DVD and VHS at major video sales outlets and through Sirena Films at www.sirenafilms.com/ takforalt/HowtoOrder.html. Visit the film's official Web site at www.sirenafilms .com/takforalt/.

Thank You and Good Night. 1991, 77 min. Directed by Jan Oxenberg. American Playhouse, Channel Four Films, P.O.V. Films, Paul Cohen, Red Wagon Films, and Theatrical Films. To procure, contact Swank Motion Pictures, Saint Louis, Mo., 63103; phone: 800–876–5577.

The Thin Blue Line. 1988, 103 min. Directed by Errol Morris. American Playhouse. Available on DVD and VHS at major video sales outlets.

The Ties That Bind. 1984, 55 min. Directed by Su Friedrich. Available on VHS through Women Make Movies at www.wmm.com/catalog/pages/c19.htm. Or contact Canyon Cinema, 22325 Third Street, Suite 338, San Francisco, Calif., 94107; phone: 415–626–2255.

INDEX

Adams, Randall, 183–84
Adorno, Theodor, 128–29
"Aetiology of Hysteria, The" (Freud), 8
alien abduction, 6, 15–16
American Psychiatric Association (APA), 3,
    12
amnesia: as characteristic of childhood
    sexual abuse, 65–66; in *Daughter Rite,*
    95; as disremembering, 17; and dissocia-
    tion vs. repression, 44–45; and historical
    meaning, xvii, xix; and recurrent mem-
    ory, 89; in *Tak for Alt,* 156
animations, 163–64, 165
Anne Frank Remembered (film; 1995), xxi
anti-Semitism: Holocaust denial and, xxi,
    139; transferential repetition of, 78–79,
    108, 131–32, 136
Apocalypse Now (film; 1979), 20
Apted, Michael, 20, 21
archival footage: absent in *Shoah,* 133, 172;
    cinema continuum and, 24, 86; in con-
    ventional vs. unconventional Holocaust
    documentaries, 171–72; direct-address
    interviews mixed with, 140–42, 147;
    experimental documentary and, 128,
    152–53; in historical compilation form,

133; in *The Last Days,* 133–34, 138; re-
    enactment vs., 27
Armstrong, Louise, 16, 74, 77
Asch, Shalom, 148
Attic Secrets (film; 1998), 21
Auschwitz (concentration camp): disposi-
    tion of, changes in, 178–79; enactments
    at, 142–44; Holocaust denial and, 176–
    77; Holocaust tourism at, 175, 184–87;
    photography of, 174; pseudomemories
    of, 5–6; reenactments of, 136–37; Spiel-
    berg's recreation of gas chambers at, 133–
    34; survivor testimonies of, 145–46,
    170–71
autobiography: feminist critical literature
    on, 23; of second-generation Holocaust
    survivors, 29; in television documen-
    taries, 190–91; in traumatic documen-
    tary films, 21–23, 59–60, 81, 82, 86–87,
    214n15. *See also specific film*
"Autobiography in Avant-Garde Film"
    (Sitney), 86
avant-garde film, 214n15

Baer, Ulrich, 173, 174
Bafaloukos, Ted, 184

Balmary, Marie, 46
Basch, Bill, 140, 141, 144
Bass, Ellen, 66, 201n43
Before the Rain (film; 1994), 20
Bellamann, Henry, 33, 45. *See also Kings Row*
Beloved (Morrison), 17–18
Beneath the Veil (TV documentary; 2001), 190–92
Bernheimer, Charles, 42
Best Kept Secret (Rush), 209–10n18
Bialis, Laura, 21, 149, 172, 219n60. *See also Tak for Alt*
Bikel, Ofra, 13, 66, 72, 76, 79. *See also Divided Memories*
Binge (video; 1987), 97, 98, 99–100. *See also Electronic Diary*
Bin Laden, Osama, xvi
Blackwell, Jason M., 14
Blair, Jon, xxi
Blair Witch Project, The (film; 1999), 177
Blake, Groverman, 45
B movie industry: childhood sexual abuse and, 94–95, 112–13, 114; exploitative practices of, 90; women characters in, 214n13
Bollock, Heidi, 21
Bomba, Abraham, 131, 134, 135
Boyle, Lisa, 90, 92–93
Breen, Joseph, 38
Brief History of Time, A (film; 1991), 183
Brill, Leslie, 206n17
Brown, Laura, 75
Burstyn, Ellen, 61
Butler, Sandra, 52, 209n8

California Senate Bill 108, 62
camerawork, experimental, 152–53, 191
Capote, Truman, 18–19
Capturing the Friedmans (film; 2003), xxi; hidden meaning in, 120–21; historiography in, 142; home movies in, 117–19; *The Last Days* compared to, 142; transferential repetition in, 115–21
Caruth, Cathy, 145
Cassandra myth, 38–40
Catholic clergy, childhood sexual assault by, 195n4, 209n6

Cayrol, Jean, 139
censorship: of incest in film, 33–41, 205n1; and narrative strategy, 206n10
Champagne, Rosaria, 65
Chelmo massacre (Poland), 79, 107–8, 135
childhood sexual assault/molestation: and B movie industry, 94–95, 112–13, 114; disremembering of, 80–81; embellished memory as symptom of, 74–75; extent of, 50–52, 212n47; extrafamilial, 195n4, 209n6; health problems associated with, 209–10n18; in *Just, Melvin*, 103–4; offender profiles, 208n5, 209n8; police response to reports of, 211n38; recovered memories of, xvii, 6–7, 12–16; satanic ritual abuse, 6, 15–16, 74–75, 77–78, 213n56; seduction theory and, 199n25; terminology used for, 198n12; true/false dichotomy and, 195n4; unreported cases of, 208n3, 211n34; victim profiles, 208–9n6, 209n8. *See also* incestuous abuse
Chronicle of a Summer (film; 1960), 133
cinema continuum, 23–27, 86, 152–53
cinema verité: in *Electronic Diary* series, 111; fiction/documentary blurring in, 24; ironic use of, 184, 187; in *Just, Melvin*, 110; mockumentary vs., 88; in *Mr. Death*, 184, 187; in *Some Nudity Required*, 89–90
Citizen Kane (film; 1941), 102
Citron, Michelle, 21; on autobiographical fiction, 82; and direct-address interviews, 96; on ethical obligations of autobiographical filmmakers, 147; family incest history of, 82–83; on home movie sequences, 88. *See also Daughter Rite*
civil rights movement, 155
Civil War, The (TV documentary; 1990), 85
Clift, Montgomery, 40
Coburn, Charles, 36
Coleman, Nancy, 36
Collins, David, 186
Committee for Historical Review, xxi
Confessions of a Chameleon (video; 1986), 21, 98, 99–100. *See also Electronic Diary*
Conspiracy of Silence (Butler), 52, 209n8
Coppola, Francis Ford, 20

experimental documentary: as antirealist, 203n60; and Holocaust disremembering, 127–28; and representational taboos, 128–29; self-discovery in, 214n15; and social historical reconstruction, 114–21; strategies of, 128, 146–48, 189–90; and vicissitudes of memory, 81. *See also specific film*

eyewitness testimony: archival footage mixed with, 140–41; contradictory, 144, 183–84; historical value of, 134, 156, 189–90; and Holocaust documentary style, 149; and *The March*, 144–49; "memory wars" and, 69; reenactment and, 172; and rhetorical patterning in, 138–44

"false memory syndrome": binaristic explanation and, xviii; definition of, 196n8; invention of, 13, 64–66; social perception vs. reality, 212n47; television bias toward, 81; therapy as cause of, 71–73

False Memory Syndrome Foundation, 6, 116; advocacy campaign of, 12–13, 200n35; establishment of, 196n8; and incest denial, xxi, 64–66; membership of, 200n35; as umbrella organization, 71

family: patriarchal, and incest, 51, 65, 101–9; therapy as threat to, 70–72, 77

Family Gathering (film; 1988), 21

fantasy: exogenous trauma and, 74; as feature of memory, 6–12, 190, 204n80; film excision of incest and, 34; and historical meaning, xix; incest denial and, 41–43; memory continuum and, 16; propping and, 200n31; reenactment and, 26–27; spelling of, 199n21; split self and, 100. *See also* psychoanalysis

Fatal Memories (TV film; 1992), 53, 57–58, 67

Father-Daughter Incest (Herman), 51

Felman, Shoshana, 127; and "event-without-witness," xx, 103–4; LaCapra on, 132; and re-forgetting of Holocaust, 108; and *Shoah*, 108, 136, 137, 217n36; and witnessing, 4–5

feminism: and autobiographical documentary films, 59–60; and "memory wars,"

xvii, 12–16, 65; and psychoanalysis, 7–12, 201n40; and psychology, 6–16; and television programming, 28–29, 49–50

Feminism and Documentary (Waldman and Walker), 82, 89

fetish objects, 164–66

fiction, continuum with documentary. *See* cinema continuum

Field, Sally, 54, 60

Fields, Betty, 35

Finkelhor, David, 51

Firestone, Renée, 141, 142–43, 144

First Person Plural (video; 1989), 21, 97–98, 99, 100, 114–15. *See also Electronic Diary*

flashbacks: cinematic, 36–37, 40–41, 46–47, 60–64, 207–8n38; psychological, 10, 11, 153, 204n80. *See also specific film*

Flashbacks in Film (Turim), 36

Fliess, Wilhelm, 42, 206n19

Ford, Maria, 90, 93–94

Fórgacs, Péter, 204n79

forgetting, 95, 148–49, 153–54, 201n43

Fortunoff Video Archive (Yale University), 5, 125, 127

Fox, Broderick, 21, 149. *See also Tak for Alt*

fragmentation: of memory, 150, 151; as rhetorical strategy, 68

Fragments: Memories of a Wartime Childhood (Wilkomirski), xvii

Frankel, Fred H., 204n80

Frank, Hans, 175

Franklin, George, 6–7, 67, 68

Franklin-Lipsker, Eileen. *See* Lipsker, Eileen Franklin

Frank, Niklas, 175

Freud (film; 1962): clinical research and, 207n23; flashbacks in, 207–8n38; incest denial in, 41–43, 206n17, 207–8n38; incest excised from, 28, 33–34; repression in, 44; structuring principle of, 40–41; textual dissociation in, 45–47; women's experience rewritten in, 54

Freud, Sigmund, 7–8, 34, 41–42, 50, 198n12, 206n19

Friedlander, Saul, xvii–xviii, 14, 22–23; and "limits of representation," 173

Friedman, Arnold, 116–21

home movies (continued)
    September 11 attacks, xvi–xvii; in televi-
    sion documentaries, 68; and transferen-
    tial repetition, 117–19; traumatic docu-
    mentaries and, 86, 191. See also specific
    film
Home Movies and Other Necessary Fictions
    (Citron), 82–83, 89, 96, 118
Horvitz, Deborah, 17
Huston, John, 28, 207n38. See also Freud
Hystories (Showalter), 15–16

incest and Holocaust discourse: compari-
    son of, xix–xxii; and forgetting, 148; and
    historiography, 126–27; and representa-
    tional taboos, 128–29
incest denial, xxi, 15–16; in Divided
    Memories, 67–81; in Freud, 41–43,
    206n17; in Just, Melvin, 105–8; in Kings
    Row, 36; and "memory wars," xxi, 64–
    66; and scientific proof, 209n7
incest survivor recovery movement, 50, 65.
    See also specific film
incestuous abuse: corroboration of, 201n38;
    definition of, 52; extent of, 50–52;
    father-daughter, 206n19; feminist writ-
    ing on, 51–52, 64–66; film excision of,
    33–41, 205n1; Holocaust compared to,
    xix–xx; home movies and, 118; television
    movies and, 49–50, 52–54; transferential
    repetition of, 108, 113–21. See also child-
    hood sexual abuse/molestation; psychol-
    ogy of trauma/memory; specific film
infantile neurosis, 42–43
"Influence of Infantile Trauma on Genetic
    Patterns, The" (Greenacre), 43
Intervals of Silence (film; 1990), 128
interviews: historiography and, 142; staging
    of, 135–36; translation of, 134–35. See
    also direct-address interviews
Into the Arms of Strangers (film; 2000), xxi
Irving, David, 180
Israel, Holocaust denial and, xxi

Jacobs, Lea, 206n10
James, David, 97–98, 214n15
Janet, Pierre, 8

Jarecki, Andrew, xxi, 117. See also Capturing
    the Friedmans
JFK (film; 1991), 20
John D., Mary D. v., 57
Journal of the American Psychoanalytic
    Association, 43
Journal of Traumatic Stress, 15
Just, Melvin, 101–9, 135
Just, Melvin (film; 2000): home movies in,
    101–2; incest denial in, 105–8; inter-
    views in, 192; reenactment in, 109–10;
    Shoah compared to, 103, 104, 107–8;
    textual dissociation in, 102, 192; transfer-
    ential repetition in, 108; and traumatic
    historiography, 29; witnessing in, xx,
    103–5, 109

Karney, Shari, 56, 57, 58, 62. See also
    Shattered Trust
Kaufman, Charles, 33
Kerrey, Bob, 28
Ketcham, Katherine, 13, 67
Kihlstrom, John, 12, 14
Kingsley, Ben, 130
Kings Row (film; 1942): incest excised in,
    28, 33, 35–40, 205n2; repression in, 44;
    textual dissociation in, 45; women's
    experience rewritten in, 54
Kinsey, Alfred, 51–52
Koch, Gertrud, 129, 133, 137

LaCapra, Dominick: on creation in post-
    traumatic condition, 129; on Maus, 167;
    and Shoah, 131–32, 137, 217n36, 218nn38,
    44
Landis, Carney, 51
Landsberg, Alison, 137
Langer, Lawrence, 127
Language of Psycho-Analysis, The
    (Laplanche and Pontalis), 198n12, 199n21
Lantos, Tom, 141, 144
Lanzmann, Claude, 29; enactment by,
    107–8, 135–36; on Schindler's List, 133;
    on Shoah as "fiction of reality," 129–30,
    218n38; and Shoah interviews, 79, 134–
    35; Williams on, 106. See also Shoah
Laplanche, Jean, 3, 9, 198n12, 199nn21, 23

and memory, 4–6; and history, 131–37. *See also* fantasy
psychology of trauma/memory, xix, 3–4, 44–45, 59, 74; feminist writing on, 6–16. *See also* memory

Radstone, Susannah, 9–10
Rains, Claude, 35
Ramona, Gary, 67
Ravett, Abraham, 29; and *Everything's for You,* 158–59, 160–66, 168–70; interview style of, 163; and *The March,* 146–48; and *Thirty Years Later,* 169–70. *See also Everything's for You; March, The*
Ravett, Chaim, 158–59, 160–66, 168–69
Ravett, Fela, 145–49, 156–57
RAWA (Revolutionary Association of Women of Afghanistan), 191
Reagan, Ronald, 35
realism: and documentary film, 82, 111–12, 127–28, 149–50; Hollywood classical, 66, 203n60; inadequacy of, 167; and *Maus/Maus II,* 167; and television documentaries, 66–68; and television movies, 58, 81
reality television, 84–85, 110
Re Covered Diary (video; 1994), 110–12, 114, 136. *See also Electronic Diary*
reenactment: in *Capturing the Friedmans,* 116–17; cinema continuum and, 24, 25–27; enactment and, 109, 135–36, 144, 172; in the *Electronic Diary* series, 110–12; experimental documentary and, 149–53, 191, 219n60; in *Just, Melvin,* 109–10; psychological impact of, 172; re-creation vs., 183–84; in *Some Nudity Required,* 112–13; in *Tak for Alt,* 25–27, 149–52; traumatic documentaries and, 86, 87, 109. *See also specific film*
Reinartz, Dirk, 174
Reinhardt, Wolfgang, 33
relics, 173–74
Renoir, Jean, 24
Renov, Michael, 25, 166
repetition, transferential: disremembering and, 192–93; historiography and, 189–90; of past anti-Semitism in the present,

78–79, 107–8, 131–32, 136, 147–48; of past incestuous patterns in the present, 108, 113–21
Representing Reality (Nichols), 25
repression: definition of, 43–44; exogenous trauma and, 74; forgetting vs., 201–2n43; incomplete, and remembrance, 95; textual excision as, 34, 43–45
resistance, 78–79, 116–17, 148
Resnais, Alain, 20
Reviere, Susan, 10, 11, 14
Revolutionary Association of Women of Afghanistan (RAWA), 191
Rewriting the Soul (Hacking), 73
Richardson, Robert, 221n35
Rivera, Geraldo, 84–85
Rody, Catherine, 17–18
Rose, Jacqueline, 10
Rose, Kate. *See* Norris, Anne
Rosenstone, Robert, 22
Rothberg, Michael, 126, 132–33, 136–37, 203n60, 217n36
Roth, James, 178
Rouch, Jean, 133
Rules of the Game (film; 1939), 24
Rush, Florence, 8, 208n5, 209–10n18
Russell, Diana, 51, 52, 65, 211n38, 213n56

Sacco, Lynn, 50–51, 65, 209n7
Sampson, Caleb, 186
Sartre, Jean-Paul, 33, 45–46
satanic ritual abuse, 6, 15–16, 74–75, 77–78, 213n56
Saving Private Ryan (film; 1998), 20, 62
Scared Silent: Exposing and Ending Child Abuse (TV documentary; 1992), 53
Scared Silent: Incest (TV documentary; 1994), 53
Schindler's List (film; 1993), 126, 129–30, 144, 154
second-generation Holocaust survivors: as celebration of survivorship, 144; disremembering by, 29; distancing and, 170–71; films/videos by, 174–75, 187–88; and generational cycle, 168–69; postmemory and, 159–60, 172. *See also Everything's for You; Mr. Death; Second Generation Video*

"memory wars" and, 67–73, 212n47;
rage therapy, 71–72; regression therapy,
69–70; in *Shattered Trust*, 61–62; in
Sybil, 54–55, 58
Thin Blue Line, The (film; 1988): musical
score of, 156; re-creations in, 183–84;
reenactment in, 20, 62, 136; Zündel and,
180–81
Thirty Years Later (film; 1978), 169–70
Thompson, *Urie v.*, 56–57
Thunderheart (film; 1992), 20
Ties That Bind, The (film; 1984), 22–23
trauma: definition of, 3, 11; as socio-politi-
cal legacy, xv-xvi, xviii–xix
Trauma and Recovery (Herman), 11
Trauma and Survival (Waites), 44
trauma cinema: cinema continuum and,
23–27; definition of, 19; feminist autobiographical documentary and, 21–23;
historiography in, 189–90; holocaustal
events in, 19–21
traumatic paradox, xviii, 4
traumatic realism, 203n60
Traumatic Realism (Rothberg), 217n36
trauma/traumatic documentary: definition
of, 84–86; direct address interviews and,
86–87; enactment in, 87; historical
documentary vs., 87; home movies as
recurrent memory in, 87–95; realist
pretensions of, 82; reenactment in, 109–
13; and social historical reconstruction,
114–21; strategies of, 86–87; textual
dissociation in, 95–101. *See also specific
film*
Triumph of the Will (film; 1935), 115, 180
Turim, Maureen, 36

Unchained Memories (Terr), 6–7
Urie v. Thompson, 56–57
U.S. Holocaust Memorial Museum
(Washington, D.C.), 126, 138, 218n51
U.S. Supreme Court, 56–57

Van Pelt, Robert Jan, 178–79, 184–86
Vidal-Naquet, Pierre, 181
video: as documentation, 177, 184–87; self-
discovery in, 214n15
Video Archive for Holocaust Testimonies

(Yale University). *See* Fortunoff Video
Archive
Vietnam: A Television History (TV documentary; 1983), 96
voice-over narration: direct-address interviews mixed with, 177, 181; enactment
mixed with, 185; and home movies, 91–
92, 93; and journalistic balance, 68, 71–
72; witnessing and, 104. *See also specific
film*

Waites, Elizabeth: and Freudian psycho-
analysis, 10, 44; and traumatic memory,
4, 11, 14, 44, 74
Waldman, Diane, 8, 9, 45–46
Walker, Janet, 8, 9, 45–46, 210n23
Wardi, Dina, 159, 173
Watters, Ethan, 13
White, Hayden, 19–21, 170
Whitney, James Ronald, xx, 29, 101–9, 114,
135. *See also Just, Melvin*
Wiener, Reinhard, 138, 197n16, 218n51
Wilbur, Cornelia, 54–55
Wilkomirski, Benjamin, xvii
Williams, Linda: on postmodern docu-
mentaries, 22, 85, 106, 108, 136; and
Shoah, 78–79, 133, 137
Winfrey, Oprah, 53
witnessing: and desire for corroboration,
46; erasure of, xx, 103–5, 197n16; false,
108; as transferential, 37–38. *See also*
eyewitness testimony
Wood, Sam, 28, 33. *See also Kings Row*
Woodward, Joanne, 54

Yad Vashem Holocaust Museum (Israel),
138
Yale University, Video Archive for
Holocaust Testimonies. *See* Fortunoff
Video Archive
Yapko, Michael, 67, 75–76
Yasui, Lise, 21
York, Susannah, 34
Young, James, 127

Zisblatt, Irene, 141, 143, 144
Zündel, Ernst, 176, 177–81, 185. *See also*
Mr. Death

Compositor:	BookMatters, Berkeley
Indexer:	Kevin Millham
Text:	11.25/13.5 Garamond
Display:	Garamond
Printer and Binder:	IBT Global